Mark Twain, Travel Books, and Tourism

Mark Twain, Travel Books, and Tourism

The Tide of a Great Popular Movement

JEFFREY ALAN MELTON

Have a great time traveling with Mark Twain !

— Jeffry Ala Melto

Oct. 16, 2010

THE UNIVERSITY OF ALABAMA PRESS

Tuscaloosa and London

Copyright © 2002
The University of Alabama Press
Tuscaloosa, Alabama 35487-0380
All rights reserved
Manufactured in the United States of America

Typeface: Bembo

∞

The paper on which this book is printed meets the minimum requirements of American
National Standard for Information Science-Permanence of Paper for Printed Library
Materials, ANSI Z39.48-1984.

Library of Congress Cataloging-in-Publication Data

Melton, Jeffrey Alan, 1962–
Mark Twain, travel books, and tourism : the tide of a great popular movement /
Jeffrey Alan Melton.
p. cm. — (Studies in American literary realism and naturalism)
Includes bibliographical references and index.
ISBN 0-8173-1160-2 (alk. paper)
1. Twain, Mark, 1835–1910—Contributions in travel writing. 2. Popular culture—
United States—History—19th century. 3. Americans—Foreign countries—History—
19th century. 4. Travelers' writings, American—History and criticism. 5. Voyages and
travels—History—19th century. 6. Travel writing—History—19th century. 7. Tourism—
History—19th century. I. Title. II. Series.
PS1342.T73 M45 2002
818.'409—dc21

2001006997

British Library Cataloguing-in-Publication Data available

For Kari

Contents

Acknowledgments   ix

Preface   xiii

1. The Success of Travel Books and the Failure of Tourism   1

2. Tourism and Travel Writing in the Nineteenth Century   16

3. Touring the Old World: Faith and Leisure in *The Innocents Abroad* and *A Tramp Abroad*   59

4. Touring the New World: The Search for Home in *Roughing It* and *Life on the Mississippi*   95

5. Touring the Round: Imperialism and the Failure of Travel Writing in *Following the Equator*   138

Notes   167

Works Cited   183

Selected Bibliography   187

Index   197

Acknowledgments

I could not have completed this project without the help and guidance of numerous people. This book began as a Ph.D. dissertation at the University of South Carolina under the direction of Ezra Greenspan, who first suggested that I start reading travel literature. In those first months of immersion in nineteenth-century travel books, when the breadth of the genre seemed overwhelming, I suspected that he held some level of contempt for me. But the journey was simply beginning, and to this day, travel books remain my preferred reading. I will always appreciate his help and continued support. The dissertation took shape with the patience and encouragement of Professor Greenspan along with the thoughtful advice of my committee: Professors Judith James, Keen Butterworth, and Kevin Lewis. The Department of English at the University of South Carolina provided a steady source of intellectual stimulation and support. In addition to the faculty and staff of the graduate program, I am forever indebted to my fellow graduate students, especially Alan Brasher, Cindy Stiles, and Amy Hudock, who helped to make an often stressful experience one that I will cherish always.

I am also indebted to several Mark Twain scholars who have shown a high level of generosity in answer to my queries and who were crucial to my progress. Thomas Tenney provided a wealth of material from which to begin. He gave me copies of travel books by Bayard Taylor and John Ross Browne as well as research material from his fine dissertation on Mark Twain and travel literature. Likewise, Victor Doyno has been consistently eager to answer questions and read draft essays for me and to voice his support for me with conviction. Also, David E. E. Sloane was kind enough not only to encourage me early in the writing process but also to acknowledge in print a paper (my first on Twain) presented at an American Literature Association conference. Such goodwill as demonstrated by these men is typical of Mark Twain scholars on the whole, and I can only hope to follow their examples. I am especially grateful to Alan Gribben, who has been tireless in his support and graciously read and edited the manuscript as it developed over the years. As a mentor and colleague, he has made an indelible mark on my work and my thinking.

This work was partially supported by two grants from the Auburn University Montgomery Research Grant-in-Aid Program. I am thankful for all of my colleagues in the Department of English and Philosophy at Auburn University Montgomery, who have provided remarkable examples of how to be teachers, scholars, and friends. I am honored to work among them. I am especially indebted to Bob Evans, who provided valuable advice on one of my early essays, and Eric Sterling, who has been a constant source of encouragement and goodwill.

It has been a pleasure to work with the staff of the University of Alabama Press. From the beginning of our association, they have consistently treated the work with a first-rate professionalism, and I am proud to have had the opportunity to work with them. Although she is no longer with the press, I would like to acknowledge Nicole Mitchell, who was the first to talk with me about my project and to encourage my progress. Special thanks go to Jonathan Lawrence, who as copyeditor helped strengthen the manuscript significantly; I am fortunate to have had his guidance.

Portions of this study have been published in several journals, and I am thankful to their editors for contributing to this work now in its final form. A section of chapter 1 appeared in *Popular Culture Review* as "The Trouble with Tourists: Authenticity and the Failure of Tourism," and it is reprinted here courtesy of its editorial board and the Far West Popular and American Culture Association. A few pages of chapter 2 appeared as part of an article published in *Studies in American Culture* as "The Tourist as Art Critic: Mark Twain and the Old Masters," and that material is reprinted here courtesy of its editorial board and the Popular Culture/American Culture Association in the South. Other segments of chapter 2 were published in *Papers on Language and Literature* as "Touring Decay: Nineteenth-Century American Travel Writers in Europe," and they are reprinted with the permission of the Board of Trustees of Southern Illinois University at Edwardsville. Also, another segment of chapter 2 appeared in significantly different form in *Thalia: Studies in Literary Humor* as "The Wild Teacher of the Pacific Slope: Mark Twain, Travel Books, and Instruction," and it is reprinted here with the permission of the Association for the Study of Literary Humor. An earlier version of the first half of chapter 3 appeared in *South Atlantic Review,* and it is reprinted here courtesy of its editorial board and under the auspices of the South Atlantic Modern Language Association and Georgia State University. Grateful acknowledgment is made to the American Humor Studies Association for permission to reprint, in modified form, "Adventurers and Tourists in Mark Twain's *A Tramp Abroad,*" *Studies in American Humor* ns 3.5 (1998): 34–47.

My parents, Otis and Esther Melton, have provided me with complete and unswerving love and support for anything I have ever attempted to do. A son could never ask for more than they have always given me. My in-laws, Wilbur and Annette Frederickson, showed an interest in my work that has been heartwarming and thoroughly gratifying. Although my baby daughter, Olivia, is yet to read, I cannot resist the chance to put her name in print here so that when she grows up, she will have this reminder that her father finds his greatest happiness in her smile. My deepest gratitude is for my wife, Kari Frederickson, whose patience, support, constant needling, and keen editorial eye have been crucial to the completion of the book, which is dedicated to her.

Preface

In *Following the Equator,* his last travel book, Mark Twain shares an anecdote about an "elderly lady and her son" who, because of a series of mishaps, have traveled well beyond their original itinerary, getting further from home all the while. "Think of it," he writes, "a projected excursion of five hundred miles gradually enlarged, without any elaborate degree of intention, to a possible twenty-four thousand" (58). This short sketch serves as an appropriate symbol for Twain's touring and travel-writing endeavors. In embarking on his own travel-book career with *The Innocents Abroad,* Twain inadvertently stepped into a world of travel writing that would carry him around the globe for the next thirty years, a beloved wandering "innocent." Furthermore, it would allow him to become an author of unparalleled success, all "without any elaborate degree of intention" —at least in the beginning. This extended "excursion" would prove fortunate for Twain and for millions of readers who have traveled with him.

To view Mark Twain as a split, often conflicted personality is a popular approach to examining the man and his literary achievement. Although it may prove distracting or even tiresome to some readers, this approach remains helpful in ongoing efforts to understand his craft. Many readers have used this premise as a springboard, citing the dualities represented by the nom de plume itself—Samuel L. Clemens versus "Mark Twain"—but readers have also recognized the identity conflicts between the genteel writer and the wild humorist, the liberal humanist and the racist, among others. I am not interested in elaborating on any of those already formidable discussions, for as Twain stated in the preface to *The Innocents Abroad,* "other books do that, and therefore, even if I were competent to do it, there is no need" (5). This study, more specifically, considers only Mark Twain, the tourist/narrator who exists within the travel books, and makes no effort to reconcile any biographical conflicts with Samuel L. Clemens or, for that matter, Mark Twain in other literary works. The narrator who introduces himself in *The Innocents Abroad* and subsequently carries readers around the world until bidding farewell over thirty years later in *Following the Equator* is our tour guide and beloved traveling partner.

My approach to Twain, however, does involve dual selves: the travel writer and the tourist. Yet these two identities depended upon one another not for establishing contrast but for complicity. Although both formed crucial parts of his literary identity, they have received relatively little notice from modern readers and critics. This travel writer/tourist Mark Twain deserves attention, and this text attempts to begin that process. Chapter 1 offers a two-part argument for this study: first, it demands recognition of travel books as central to Twain's professional career and as worthy of study in their own right, not simply as practice work for his fiction; second, it proposes tourist theory as a controlling critical perspective from which to read the individual narratives. This chapter thus lays out the framework indicated by the title of this work: Mark Twain, travel books, and tourism. Chapter 2 dissects the conventions of the genre prominent in the mid–nineteenth century and illustrates Twain's application of them in juxtaposition to his travel-writing peers. Although it may not be surprising to discover that Twain worked within as well as outside conventional demands, this is the first attempt to define those conventions and apply them to his work directly and substantively. The remaining chapters examine the five narratives individually, grouped by geographical itinerary rather than publishing chronology. Chapter 3, focusing on *The Innocents Abroad* and *A Tramp Abroad,* follows Twain to the Old World, wherein he confronts the limitations of tourist experience and explores the power of imagination and self-delusion. Chapter 4, focusing on *Roughing It* and *Life on the Mississippi,* tours the New World as Twain seeks to reconcile his outsider identity as tourist with a symbolic search for home. Chapter 5 considers *Following the Equator* as the tourist searches for escape from an inevitable imperialistic reality.

All of Twain's five travel books are closely linked, not just by the author's masterful use of the genre's conventions, but also by his intuitive recognition and manipulation of emerging touristic sensibilities. This study considers how these influences converged to make Mark Twain, travel writer and tourist. All five travel books are also linked in that the four which followed *The Innocents Abroad* were all consciously created sequels to it. Although Twain never matched its popular success in sales, he was able to enjoy a consistent remuneration that exceeded his other literary efforts (not to mention his entrepreneurial enterprises). Moreover, he succeeded artistically and, in so doing, captured the nuances of an emerging Tourist Age that would increasingly define how Americans would view the world and themselves.

Mark Twain stands at the beginning of the great social tide of American tourism, heralding its beginning in *The Innocents Abroad* and acknowledging the close of its "innocent" first phase with *Following the Equator.* As the striking differences between *The Innocents Abroad* and *Following the Equator* reflect, the significant changes in the political and cultural power of the United States and its increasing muscularity would place the nation at the center of the global stage. Mark Twain, the travel writer and tourist, would be its leading actor.

Mark Twain, Travel Books, and Tourism

I

The Success of Travel Books and the Failure of Tourism

Captain Duncan desires me to say that passengers for the *Quaker City* must be on board to-morrow before the tide goes out. What the tide has to do with us or we with the tide is more than *I* know.

Mark Twain

THE TRAVEL WRITER

For readers in the late nineteenth century, Mark Twain was first and foremost a travel writer instead of a novelist.[1] He earned the greatest patronage from his contemporaries as the endearing narrator of *The Innocents Abroad,* his most popular book and the best-selling travel book of the century, rather than as the author of *Huckleberry Finn* and *Tom Sawyer,* as most modern readers assume. Excluding collections of short stories and sketches, four of Twain's first seven books published in the United States were travelogues: *The Innocents Abroad* (1869), *Roughing It* (1872), *A Tramp Abroad* (1880), and *Life on the Mississippi* (1883). He would bring out his fifth and last travel book, *Following the Equator,* in 1897.

It was no coincidence that Twain made such extensive use of the genre or that so many readers loved these narratives. Twain recognized early the lucrative sales potential of travel books and capitalized on it throughout a varied and formidable career. Consistently, his travel books proved to be his best-sellers, especially in his formative years as a professional author. In its first three years of publication, *The Innocents Abroad* sold over 100,000 copies, just over 70,000 of them in the first year (Hill, *Twain and Bliss* 39).[2] *Roughing It* sold over 76,000 copies in its first two years and 96,000 by 1879 (63), and *A Tramp Abroad* sold 62,000 in its first year (152). *Life on the Mississippi* was the only one of the four to struggle—but only comparatively, selling over

32,000 copies in its first year (Hill, *Twain's Letters* 164). The popular success of his three fictional works of the same period varied, but none matched that of his travel books. *The Gilded Age* (1873), co-written with Charles Dudley Warner, took more than six years to sell 56,000 copies (Kaplan 167–68), and *The Adventures of Tom Sawyer* (1876) sold only 24,000 copies in its first year (200).[3] *The Prince and the Pauper,* published in 1882, sold around 18,000 copies in its first few months, according to Twain's estimate, but sales dropped off dramatically soon after the brisk start and became so disappointing that Twain was uncharacteristically tempted to abandon subscription sales and dump the work on the trade market (Salamo 17).[4]

For a writer who had earned worldwide acclaim with his first travel book, the reception of his fiction must have been a letdown. *The Innocents Abroad* sold well over three times as many copies in its first year as *The Adventures of Tom Sawyer* sold in its first year, yet Twain's best-selling book in his lifetime has been largely forgotten by most current readers. This is a shame and a loss to our understanding of both Twain's literary craft and the genre that made his career possible.

Always highly conscious of the desires and expectations of his readers, Twain confidently believed, for the most part, in his ability to fulfill them. Many of his genteel contemporaries criticized him for being irreverent, indecent, and even vulgar, and he proved sometimes sensitive to such assertions, but he understood well the tastes of those who read his works.[5] In an often-quoted letter to Andrew Lang, Twain commented on his intended audience: "Indeed I have been misjudged, from the very first. I have never tried in even one single instance, to help cultivate the cultivated classes. I was not equipped for it, either by native gifts or training. And I never had any ambition in that direction, but always hunted for bigger game—the masses" (Paine 2: 527).[6] Throughout his career Twain sought to capture the devotion of "the masses," and despite occasional bouts of insecurity regarding his literary reputation among "cultivated" readers (the Whittier birthday speech episode being the best-known example), he carefully established and nurtured a rapport with "uncultivated" readers, who, in turn, made him world-famous.[7] Referring to a critic's comment that his work was not "high & fine," Twain, in a letter dated 15 February 1887, admitted to his longtime friend and literary confidante William Dean Howells that "high & fine literature is wine, and mine is only water; but everybody likes water" (Smith and Gibson 2: 586–87).[8] Twain's assertion that "everybody" liked his work is not simply a clever or defensive retaliation to criticism; it directly reflects how he perceived his art and, more importantly to Twain, how he consistently valued the patronage of the masses over that of the highbrows.

Modern critics have yet to examine the expectations of Twain's contemporary readers or how he carefully catered to them. Throughout his career, he successfully stalked his "bigger game" by capitalizing on the vastly popular genre of travel literature, which proved an ideal vehicle for his wit and literary propensity. By studying how Twain used the formulas of the travel book, we can understand better how he fulfilled his readers' common expectations. In other words, we may learn how he created that liquid sustenance everybody liked to drink. Moreover, our grasp of Mark Twain as an author would benefit from examining his travel narratives from two perspectives: first, how he sought to please his contemporary readers with a finely tuned adherence to travel-book conventions, and second, how he sought to fashion his work within the inextricable context of an emergent Tourist Age.

Scholars have not ignored Twain's travel writing by any means, and a formidable body of scholarship exists that illuminates it. Richard Bridgman's *Traveling in Mark Twain* (1987) is the only published book-length examination of Twain's travel writing. In this insightful study, Bridgman considers how the travel texts reflect the psyche of their author; as such, he does not concern himself with the contexts of the genre beyond the narrative freedom the form allows writers. Within this specific focus, Bridgman correctly points out which features of travel writing allowed Twain to tap into his native talent: "All that the form demanded Twain had in abundance: curiosity, a reactive intelligence, and stamina" (3). Although Bridgman may oversimplify the demands, his framework nonetheless allows for helpful readings of how travel encouraged Twain's powerful associative ability, which in turn led him to produce his most compelling writing. In *Return Passages: Great American Travel Writing, 1780–1910* (2000), Larzer Ziff places Twain in context with other travel writers, and although he has only a chapter with which to examine Twain, he offers a strong overview of Twain's travel books. Ziff follows Bridgman by emphasizing Twain's personal recollections, noting that "travel writing was a perfect vehicle for Twain's imagination" (174).[9] Both of these scholars, among many others over the years, have elicited from Twain's travel writing a wealth of insightful and often provocative interpretations.[10]

The problem remains, however, that no critics have analyzed Twain's travel books as products of a specific genre with its own demands and expectations. Too often travel books have been lumped together with novels and criticized according to novelistic conventions rather than those of travel literature.[11] This is not to say that Twain's travel books should never be discussed in relation to his novels and other works; such criticism has been and continues to be highly beneficial. It is unfair, however, to place demands on Twain's travel books that were simply foreign to his understanding of the genre itself. After all, he wrote to sell books, and his contemporary readers, it seems clear by their purchasing fervor, accepted that quite well.

To ignore the conventions of the genre is to invite misunderstanding. Since twentieth-century readers preferred fiction, it is not surprising that the travel books have generally been seen as failing to meet inapplicable standards. In short, Twain's travel books have been analyzed as failed examples of fiction or as practice pieces that served only to illustrate his development into a "better" writer—that is, a novelist. Twain himself recognized the inability of many critics to take into account the expectations of his intended audience. In the letter to Andrew Lang quoted above, Twain also claimed that he always wrote for the "Belly and the Members" rather than for the "Head," and closed with a plea that "the critics adopt a rule recognizing the Belly and the Members, and formulate a standard whereby work done for them shall be judged" (Paine 2: 528). The time has come to grant Twain his wish by reading his most popular works along the same lines that his contemporary audience did. The present study endeavors to begin this process.

THE TOURIST

In addition to his role as a travel writer, Twain also serves as a prototypical modern tourist, and it is this controlling identity that provides the figure in the carpet of his work. In the opening chapter of *The Innocents Abroad,* Twain rejoices in his upcoming journey to the Old World. "During that memorable month," he writes, "I basked in the happiness of being for once in my life drifting with the tide of a great popular movement. Every body was going to Europe—I, too, was going to Europe" (27). In addition to its purpose of creating enthusiasm for the narrative and setting up a central theme of disappointed expectations, this comment reveals an important cultural context. This "great popular movement" into which Twain insinuates himself and his readers parallels the beginnings of what can be termed the Tourist Age. Americans were on the move, and Twain was caught in their growing tide. He notes that "steamship lines were carrying Americans out of the various ports of the country at the rate of four or five thousand a week, in the aggregate" (27). Although Twain depicts himself as "drifting" with this tide, his travel books and his tourist experiences clearly indicate he was more accurately riding the *crest* of a tourist wave—in the forefront both as a travel writer helping to popularize its seductive, engulfing power *and* as a tourist participating in one of its earliest leisure cruises, a form of tourism that has since become definitive of mass touristic behavior. The inevitable drag swept along everyone in what amounted to a large-scale cultural shift. As the tide swelled, Twain, ever an astute and opportunistic writer, quickly recognized a way to capitalize on the movement. He thus gives us a record of the birth of the Tourist Age for which he was both a creating, defining force and a prototypical participant.

THE TOURIST EXPERIENCE

"Don't be a tourist," advises a high-rotation commercial for *The Travel Channel,* a popular cable television network that offers travel documentaries, promotions, and information. These words convey two messages simultaneously: the more direct one encourages viewers to tune into *The Travel Channel* to learn about foreign cultures and thereby avoid mistakes and embarrassing situations while traveling; the indirect one encourages viewers to stay at home and watch the rest of the world from the comfort of their armchairs. "Don't be a tourist," indeed. We need also to consider a third implication, a message that has been intertwined with tourist mentality since the beginning of that boom in the mid–nineteenth century. The subtext of the direct message reads: by learning of foreign cultures—by watching television, in this case—one can transcend being a "tourist" (a lowly creature) to become a "traveler" (an altogether impressive creature). The promotion is a clever one; it easily taps into one of the most pervasive and powerful sentiments of this touristic era: everybody wants to travel, but nobody wants to be a tourist, at least conceptually. And there is the rub—a "great popular movement" in which hordes of people want to participate but for which the same people refuse to admit their participation. As Dean MacCannell, in his seminal study *The Tourist* (1976), wryly states, "tourists dislike tourists" (10).

Tourism continues to thrive and reshape the world's economic and social makeup, and the tide shows no sign of abating well over a hundred years since Mark Twain heralded its beginning. Our cultural ambivalence toward tourism—embracing the trappings of it in practice while denying our complicity in theory—has engendered, then, an ongoing battle between "travelers" and "tourists," a struggle for self-identification that ultimately exists only semantically. For most people, there is no resolution in the foreseeable future.

It is important to remember, however, that this phenomenon is not a late-twentieth-century (or twenty-first-century) creation; the conflicts over travel identity were well in place by the time the tourist boom in America began in earnest after the Civil War. The word *tourist* itself has been around for quite awhile (the *Oxford English Dictionary* cites the earliest reference in 1780), yet it did not begin to take on widespread negative connotations until the mid– to late nineteenth century, thereby coinciding (it should come as no great surprise) with the increased numbers of tourists moving energetically around the globe. *Blackwood's Magazine* in England, for example, provides one of the most aggressive attacks upon this supposedly new breed of traveler. In an article titled "Modern Tourism" (1848), the editors note that technological advances in travel have had beneficial social effects but have also initiated a decidedly unfortunate one: "They have covered Europe with Tourists" (185). The article continues by noting that this mass traveling "spoils all rational travel; it disgusts all intelligent curiosity [*sic*]; it repels the student, the philosopher, and the manly investigator, from subjects which have been thus trampled into mire by the hoofs of a whole tribe of travelling bipeds, who might rejoice to exchange brains with the animals which they ride" (185). In short, tourists are mindless, brutish "bipeds" with an undeniable herd instinct and "hoofs" that trample underfoot places that more properly exist as "subjects" for true-thinking travelers. In an effort, it seems, to be fair to other herd animals, the editors generously imply that tourists are less intelligent than the quadrupeds upon whose backs they ride. A generation later, as the tourist movement became firmly rooted in the United States, cultural critics echoed *Blackwood's* disgust. Henry James, in his "Americans Abroad," regrets the tourist boom and laments how, in his view, it reflects poorly on the nation as a whole. "A very large proportion of the Americans who annually scatter themselves over Europe are by no means flattering to the national vanity," he writes. "Their merits, whatever they are, are not of a sort that strikes the eye—still less the ear. They are ill-made, ill-mannered, ill-dressed" (209). Thus begins the notion of the "ugly American." Interestingly, James goes on to note that the American tourist travels to Europe as "a provincial who is terribly bent upon taking, in the fulness of ages, his revenge" (209). Perhaps James is correct; if so, the American "revenge" upon Europe in the Tourist Age continues well over a hundred years later, perhaps best evidenced by Euro-Disney.

The great movement created its own self-loathing. Critics have long recognized this struggle and illustrate the deep, abiding desire to distinguish between desirable travelers and undesirable tourists. Among twentieth-century cultural critics, Daniel Boorstin, in *The Image: A Guide to Pseudo-Events in America* (1985), provides the most compelling and energetic discussion of the nature of tourism, and he aggressively defends the separation of traveler and tourist identity.[12] By emphasizing the historical connections between *travel* and *travail,* he reminds us that to travel is, in effect, to work, thus making a crucial distinction: the traveler is active, while the tourist is forever passive. Travelers seek and earn experience, while tourists sign up for a program and sit back to wait for experiences to come to them. For travelers there is work to be done; it will not be easy, but it promises rewards worth the discomfort. This image is powerful and attractive; it is also romantic—the lone traveler enduring trials and tribulations because he or she *has* to, "because it's there." Many of us are up for the ideal, but few, really, are up to the actual physical and emotional challenge such a self-image requires in praxis. The tourist identity, in the end, can only suffer in contrast to such a romantic ideal. For tourists, there is little work to be done; it will be easy, and it promises comfort. Although this image may attract our more hedonistic urges, it nonetheless suffers aesthetically in comparison to the romantic traveler.

Another cultural critic, Walker Percy, in his essay "The Loss of the Creature," offers an interesting appraisal of the dilemma facing modern tourists. He questions whether any of us can approach the same sense of wonder—the authentic sense of discovery—that the first Spanish explorer to see the Grand Canyon, García López de Cárdenas, felt upon his encounter. Using "P" to denote the value of the authentic discovery, Percy asserts: "If the place is seen by a million sightseers, a single sightseer does not receive value P but a millionth part of value P" (46). The primary reason for this devaluation is not necessarily the number of tourists but the amount of information that we unavoidably carry with us as we go to the canyon. We bring along a complex, deeply rooted collection of data that creates in us expectations of "The Grand Canyon"—an image, an idea, in addition to a geological phenomenon. Cut by the churning of the Colorado River, this remarkable canyon itself changed in human perception when it became "grand." We can see the canyon, therefore, not for what it is but for what we have been told it is. The "symbolic machinery" that creates our expectations and informs us also causes a "loss of sovereignty." We are, as a result, no longer in charge of our experience, and the more we travel, the more we lose the horizon. Although we should probably apply the value "P" not to a Spanish explorer but to an unknown Native American, Percy's example still illustrates intuitively that the trouble with tourism, in this sense, is the trouble with travel. It affects anyone who follows another, and we are, with very few exceptions, followers. (Even Neil Armstrong, in taking his first small step on the moon, was filled with expectations derived from extensive training and based on copious advance research.) Again, this frustration is not a new one. Twain, in *The Innocents Abroad,* confronts the issue as he tours Rome: "What is it that confers the noblest delight? What is that which swells a man's breast with pride above that which any other experience can bring him? Discovery! To know that you are walking where none others have walked; that you are beholding what human eye has not seen before; that you are breathing a virgin atmosphere. . . . To be the *first*—that is the idea" (266). Twain, in celebrating the thrill of discovery, also recognizes that for the tourist—even at the beginning of the Tourist Age—such a feeling is unavailable. He continues: "What is there in Rome for me to see that others have not seen before me? What is there for me to touch that others have not touched? What is there for me to feel, to learn, to hear, to know, that shall thrill me before it pass to others? What can I discover?—Nothing. Nothing whatsoever" (267).

It is no wonder that many of us wish to distance ourselves from such an unpleasant demarcation as that of the tourist. The frustration that comes from being removed from true discovery is real and immediate. But in so doing, we misrepresent ourselves and our behavior in this age. Moreover, we deny the effects of our travels on ourselves and the world at large. Jonathan Culler observes that by denying our complicity in tourism we inadvertently become what we fear. "Ferocious denigration of tourists," he writes, "is in part an attempt to convince oneself that one is not a tourist. The desire to distinguish between tourists and real travelers is a part of tourism—integral to it rather than outside it or beyond it" (156). Their need to distance themselves from one another creates an interesting phenomenon. While partaking in a thoroughly communal activity—notions of the lone, romantic soul notwithstanding—the individual participants are encouraged to feel hostility toward their partners in the process and deny their connections wholly or partially. Culler makes a provocative connection between travelers and tourists. Any tourist can always find someone with *more* touristic characteristics to hate. The backpacker looks down on the man in a rental car, who in turn looks down on the crowds in a tour bus, and these people, also in turn, may look down on those who stay at home watching *The Travel Channel.* All of these people are travelers, and all are tourists; the words are synonymous.

No matter what term we choose to describe ourselves as we travel, all tourists in one form or another seek to escape from their daily lives, but it remains unclear precisely what it is they escape *to.* How do the backpacking tourists, the automobile tourists, the bus tourists, and even the vicarious tourists at home respond to their travels? The definitive study of the behaviors and assumptions implicit in mass tourism is MacCannell's *The Tourist,* which remains invaluable in examining how we define touristic experience. As such, it provides the primary theoretical grounding for this study.[13] Rejecting any reductive dismissal of touristic behavior, MacCannell refers to tourists as "sightseers" who spread throughout the world to search for experiences that they consume voraciously. Their search is genuine and deserving of critical attention rather than condescension. Moreover, this search is definitive of modernist Western culture, and as such it offers an opportunity for deeper understanding. He notes as well that despite the protestations from the good-old-days-of-travel camp (represented here by Boorstin and Percy), *all* tourists seek "deeper involvement" with the cultures they visit "to some degree" (10). The phrase "to some degree" is a crucial one. For those who insist on a definitive and absolute distinction between traveler and tourist, MacCannell allows for some solace. Yes, everyone is a tourist, but there are variations of behavior within that realm.[14] One tourist's desire for "deeper involvement" with the Grand Canyon, for example, may be satisfied by a cursory glance over the edge before a return to the gift shop; another's degree of interest may only be met by a ten-day hike down into the canyon itself.

We need also to recognize that another factor influences how we seek "deeper involvement," and that is the desire for comfort. Widespread tourism, after all, derives from a social structure that promotes leisure as a goal.[15] Tourists have often balanced the desire for experience against the desire for comfort, and this has always been the case, even well before the tourist explosion of the mid–nineteenth century. If these two impulses are not diametrically opposed, they are at least very often in practical conflict. Continuing with our example, as beautiful as much of the Grand Canyon landscape is, it remains, after all, a desert. It is hot. It is dry. The gift shops, however, have air-conditioning and ice cream. The tourist at the Grand Canyon who has little interest in moving beyond the ready-made, programmed sights from the rim prefers to remain always near a comfort level that closely resembles home. The tourist who chooses to hike deeply into the canyon itself, by contrast, prefers to forego his or her normal amenities and escape from the solace of home, momentarily. They are both tourists, but the question remains: How should we define their disparate experiences? Is one more "authentic"—more real—than the other?

Henry David Thoreau can help us with this query. According to *Walden* (1854), one of the most provocative and challenging travel books ever written, Thoreau went to the woods to "live deliberately" and thus avoid coming to the end of his life only to realize, too late, that he "had not lived," that he had remained too passive, too comfortable (90–91). By expressing his desire "to suck out all the marrow of life," Thoreau perfectly encapsulates the ideal of the romantic traveler. Regardless of how short the physical journey, it would be work, and it would be hard. It would also be original. Still, it is important to remember that Thoreau had plenty of help, being only a few miles from Concord, and that his stay was temporary, a limited tour. In any case, is such an experience truly still available? We may appreciate Thoreau's rather local traveling and his twenty-six-month experiment on Walden Pond, but few modern readers opt for his brand of travel even if they embrace his desire to "live deliberately." Moreover, there are few ponds like his Walden around (Walden itself perennially faces the prospect of development), and few of us, for that matter, have a friend like Ralph Waldo Emerson who owns lakefront property. Still, we crave—to some degree—matching at least Thoreau's basic desire to touch the "essential facts of life," and this craving manifests itself most often in the Tourist Age as a search for authenticity. MacCannell argues that this quest is definitive of modernity and belies an intuitive belief that life in Western civilization is devoid of authentic experience. Tourists, then, seek it elsewhere. Herein is the key to the ultimate and inescapable failure of tourism: no matter how often it promises authenticity, it can never fulfill that promise; moreover, it never did, even when tourists called themselves travelers, even when the trees grew dense and undisturbed on the shores of Walden Pond.

So what is the tourist to do? To try to answer this question, we can begin by altering one of Shakespeare's most memorable lines and applying it to the Tourist Age: All the world's a sight, and we are merely tourists. This petty theft may help illustrate an important point about the nature of touristic experience—that, as with Shakespeare's original assertion that the world is a "stage" and we are "players," sights and tourists require playacting.[16] The search for authenticity relies on—for better or worse—careful staging and meticulous production design. Tour promoters and sight marketers, among others, have long recognized the drawing power of "authenticity," and they have touted it accordingly—"See live killer whales!" (in a concrete pool) or "Watch a real Hawaiian luau!" (in the hotel courtyard).[17] Authenticity is a commodity of the Tourist Age, and its presentation is a cultural production, always. Consider, for a moment, a reenactment of the 19 April 1775 battle between colonial minutemen and British regulars, a popular tourist production in Concord, Massachusetts. If this "play" is *real* enough, then the onlookers have gained a typical touristic experience and the cultural production is complete. Of course, different tourists may have different standards of authenticity (as in the example of the Grand Canyon), and their reactions could easily range from "I could feel the tension of the battle" to "I really doubt that the minutemen wore watches." In either case, the show must go on, and so must the tourists. The next "battle" will be in a few hours, and the next sight is just down the road at a pond called Walden.

The Concord battle reenactment may garner another reaction from the tourist, one that is more directly fundamental to the nature of touristic experience: "It's just as I had imagined the battle to be." The expectations we have when we visit a sight cannot help but influence our reaction to it. But it is difficult to separate our imagination from our concept of the *real,* especially when it comes to historical reenactments, wherein tourists are separated not only from a place but also from a time. And until someone invents real time travel, we simply cannot touch the original experience of the battle in Concord, and we can never hear the "shot heard around the world." Even if someone perfects actual time travel, we could only witness the event distanced by our knowledge of how the day turns out. So we are stuck, and we can only try to gather as much information as we choose to, and then, as spectators, imagine the experiences of others. This battle reenactment, what Boorstin would call a "pseudo-event," is central to tourism, and although it is a staged production, a "play," it becomes associated nevertheless with the authentic, not because of its accuracy so much as because many people see it.[18] The authenticity of any sight, then, increases with each tourist moving through the turnstiles. Sights gain weight and authority by being seen, and the masses over time thus help authenticate them. Sticking with the battle example, we can see that tourists do not simply travel to Concord to see the reenactment and experience the actual day of 19 April 1775. More significantly, they go because of all that has followed that original event—the starting of the Revolutionary War, the founding of a nation, *and* the founding of a tourist sight and the building of an elaborate tourist apparatus—roads, guide maps, hotels, historical markers, and so forth—of which the reenactment is but a part.

Any touristic production, in addition to asking for imaginative leaps from the audience, also implicitly asks for what I call touristic faith, a phrase adapted from Coleridge's "poetic faith," wherein readers experience a "willing suspension of disbelief." Touristic faith, likewise, implies that tourists ignore that they are watching a production, that they willingly dismiss their skepticism and pretend to believe, at least for the moment, that they are gaining an authentic experience. Erik Cohen notes that tourists' enjoyment level "is contingent on their willingness to accept the make believe or half-seriously to delude themselves. In a sense, they are accomplices of the tourist establishment in the production of their own deception" (184). Of course, tourists may vary in how much amusement they take in the make-believe and in how much consciousness they have of the play. Their actions, nonetheless, are akin to ritualized behaviors, a series of obligatory acts derived from devotion—however reluctant—to established conventions. Some tourists may alter the form and diverge from the masses (and boldly call themselves "travelers"), but they are part of the ritual nonetheless. If a few tourists seek to reject the cultural production, they are put in a difficult position since few sights remain off the beaten path. What are their options? Should they avoid the battle reenactment in Concord, the Statue of Liberty in New York, the Great Sphinx in Egypt—all highly ritualized sights? Even if these tourists eschew such well-marked sights, the question remains: Why? Are they rebelling against programmed travel? If so, the program still shapes their itinerary as they consciously (desperately) try to avoid it. Or there may be another way to get around the program. For example, a tourist may live with a family in the Yucatán—eat, sleep, and work with them. She may be like a chameleon and change from tourist, to guest, to friend, and come much closer in the process to an authentic experience. Yet one day—in a week, a month, or a year—she will return home. She knows this all along the way, and so do her hosts. This knowledge alone alters the experience, distinguishes her from everyone else. Because tourists are by definition outsiders, they can never meet pure authenticity. The essence of any touristic experience, that it is a temporary condition, will inevitably reenter her consciousness, and the illusion of authenticity, however strengthened by extended personal, even intimate, contact, will be shattered. There is no escaping this reality of the Tourist Age.

Although Percy is optimistic about our innate ability to step aside from the beaten path and find our own moments of pure discovery, we should acknowledge that the "symbolic machinery" is comprehensive and overwhelming. Our only refuge is in the play and our willingness to act our parts. Fortunately, tourists rarely have authenticity as their only goal.[19] If they do, they will always meet with disappointment and failure, and that failure will be absolute. We have forever enjoyed travel as a metaphor for life, one in which we move through an often strange landscape and in the process see, hear, smell, and touch new things. We learn and grow wiser. Ostensibly, that is why we want to travel, whether we move across oceans or ponds. We all want, at least aesthetically, to suck the marrow from life. Implicit in this desire, however, is the assumption that such experiences reenacted as tourists are innately authentic simply because they stand in seeming opposition to modernity. They are not. No intellectual meditation or wordplay between "traveler" and "tourist" can change this definitive fact of the Tourist Age.

Tourism is an ever-expanding collection of cultural productions, staged in varying forms and contexts around the globe, all promising authenticity but at the same time remaining unable to provide it. Whether outfitted with a well-worn copy of *Walden* and a rugged knapsack or a well-worn American Express card and a new camcorder, we all search in vain for the *real* in our travels. Because of this paradox, promoters of any tourist sight, writers of any travel book, and directors of any filmed travelogue must structure experience to convince us that we are witnessing the authentic, and we must comply faithfully in order to enjoy the illusion. Mark Twain was the first travel writer to recognize this phenomenon, and as his five travel books demonstrate, he would become for tourism and for travel writing the first great negotiator of the spaces between reality and dream.

THE DRIFTER

It is within this literary and theoretical context that this book examines the travel literature of Mark Twain, the nineteenth century's most versatile travel writer, and its most masterful. To ensure his success, Twain had to be more than a clever author; he also had to be a clever tourist. Like no other figure in American cultural and literary history, he captures the birth and growth of a new creature who would go on to change the map of the world, the American tourist. With his travel narratives as a guide, modern readers—tourists all—can take their own grand tours through the early days of the Tourist Age.

In *The Innocents Abroad,* Twain's description of the *Quaker City* pleasure excursion may also apply to the tourism boom of which it was a part; it would be a "picnic on a gigantic scale." After the Civil War, as the tourist tide became a tidal wave, America could no longer define itself through its frontier alone—its ample geography waiting for poetic meters. The new American had to travel, to move outside that vastness and around the rest of the world, and this new American, true to the new age, could only go as a tourist. His travel books put Twain as the tourist both at the crest of the wave enjoying the ride of a lifetime and at its trough desperately spinning in its tumult. What makes Twain special in this regard are not the experiences themselves but how he responded to them in his travel books. Although he implied that he was "drifting" with this "great popular movement," Twain was by no means a drifter. Through his five narratives, he actively helped shape and direct the tide. In the quote that serves as the epigraph for this chapter, Twain, upon the imminent departure of the *Quaker City,* comically plays with the notion of the uncertain connection he and his fellow passengers have to the ocean tide.[20] For the joke, Twain pretends to be oblivious to the fact that not only the captain but also the ship's passengers depend on the certain movements of ocean tides. The symbolic movement of the cultural tide, as Twain would learn, was no less certain. His feigned innocence aside, Twain's subsequent travel-writing career and his developing understanding of the Tourist Age would illustrate consistently for thirty years that Mark Twain, indeed, knew quite well how to ride with the tide.

2

Tourism and Travel Writing in the Nineteenth Century

No other genre of American literature enjoyed a greater popularity or a more enduring prominence in the nineteenth century than travel writing. Essentially, it had been intertwined with the development of America's literary identity from its beginnings, as the first European explorers recorded their experiences for readers back home. By the mid–nineteenth century, the passion for traveling as both tourist and reader touched most sectors of American life. Published by canonical and minor writers, travel books provided crucial income for many of the century's authors. At one point or another in their careers, almost all of the era's prominent literary figures availed themselves of the freedoms and benefits of travel writing. Often, as in Mark Twain's case, that decision proved highly profitable. Although most modern readers have ignored this vibrant genre of American literature and its vital connection to the century's finest authors, the numerous and now-forgotten career travel writers who defined its development and pushed its popularity were among the more prominent literary personalities of their time.[1]

Midway in the century, the interest in both tourism and travel literature had evolved into an outright phenomenon. In the May 1844 issue of *United States Magazine and Democratic Review,* for example, Henry Tuckerman notes: "Our times might not inaptly be designated as the age of travelling. Its records form no insignificant branch of the literature of the day" (527).[2] The American curiosity for faraway lands combined with the increasing availability of quicker and cheaper transportation to create a boom in foreign travel. Physically and economically, more Americans were able to travel abroad, and as the number of commercial and passenger ships sailing the Atlantic Ocean multiplied, so did the number of tourists who could afford to make the trip to the Old World. Christof Wegelin notes that the steadily increasing numbers from 1820 to 1849 exploded by 1860. The number of U.S. citizens returning yearly to Atlantic and Gulf ports, according to Wegelin, "rose from 1,926 to 2,659" in the three decades following 1820, but in 1860 the returning tourists in the four largest Atlantic ports alone numbered 19,387 (307).[3] With the dramatic technical advances in steam-powered ships, voyages between the continents became commonplace. "Steam is annihilating space," Tuckerman continues. "The ocean, once a formidable barrier, not to be traversed without long preparation and from urgent necessity, now seems to inspire no more consideration than a goodly lake, admirably adapted to a summer excursion" (527). By the post–Civil War era, the travel contagion had become a full-fledged social upheaval. "If the social history of the world is ever written," observed *Putnam's Magazine* in May 1868, "the era in which we live will be called the nomadic period. With the advent of ocean steam navigation and the railway system, began a travelling mania which has gradually increased until half of the earth's inhabitants, or at least of its civilized portion, are on the move" ("Going Abroad" 530–31). Indeed, Americans were "on the move" in unprecedented numbers, and as an inevitable result, supply-and-demand economics gradually took hold as the industry and ancillary business ventures matched public interest. For the first time in history, tourism was beginning to become the norm for a significantly broader segment of the population, and traveling became associated more often with economic forces than with aesthetic ones.[4]

The corresponding interest in travel literature swelled as well, both for readers who planned to make their own journeys and for those who simply wanted to gain the experience vicariously. For every actual tourist, there were hundreds more who were fascinated by the experience offered by reading travel books—virtual reality for the nineteenth century. In *Trubner's Bibliographic Guide to American Literature* (1859), Benjamin Moran writes: "This would seem to be the age of *travel literature*, judging from the many narratives now published, and the general excellence of such works. No nation has given more good books of this class to the world since 1820 than the United

States, considered with regard to styles or information" (lvi). Sales figures encouraged writers and publishers to fill the seemingly insatiable demand aggressively, and the result was a plethora of travel texts with a wide array of points of interests and narrative styles. Harold Smith, whose *American Travellers Abroad: A Bibliography of Accounts Published before 1900* (1969) is the only attempt to provide a comprehensive listing of travel narratives, cites just under two thousand travel books published in the United States. Although this number is astounding, it is actually quite conservative, since Smith excludes all books concerned with journeys made within the continental forty-eight states (whether or not the states existed as such at the time of publication), which in fact constituted a substantial portion of the genre. Moreover, although they are not within the scope of his study, virtually all periodicals and newspapers featured travel sections that served as outlets for travel writers throughout the nation—Mark Twain, of course, being one of them.[5]

Since travel literature attracted writers and readers in unprecedented numbers, it may be helpful to consider why the genre appealed to so many people. Early in the nineteenth century, the United States had yet to establish itself either externally in relation to the rest of the world or internally in relation to its own borders. As the nation approached midcentury and survived the gruesome challenge of the Civil War, however, the country at large was eager to reach out into the outer world with a newly formed and somewhat tenuous confidence. Nineteenth-century Americans searching for their cultural identity increasingly turned to travel writing, which served a vital aesthetic and practical purpose by helping readers to understand themselves as they encountered a variety of cultural behaviors and assumptions foreign to their own.[6] In short, the writers and readers of travel sought other parts of the world to learn about themselves, and travel narratives thus voiced the anxieties and assurances, the successes and failures, of this massive social quest.

For those who could not (or chose not to) experience tourism firsthand, travel writers provided an ideal solution. These readers could learn everything they felt they needed to know from someone they trusted and thus gain a worldliness of sorts without putting themselves to much expense or discomfort. In an age of a democratization of knowledge that glorified self-improvement, the burgeoning, literate middle class clamored for anything perceived as educational.

William Ellery Channing effectively captured the growing mood in his "Address on Self Culture," a lecture first given in Boston in September 1838. Although his comments predate the tourist boom by thirty years, the concepts endured well into the late Victorian period and serve as helpful points of reference for understanding the social impetuses for post–Civil War tourism. Defining "self culture" as "the care which every man owes to himself, to the unfolding and perfecting of his nature" (354), Channing insists that the goal of the American people should be "to fasten on this culture as our Great End, to determine deliberately and solemnly, that we will make the most and best of the powers which God has given us" (371). This social and individual desire for perfection helped to create a large market for informational texts; the demand for histories, biographies, and travel books was accordingly heavy and remained so throughout the century. The time-honored and socially respected art of traveling, in and of itself, connoted self-improvement, whether or not tourists actually changed substantially or learned anything. Tourists could always say— once back at home—that they had been there, wherever "there" was, and no matter the nature of the experience, that fact alone could hold sway in any salon discussion or social occasion. Following the Civil War, middle-class tourists were hungry for the worldliness that travel promised and eagerly embraced earlier generations' notion of "self culture," but in practice their attempts at self-improvement most often mimicked consumer culture and became adornments to display, souvenirs to show friends. Traveling to learn, at least ostensibly, therefore established itself as a valuable part of touristic performance.[7]

Touring East, Touring West

The Old World, especially Europe, offered the strongest lure for American travel writers and readers (the overwhelming majority of texts were penned by writers of Euro-American heritage), who sought to understand where they came from in order to decide where they were going.[8] America had successfully separated itself politically from England, but it had yet to sever the undeniable emotional and intellectual ties to European cultures and institutions at large. The European travel experience, then, helped these tourists reconcile opposing impulses: to reject the past by concentrating only on an American present and implied destiny, or to embrace that legacy and the rich associational identity it fostered. By traveling to Europe, Americans could wander among the accomplishments of their ancestors, and celebrate them, all the while affirming their belief through direct comparison that America was a land of the future and Europe of the past.

One of the earliest writers to express this American view of Europe was Washington Irving. In "The Author's Account of Himself," the introduction for the monumentally successful *The Sketch-Book* (1819–20), Irving wistfully captures a prevailing and enduring sentiment through the voice of his fictional narrator, Geoffrey Crayon:[9]

> But Europe held forth the charms of storied and poetical association. There were to be seen the masterpiece[s] of art, the refinements of highly-cultivated society, the quaint peculiarities of ancient and local custom. My native country was full of youthful promise: Europe was rich in the accumulated treasures of age. Her very ruins told the history of times gone by, and every mouldering stone was a chronicle. I longed to wander over the scenes of renowned achievement—to tread, as it were, in the footsteps of antiquity—to loiter about the ruined castle— to meditate on the falling tower—to escape, in short, from the common-place realities of the present, and lose myself among the shadowy grandeurs of the past. (14–15)[10]

Irving makes interesting word choices as he describes the attractions of Europe: "Her very ruins," "times gone by," "mouldering stone," "ruined castle," "falling tower," "shadowy grandeurs of the past." Taken together, these not-so-subtle associations encouraged readers to view Europe as a culture long past its prime, described with the tone of a romantic dreamer touring a cemetery that was aesthetically charming, perhaps, but marked by death nonetheless. Irving was by no means alone in such characterizations, and subsequent generations of travel writers in overwhelming numbers would likewise lose themselves among "shadowy grandeurs," many whistling along the way as they echoed his language and mimicked both his enthusiasm and his undeniable "youthful promise."

While travel writers and readers looked eastward to the past of the Old World, they looked westward to their implicit future. Travel literature based on the American West and the Pacific South Sea Islands made up a significant and popular portion of the genre. If Europe represented the "treasures of age," then the West and the Pacific Islands promised an "image of perpetual juvenescence" (15), as defined by travel writer James Jackson Jarves in *Scenes and Scenery in the Sandwich Islands* (1843). The Pacific Islands embodied the Edenic possibilities of the New World in much the same manner as the eastern coast beckoned to the early explorers, and the West itself offered evidence of America's supposed manifest destiny. Symbolically, one of the most popular travel writers of the century, Bayard Taylor, named his narrative of his journey to the Pacific coast *Eldorado: or, Adventures in the Path of Empire* (1850).[11] Tourists and readers alike could take part in this cultural production with a confident imperialistic tone, thereby becoming part of the manifest tide as they explored the streets of Nevada City, crossed the Isthmus of Panama, or climbed atop Kilauea volcano. The American quest for cultural stability influenced the popularization of travel books on the whole; moreover, the slow but steady American conquest of the West gave epic significance to any journey through the region.

Both traditions—looking eastward, looking westward—helped to nurture a strong American popular identity for tourists and readers alike, but it is important to note also that travel writing at large appealed to its producers as well. Early in the nineteenth century, many authors quickly recognized the lucrative potential of travel writing. The genre provided another forum for an indigenous literature. The American struggle for identity so prevalent in popular culture was no less evident in the development of American literary identity for writers. Cultural and literary critics were impatient to establish a viable native literature competitive with that of Europe.[12] Lacking national and international respect, potential authors were separated from the public by a barrier that was difficult to define but often discouraging. This uncertainty, combined with inadequate copyright laws, greatly hampered the grooming of American literary talent. Publishers, in short, more often chose to publish well-established literary giants of Britain, who represented sure bets in regard to sales and, moreover, could not claim royalties. Few observers believed an American writer could support him- or herself consistently in such a competitive and adverse publishing market. Washington Irving, however, proved otherwise, and he did so largely in the guise of travel literature.

Irving achieved America's first sustained success for the profession of authorship, and his popularity demonstrated to readers, publishers, and other writers that Americans could produce entertaining and informative books, that they could sell in impressive numbers, and that authorship could be a viable career.[13] The key, of course, was to write a book readers liked, which was no easy task. It is no surprise, then, that America's first professional writer achieved his first great success with a travel book.[14] Irving effectively capitalized on the reading public's vast appetite for tales of foreign travel in *The Sketch-Book,* demonstrating the opportunities for a good American writer and, more specifically, the potential of the travel book as a vehicle.[15] Irving's contribution to the genre was crucial. His prestige helped raise the stature of travel writing in a nation struggling for self-identity and literary respect, and he also, indirectly, demonstrated the viability of a heretofore unrecognized publishing market that only *American* writers could satisfy. If American authors were disadvantaged by the prominence of their British counterparts, they could also benefit, it would seem, from that exclusion. American travel writers could fill a need in American readers' psyches that could never be addressed by British masters; they could offer views of the world from an avowed *American* perspective. Scott and Dickens might entertain a massive audience with their novels, but they could never give American readers the picture of an English countryside or the "real" London that an American travel writer like Irving could. This is Irving's primary contribution to the genre; he demonstrated to the reading public, publishers, and writers alike that a rich vein of indigenous literary ore was ready to be mined. The thoroughly self-conscious American point of view proved to be refreshing and seemingly irresistible, and many travel narratives would follow upon *The Sketch-Book.* Although American readers were already familiar with the genre at large, they were eager to embrace a new type of travel writer, one with a distinctive, fresh perspective. The nation and the world were thus primed to be defined through American eyes.

TOURING CONVENTIONS

Travel literature is a varied and overlapping genre that combines the characteristics of journalism, autobiography, fiction, history, anthropology, and political analysis, among others, into a smorgasbord of interpretation and experience. As a composite literary form, it resists neat categorization and isolation. It does, however, exhibit certain forms and conventions that set it apart from other, more focused forms of writing with which it shares mutual influence, and by extension it creates reasonable expectations in its numerous readers. In the case of nineteenth-century America, patterns and themes emerged that provide a valuable record of the genre and its readers' implicit expectations.

Travel writers could not travel in a vacuum separate from the tourists who preceded them, nor could they presume to ignore established mores of the genre.[16] The travel book, however, was often victimized by its own simple though flexible formula, especially as worked by inferior writers, of which there were many. Its structure yielded to repetitiveness, which eventually created obvious patterns as more and more writers trod the same ground. Their weight, like the weight of their tourist peers, wore down the literary turf underfoot and in doing so created ruts that were all too easy to follow. As the century progressed and tourists' numbers expanded, redundancy was inevitable. The problem was certainly not uniquely American, and Frederick Marryat, a successful British travel writer, captures best the pervasiveness of formulaic approaches to the genre. In his whimsical "How to Write a Book of Travels," the struggling narrator, Ansard, receives advice from a mentor, Barnstable, on how to organize a travel book. Barnstable gives to the younger writer the framework for any single travel-book chapter: "Traveling—remarks on country passed through—anecdote—arrival at a town—churches—population—historical remarks—another anecdote—eating and drinking—natural curiosities—egotism—remarks on women (never mind the men)—another anecdote—reflections—an adventure—and go to bed" (529). Despite its comic overstatement as well as the British subject matter, Marryat's satire could aptly apply to almost any chapter in a multitude of travel books produced in the United States. Twentieth-century critic Willard Thorp echoes Marryat's disdain for the travel-book formula, noting several tired conventions:

The author must begin with the excitements of the ocean voyage itself and devote at least a portion of a chapter to the thrill, so long anticipated, of setting foot on foreign soil. From this point on he should mix architecture and scenery with comment on philanthropies, skillfully work in a little history cribbed from Murray's guides, taking care to add a touch of sentiment or eloquence when the occasion permitted. If the essay or book required a little padding, it was always possible to retell an old legend or slip in an account of dangers surmounted in crossing the Alps. (831)

Significantly, while both critics lampoon the genre, they also indirectly validate its essence as a mix of varied narrative points of focus and interest, the very characteristics that readers appreciated. The rules rendered absurd and mind numbing by Marryat and Thorp could potentially produce enjoyable and lively reading experiences that mimic ideal tours. While acknowledging that some writers undoubtedly stuck to safe forms and perpetuated simplistic patterns, we may profit more significantly by considering why certain conventions prevailed, how travel writers employed them, and what they reveal about the expectations of the genre.[17]

Preparing to Leave

Although the travel book resists a tight, infallible definition, if we were to jump back to any decade of the nineteenth century, go to the bookstore or library in any city, and open a book of our choice, we could do so with a comfortable confidence in several basic expectations.[18] One of the most important of these would be the author's attempt to welcome us to a journey and to invite us along for the tour. A close relationship between travel writers and their readers was vital, and the best writers carefully cultivated and catered to readers to encourage at least the feeling of comradeship. It was a shared journey, and the most effective travel writers consciously allowed their readers to join the tour as active partners. As with any tour, we would need some sort of preparation, which could take the form of a formal preface or introduction or a more informal greeting in the opening paragraphs of the first chapter. Such introductory material, no matter its placement, reveals much not only about the genre but also about the relationship between writer and reader as touring companions. In the process of introducing themselves to readers, travel writers often bow to well-established traditions. In short, the openings of travel books serve as contracts between the two parties—and like most contracts, they contain basic forms and templates.

Writers, as their introductions often indicate, assume that their potential touring partners respect humility. Wilbur Fisk, for example, in his popular *Travels in Europe* (1838), which went through five editions in nine months, provides an outright apology for endeavoring to write a travel book in the first place: "What! Another book of travels! And that, too, describing the ground over which so many have travelled before! What good reason can a man of principle and of sound judgment give for such a publication?" (iii). Even as early as 1838, the pressure to justify adding to the pile of travel narratives to Europe compelled writers to acknowledge that they were part of a growing tide. This humble apology, however, was even then a stock one, and it encouraged, in turn, a standard justification. Fisk continues:

> If mere pleasure were to be communicated, I should not write on these subjects, which others can adorn more tastefully than myself; if mere description of foreign objects were the design, I should not delineate scenes which have been so often delineated and by pencils far more skilful than mine. But if any important truths, any facts connected with politics or morals, education or religion, can be wrought into the incidents of a journal so as to make them readable or acceptable, this is [the] most that I can hope. (v)

In his humble greeting, Fisk also reiterates one of the primary purposes of a nineteenth-century travel book: to instruct. We open a travel book to learn something about the world around us, and although other motivations enter our minds, the potential educational value remains paramount (the instruction convention is discussed below). Specifically, Fisk emphasizes that "pleasure" is not his concern, nor is simple "description" of objects, not because they have no inherent value but because he lacks the talent to render them effectively.

Bayard Taylor, the most prolific and adored travel writer of the mid–nineteenth century, masterfully establishes an inviting rapport with his readers. Like Fisk before him and Twain after, he graciously offers himself to readers, per convention, as the ever-humble narrator throughout his lengthy career. In the opening to *A Journey to Central Africa* (1854), for example, Taylor writes: "Although I cannot hope to add much to the general stock of information concerning Central

Africa, I may serve, at least, as an additional witness, to confirm or illustrate the evidence of others. Hence, the preparation of this work has appeared to me rather in the light of a duty than a diversion, and I have endeavored to impart as much instruction as amusement to the reader" (1–2). Taylor, while reiterating the need for information within his proposed tour, presumes no inherent value, no originality in that he promises only to corroborate other tourists' observations. He gives us this knowledge "in the light of a duty" rather than for his own benefit. Mark Twain would echo Fisk's and Taylor's conventional introductory format. In *The Innocents Abroad* he elevates pleasure as the primary goal of his proposed tour: "This book is a record of a pleasure-trip. If it were a record of a solemn scientific expedition, it would have about it that gravity, that profundity, and that impressive incomprehensibility which are so proper to works of that kind, and withal so attractive" (v).[19] Although his admitted purpose stands in opposition to that of Fisk, who attempts to offer "important truths," Twain also, it is crucial to note, recognizes conventional expectations of readers and graciously and humbly—if ironically—clarifies the type of tour to which he invites them.

Although these three writers are separated by intervals of roughly fifteen years (1838 to 1854 to 1869), they sound similar notes. Twain, by focusing on pleasure, does not negate the assumptions of instruction more explicit in most earlier texts; he merely chooses to set a different tone in his greeting, a tone that benefits from readers' familiarity with the more common and staid approaches of writers like Taylor and Fisk. Also, as the text of *The Innocents Abroad* bears out (as we will see later), Twain knew how to provide his touring partners with a wealth of instruction while also keeping them thoroughly amused. Such introductions allow authors to achieve two seemingly disparate but intertwined tasks: establishing authority while denying it. These humble narrators hope to win our approval by avoiding any indication that they will impose any dominion over us during what they hope will be, aesthetically, a shared tour.

In addition to finding a humble narrator as we open a travel book, we could also expect to meet an honest one. Trustworthiness and fidelity to fact were essential characteristics for any touring partner, and most writers would communicate their sincerity right away. Caroline Kirkland, in *Holidays Abroad* (1849), provides a helpful example: "My aim has been to give a simple, personal narrative, in order that, taking the reader with me through the medium of sympathy, I might succeed in suggesting what may be advantageously accomplished by the traveller. One should be willing sometimes to be a warning, though it is pleasanter to be an example; and telling the plain truth is apt to end in making us the one or the other" (1: v). "Truth," like "authenticity," advances a strong selling point for any tour. "Telling the plain truth" is an unparalleled virtue in travel writing, and examples of such claims are effusive. Like Kirkland, Taylor in *A Journey to Central Africa* proposes an honest touring experience: "My aim has been to furnish a faithful narrative of my own experience, believing that none of those embellishments which the imagination so readily furnishes, can equal the charm of the unadorned truth" (2). Travel writers were early proponents of realism (or at least the pretense of it); in fact, their livelihood depended on the impression that they delivered realistic presentations. As the similarities between Kirkland and Taylor help show, the promise of unsullied and uncompromising fidelity to fact was necessary. James Jackson Jarves provides an interesting and clever twist on the convention in the preface to his *Parisian Sights and French Principles Seen through American Spectacles* (1852): "I wish to take off my hat to my reader. A French bow would be more graceful, but it will take more time, and a greater flourish. I prefer to make his acquaintance with the plain but sincere Yankee nod. In bidding him good morning, I have only to say, that if he read these pages, he will find some truths frankly told, and some opinions frankly expressed" (5). Whether or not his audience would forgive Jarves his "frank(ly)" puns on the French, most likely they would appreciate his promises of truthfulness. His, and by extension his readers', identity would remain secure as he viewed always "with American spectacles" and maintained a "sincere Yankee nod" amid the flourishes of French society. Twain, again in the preface to *The Innocents Abroad,* reworks the honesty pose and, like Jarves, creates a strong sense of affiliation in his readers by emphasizing his honesty (and humility, for that matter):

> I make small pretense of showing any one how he *ought* to look at objects of interest beyond the sea—other books do that, and therefore, even if I were competent to do it, there is no need.
> I offer no apologies for any departures from the usual style of travel-writing that may be charged against me—for I think I

have seen with impartial eyes, and I am sure I have written at least honestly, whether wisely or not. (5)

As we have already touched on, standard practice—and good marketing sense—dictates that a travel narrator adopt a humble point of view in relation to his or her readers, and Twain accomplishes this task adroitly by insisting not only that he will not presume to condescend to us but also that he will not attempt any dissertation for which he may not be "competent." Although this passage contains evidence of Twain's rebellious character—an American defiantly taking "departures from the usual style" (read "usual" as *romantic*)—it also places him firmly within conventions established by his predecessors and contemporaries, the vast majority foregrounding their honesty and claiming their own "departures."

Sometimes the promise of honesty would tap into our more scurrilous interests while also being sensitive to genteel sensibilities. In one of the most widely read sea-adventure travel books of its time, *Two Years before the Mast* (1840), Richard Henry Dana, Jr., uses the preface to warn readers: "I have been obliged occasionally to use strong and coarse expressions, and in some instances to give scenes which may be painful to nice feelings; but I have very carefully avoided doing so, whenever I have not felt them essential to giving the true character of a scene" (1: xxii). Dana accomplishes two tasks here: first, he follows form and dutifully promises honesty, and second, he piques our interest by indicating that his rectitude demands potentially shocking content. John Ross Browne, in *Etchings of a Whaling Cruise* (1846), uses the same formula, writing that "a due regard to fidelity induces me to present the incidents and facts very nearly in their original rude garb. I have no faith in softening or polishing stern realities. Let them go before the world with all the force of truthfulness" (v). Invoking the virtue of honesty allowed nineteenth-century travel writers unprecedented latitude in a timid age, a freedom certainly not afforded to other genres. Travel writing's status as nonfiction combined with demands for authenticity to give writers an almost automatic integrity as well as virtual freedom to shock and appeal to sensational interests.

So far we have entered a tour with a humble and honest partner. There remains one more characteristic that we would require for the promise of a good experience: comradeship. Writers were willing to offer loyal friendship in abundance on the tour. Jarves, for example, closes the preface to *Parisian Sights* with the following invitation: "Having brought you, gentle reader, to the threshold of my apartment, your courtesy will not allow you to do less, for my hospitality, than to take off your hat, also, and walk in" (5). As welcome guests, we are encouraged to enter Jarves's home, to enter his narrative. Upon such a courteous gesture, we, Jarves would hope, cannot help but turn the page and thus begin our tour in the company of our newfound friend. Browne, likewise, offers another masterful greeting that, while sharing goodwill, also places readers on equal footing, thus reemphasizing the implied partnership of travel writing. His opening words in *Adventures in Apache Country* (1868) deserve quoting at length:

> I have almost forgotten through what uncomfortable part of the world the obliging reader and myself performed our last exploit in the way of a pleasure trip.[20] A foggy remembrance comes over me that it was over the barren *fjelds* of Norway, and through the treacherous bogs of Iceland. Assuming that we parted on friendly terms, and that we still entertain a kindly recollection of each other, I have now to offer a new programme of exploration and adventure, very different indeed from our last, but possessing the peculiar charms in the absence of accommodation for travellers, and extraordinary advantages in the way of burning deserts, dried rivers, rattlesnakes, scorpions, Greasers, and Apaches; besides unlimited fascinations in the line of robbery, starvation, and the chances of sudden death by accident. From the borders of the Arctic circle to Arizona the transition will at least afford us a new sensation of some sort; and if we fail to make the trip remunerative either in novelty of scenery or incident it will be our own fault. (11)

Throughout his formidable career, Browne was an especially adept touring partner who went to prodigious lengths to ensure in his readers a strong sense of personal and active involvement as they turn the pages of his narratives. His repetition of "our" and "we" helps to emphasize the partnership. In an additional bit of marketing genius, Browne plugs an earlier travel book, *The Land of Thor* (1868), by commenting on "our last exploit." This reference accomplishes two helpful tasks: first, if we did indeed take the previous tour of Scandinavia and the North Atlantic, then we are graciously welcomed on board for another tour and cannot help but enjoy the nostalgic connection between fellow tourists; and second, if we did not take the previous tour, we may then be encouraged to do so, and thereby join the community of tourists who "entertain a kindly recollection of each other." This is one of the distinct advantages that travel writers and readers have over their peers who make actual journeys rather than virtual ones; the virtual tourist can, indeed, go to *The Land of Thor* anytime he or she chooses. Browne's "programme"—a word often associated with a package tour—is thus timeless and wonderfully elastic. Browne closes this opening paragraph with a strong reiteration of the basic attachment potential of any travel book: the ability, at least aesthetically, to link writer and reader together in direct partnership. If we accept Browne's "programme," we can expect to share the freedom and the responsibility to make our virtual trip "remunerative either in novelty of scenery or incident," and if the tour fails, "it will be our own fault." Through this partnership, so often implied in the introductory paragraphs of travel books and reinforced within the texts themselves, both writers and readers benefited as they traveled the world. Writers could help build a loyal and supportive reading public, and readers could tour vicariously, in the company of a humble, honest, attentive friend.

Once we have made our introductions, we can move our hypothetical tour of travel-book convention into the texts proper. Having established a rapport with us, the travel writer, no matter the specific contexts of the narrative, must adhere to basic and overriding conventions that serve to define the genre. As the foregoing examples have implied, the travel book has three central requirements: to instruct, to entertain, and to comfort. The first two are the ostensible goals, but the more tacit need of readers for comfort as they travel the world is nonetheless vital to the popularity of the genre.

Instructing Readers

As we have seen briefly in the prefaces, writers knew well that, above all else, readers expected a travel book to educate. As a result, travel books in the nineteenth century were heavily laden with factual information—heights, weights, distances, populations, expenses, temperatures, and so forth—anything from average yearly rainfall in the

Holy Land to the number of cats in Constantinople. Although the pervasiveness of such material, often encyclopedic in presentation, distances or even annoys certain modern readers, we must recognize how central it was for nineteenth-century readers. In most cases, it does *not* amount to padding. The examples of instructive information are as numerous as the pages in travel books; one need only pick up any book and turn to any chapter. A few passages, nevertheless, may be helpful here. Taylor's *The Lands of the Saracen* (1855) contains a wealth of information, and one quick example may illustrate how Taylor, one of the best travel writers of his age, incorporates instructive material. In describing the Temples of Baalbec he writes: "The platform itself, 1,000 feet long, and averaging twenty feet in height, suggests a vast mass of stones, but when you come to examine the single blocks of which it is composed, you are crushed with their incredible bulk. On the western side is a row of eleven foundation stones, each of which is thirty-two feet in length, twelve in height, and ten in thickness, forming a wall three hundred and fifty-two feet long!" (168). It is hardly likely that Taylor carried with him a measuring tape; however, he clearly recognized that his readers wanted this specific information, even if cribbed from a guidebook or local guide. Taylor attempts, moreover, not only to impress upon his touring partners the immensity of the structure via its measurements but also to convey that the enormous blocks make "you" feel "crushed with their incredible bulk."

Factual information was not limited to guidebook recitations of dimensional details; it could also take the form of basic descriptions or how-to explanations. We could learn how to avoid certain customs regulations in Italy, how to find the best bargains in India, or, as in Francis Parkman's *The California and Oregon Trail* (1849), how to hunt buffalo in the American West. Parkman writes that the "method of hunting called 'running' consists in attacking the buffalo on horseback and shooting him with bullets or arrows when at full speed. In 'approaching' the hunter conceals himself, and crawls on the ground towards the game; or lies in wait to kill them" (71). With the goal of sharing discovery with readers and opening foreign cultures to them, writers could dismiss no bit of data out of hand as useless or negligible; therefore, readers could expect a wide variety of information, much of it subjective, much of it wholly dependable. In that context, travel books serve as valuable repositories of knowledge.

Often, if they could not fit certain information within the narrative itself, travel writers would use appendices, a common practice that nineteenth-century readers expected yet one for which Twain has received criticism from modern critics. Again Browne provides a helpful illustration. In *Etchings of a Whaling Cruise,* he adds a "History of the Whale Fishery" and a plethora of nautical terms and practices as well as how-to sections on the basics of whaling.[21] He justifies his decision to provide the lesson within the demands of the genre: "No correct idea can be formed of the process of capturing whales and trying out their blubber, without some knowledge of the instruments employed. I shall take pains to make my information on this subject as intelligible as possible to the 'unlearned' landsman, taking it for granted he is not versed in the mysteries of the craft" (51). Browne begins the lesson, complete with diagrams, by describing the harpoon and continues in depth for six pages. He also diligently explains the various processes of obtaining oil from a whale and offers extensive descriptions of the "try-works" and "cutting in." His explicit goal, of course, is not to turn readers, his partners, into whalers, but to allow them as much access as possible to that world, and travel books consistently assume that such instructive information is the vital key to such a goal.

Factual data and description did not provide the only devices for instruction; local history, legends, and anecdotes also helped to fill in the touristic experience. The best travel writers were able to weave such information into their chronicles without harming the flow of the tour itself. These narrative "asides," a term that seems the most helpful way to think of them, broaden the learning experience by moving beyond the singular activities of the narrator. By offering breaks in the journey, the anecdotal, historical, or cultural information could create a more complete picture of a specific location. Although they are most often too lengthy to quote here, asides were common practice and are easily found in any travel book. For general examples of the types of asides prevalent in texts, we could expect to encounter versions of famous historical events at the corresponding location—the eruption of Mount Vesuvius at Pompeii, the killing of Julius Caesar in Rome, the crucifixion of Christ in Jerusalem, and the death of Captain Cook in the Sandwich (Hawaiian) Islands—as well as famous (and not-so-famous) legends, ghost stories, and even jokes. All such information moves the text beyond the personal experience into a more textured picture of a place.

Twain proved to be especially adept at meeting the convention of instruction throughout his travel-writing career. Knowing well the importance of catering to reader expectations, he carefully incorporated educational material within all of his narratives. Although he readily accepted and even embraced standard travel-book formulas, he was by no means simply a conventional writer, choosing often to manipulate expectations for his readers' entertainment and his own satirical interests. He thus achieves a tenuous balance between following form and snubbing it. We have already examined how the preface to *The Innocents Abroad* matches common practice by establishing a humble and honest narrative stance from which to begin a tour. The preface for *Roughing It* also takes a customary tack:

> This book is merely a personal narrative, and not a pretentious history or a philosophical dissertation. It is a record of several years of variegated vagabondizing, and its object is rather to help the resting reader while away an idle hour than afflict him with metaphysics, or goad him with science. Still, there is information in the volume; information concerning an interesting episode in the history of the Far West, about which no books have been written by persons who were on the ground in person, and saw the happenings of the time with their own eyes. (iv)

If we had followed Twain from the earlier Old World tour in *The Innocents Abroad,* we would recognize certain elements in this preface. Once again he highlights his "eyes"; this time, however, in addition to reminding readers that he will serve sincerely as their eyes, he notes his special expertise. Twain was, after all, one of those who were "on the ground in person." Also, once again, he implies that the narrative avoids pretension and is a light volume—the picnicking of *The Innocents Abroad* has become "vagabondizing" in *Roughing It.* Even though he promises casual fare, he points out that the text does contain valuable information that has never been adequately recorded. Up to this point, Twain follows travel-book convention with precision. However, he continues, tongue in cheek: "Yes, take it all around, there is quite a good deal of information in the book. I regret this very much; but really it could not be helped: information appears to stew out of me naturally, like the precious ottar of roses out of the otter" (iv). Twain goes on to wish he could stop himself, but unavoidably he cannot help but "leak wisdom." His humorous manipulation is a telling one; of course it is simply one of countless examples of his engaging wit, but it is also evidence of his astute grasp of travel-book convention. He needs to "regret" the presence of information within *Roughing It* in order to set up his joke, strengthened by his readership's knowledge of convention, but we must also recognize that the information "stew[s]" out of him not "naturally," as he claims, but because the basic nature of the genre within which he is writing demands it. This passage nudges the convention gently without denying its relevance to the text.

Within his travel books, Twain uses this narrative ploy of both following and mocking the convention requiring instruction as a conscious strategy. A letter to Dan DeQuille (4 April 1875) illustrates that Twain did not disdain the use of information, material he often called "dry." In advising DeQuille how to write his own book, *The Big Bonanza* (1876), Twain states confidently: "Bring along *lots of dry statistics*—it's the very best sauce a humorous book can have. Ingeniously used, they just make a reader smack his chops in gratitude" (qtd. in Lewis xix). Like other travel writers, Twain splices a wealth of informative material into his narratives, and we can pick almost any page to find examples. In one instance from *The Innocents Abroad*, he writes a typical description of the Milan Cathedral: "I like to revel in the dryest details of the great cathedral. The building is five hundred feet long by one hundred and eighty wide, and the principal steeple is in the neighborhood of four hundred feet high. It has 7,148 marble statues, and will have upwards of three thousand more when it is finished. In addition, it has one hundred and thirty-six spires—twenty-one more are to be added" (180). Twain did not have a tape measure any more than Bayard Taylor did in the passage discussed earlier, and he certainly did not count the spires. He includes such data, however, not as filler, as modern readers too often assume, but as context and texture. Twain's accounts of well-known landmarks are extensive and precise for the most part, and the "details" of the Milan Cathedral represent a large and vital portion of his narrative tour. Like other writers, Twain incorporates a variety of instructive material beyond simply stated "dry statistics." In the same manner as Dana and Browne cited above, he provides textbook information. For example, in an addendum at the end of chapter 61 of *Roughing It,* Twain writes: "Some of the phrases in the above are mining technicalities, purely, and may be a little obscure to the general reader" (443). He follows by methodically defining the terms for all readers. Despite such faithful bows to convention, he was adept at satirizing them as well. On the same page as the addendum, he closes the chapter with the following: "Our wanderings were wide and in many directions; and now I could give the reader a vivid description of the Big Trees and the marvels of the Yo Semite—but what has this reader done to me that I should persecute him? I will deliver him into the hands of less conscientious tourists and take his blessing. Let me be charitable, though I fail in all virtues else" (443). Perhaps Twain did not care to write the description and was satisfied with the length of the chapter as it was, or perhaps he found it too well performed by his predecessors; in either case, the passage skirts the convention by stating that elaborate factual material would simply "persecute" readers. Such playful manipulations of convention prove highly effective for readers aware of the basic expectations targeted by his parody. This is a central pattern that Twain sets up in his preface. Another brief example may clarify his method. At the beginning of chapter 52, which centers on the science of silver mining in Nevada, Twain opens: "Since I desire, in this chapter, to say an instructive word or two about the silver mines, the reader may take this fair warning and skip, if he chooses" (376). Twain pretends disdain for dry facts, yet as a travel writer he wants to instruct just as much as his readers want to learn, so he includes in the chapter what he considers valuable information on silver mining, managing to accomplish two tasks: to provide "an instructive word or two" and to tease about normal reader expectations.

Such approaches are certainly not confined to *Roughing It.* In one instance, for example, in *The Innocents Abroad,* as Twain tours the Holy Land, specifically the village of Jaffa, he uses a variant of the same joke: "Jaffa has a history and a stirring one. It will not be discovered anywhere in this book. If the reader will call at the circulation library and mention my name, he will be furnished with books which will afford him the fullest information concerning Jaffa" (606). This time, rather than warn his readers about an upcoming chapter, Twain deletes the information altogether. He avoids giving readers the information they could rightly expect, but instead of ignoring the deletion, he mocks the convention that demands it. Moreover, he acknowledges readers' desires for such material (which is "stirring"), and in not satisfying it he covers himself, drolly, by referring to other sources. They need only mention his name to obtain it, so he is still, by proxy, providing instructive material; however, readers must do some of their own legwork.

Narrative asides proved to be Twain's favorite method to meet and simultaneously thwart instruction convention.[22] Twain rarely trusted the accuracy or validity of local anecdotes and legends, and he often mocked them within the narratives and questioned their authority. However, his skepticism did not prevent him from passing on to his readers an assortment of stories (from factual to fanciful, and all points in between) as instructive and entertaining material. One of the most engaging examples of such manipulation occurs in *A Tramp Abroad* as he shares with readers the legend pertaining to the origins of Frankfort, Germany:

> Frankfort is one of the sixteen cities which have the distinction of being the place where the following incident occurred. Charlemagne, while chasing the Saxons, (as *he* said,) or being chased by them, (as *they* said,) arrived at the bank of the river at dawn, in a fog. The enemy were either before him or behind him; but in any case he wanted to get across, very badly. . . . Presently he saw a deer, followed by her young, approach the water. He watched her, judging that she would seek a ford, and he was right. She waded over, and the army followed. So a great Frankish victory or defeat was gained or avoided; and in order to commemorate the episode, Charlemagne commanded a city to be built there, which he named Frankfort,—the ford of the Franks. None of the other cities where this event happened were named from it. This is good evidence that Frankfort was the first place it occurred at. (18)

For Twain, the actual facts behind the anecdotal legend are irrelevant. Tourists (and writers) will perpetuate the story nonetheless. This particular legend, seemingly omnipresent to Twain, provides fertile ground for his satirical plow, and he methodically deconstructs it by acknowledging multiple versions. His humorous treatment notwithstanding, the Charlemagne story is an interesting one—if unreliable —and, for those willing to believe any or all of it, an instructive one. The repetition of faulty legends or anecdotes served as a common target for Twain, and understandably so. Such asides allowed him to enjoy the best of both worlds. He could mine them for ironic treatment, and he could all the while fulfill his obligations to readers who craved such instruction.[23]

All in all, touring with Twain can be a highly instructive experience, and although he often uses his readers' desire for such information to set up his witticisms, he does so as he pays heed to the basic travel-book convention that requires instruction. His protestations against "dry facts" and his promises of light, pleasurable fare within his narratives merely whet his readers' appetites for what follows.

Entertaining Readers

In addition to expecting a travel book to teach, readers certainly wanted the experience to be an enjoyable one, so travel writers typically included as much emotional and physical stimulation as possible. Of course, instructive material, as we have seen, holds an explicit value in and of itself, especially for readers concerned about mastering basic information. Many of these readers would, perhaps, disparage obvious attempts to play to their lighter interests in amusements and fancies. Nonetheless, the best writers built into their narratives material designed to appeal to readers' conscious and subconscious needs for pleasure. Unlike instructive conventions, entertainment conventions offered narrators opportunities to establish personality and reinforce their role as touring partners who have a passion for life. Writers adept at establishing an enthusiastic and emotional tone could effectively bring any tour alive for their armchair partners.

One of the most popular entertainment conventions was the romantic reverie, for want of a better phrase. An effusive romantic reverie could be sparked by a plethora of visual stimuli. Natural wonders were the most popular, especially in tours of the American West and South Seas as well as the European Alps. Specifically, writers dutifully recorded their impressions in language that attempted to match the splendor of the natural scene itself. As early as 1827, the *American Quarterly Review* complained of the tendency of writers to overindulge in such reveries: "For those who write travels, there is a forcible temptation or apparent necessity to launch into raptures, or be struck motionless or dumb with amazement, at certain famous exhibitions of the picturesque in mountain or lake scenery; and they repeat ecstacies often before expressed in similar terms" ("Carter's" 552). There would be many more ecstasies to follow, many "expressed in similar terms." When it came to describing nature, writers rarely relied on subtlety or understatement, for they were trying to fascinate readers who depended on them to enliven any wondrous scene. The touring partners back home had only their narrators' eyes to see the world, and they certainly appreciated impressionistic musings, even if fanciful or over the top. Although many writers whose narratives contained illustrations could depend in part on the complementing woodcuts and engravings to help convey visually stunning scenes, ultimately they had to use their words to reflect emotional content. This was not a moment for minimalist sensibilities; it was show time. In his *Scenes and Scenery in the Sandwich Islands,* Jarves provides a typically abstract example of romantic reverie as he pictures for his touring partners a view from the mountains of Kauai:

> It was a spectacle that would have repaid the greatest toil; and was, doubtless, one of those rare combinations in the natural world, of the serenely grand and beautiful, shadowing forth the mysteries and sublimities of the all-creating power, which ever awaken a holy sentiment even in the coldest heart. The effect was overwhelming, and we gazed, spell-bound, in silent praise and admiration. . . . But we were resting on one of the sublimest monuments of God's creative fiat, far beyond the works of man. Around us, above and beneath, rose the mighty pinnacles of nature's glorious temple; the lovely and stupendous, the pleasing and terrible commingling in most perfect harmony. It was as if all spirits, pure and great, fair and base, had involuntarily united in an anthem to the Almighty. (226–27)

Such poetic euphoria and hyperbole were commonplace, and although Jarves and many others profess their "silent admiration," as writers they cannot remain silent; their touring partners depend on their articulation of feelings engendered by the scenery.[24] If ultimately no words can suffice, the travel writer is nevertheless under an obligation to try. Overwriting was thus a natural by-product of the genre's unremitting demand that writers dare not err on the side of cautious understatement as they bring the world to their readers.

As he did with instruction conventions, Twain worked within common entertainment patterns, using many standard gimmicks and often relying on trite romantic reveries.[25] Sentimental, exceedingly ornate descriptions of natural and human-made landmarks were standard fare, and although Twain often mocked such content (his most aggressive parody of mawkishness is his extended attack on "Grimes" [William Prime] in *The Innocents Abroad*), he also had his own enthusiasm and exclamation points ready for service. In *The Innocents Abroad,* in particular, Twain offers readers his most romantic impressions. France especially captured his imagination. For example, in describing the French countryside, he writes: "What a bewitching land it is!—What a garden!" After expounding rapturously on the beautiful orderliness of the landscape, he continues: "We had such glimpses of the Rhone gliding along between its grassy banks; of cosy cottages buried in flowers and shrubbery; of quaint old red-tiled villages with mossy mediæval cathedrals looming out in their midst; of wooded hills with ivy-grown towers and turrets of feudal castles projecting above the foliage; such glimpses of paradise, it seemed to us, such visions of fabled fairy-land!" (105). Twain's narrative reaction may match his touristic one; still, his description is stock romantic reverie shared with readers who desired that sort of enthrallment. He approaches Versailles in much the same manner: "Versailles! It is wonderfully beautiful! You gaze, and stare, and try to understand that it is real, that it is on earth, that it is not the Garden of Eden—but your brain grows giddy, stupefied by the world of beauty around you, and you half believe you are the dupe of an exquisite dream" (153). The French countryside is a "fairy-land" and Versailles a "Garden of Eden," and if Twain's writing seems to go a bit "giddy," we should understand that such emotional energy, even if appearing silly to stern critical eyes, can also be contagious for his readers, and thus entertaining. Such romanticism need not stand in opposition to Twain's realist credentials. Rather, these passages among others testify to his artistry. By balancing his shrewd cynicism with a dreamlike exuberance, Twain ensures that readers trust him on both counts.

Twain also recognized the comic potential of such romantic reveries, and he takes them on often in the Holy Land sections of *The*

Innocents Abroad, most notably in his use of William Prime and in his disdain for other "pilgrims." His mock sentimentality at the Tomb of Adam illustrates his satirical treatment of the same convention. Twain *gives way,* as he puts it, to "tumultuous emotion": "I leaned upon a pillar and burst into tears. I deem it no shame to have wept over the grave of my poor dead relative. Let him who would sneer at my emotion close this volume here, for he will find little to his taste in my journeyings through the Holy Land" (567). The last sentence, taken word for word from Prime's *Tent Life in the Holy Land* (1857)—a passage Twain quoted earlier—provides an outlandish mockery of what Twain considered to be truly mawkish sentimentalism. It is important to recognize that Twain does not disdain emotionalism so long as it comes across as sincere, but for him, Prime's language was too slippery with tears to be taken seriously, and it was thus open for parody. Another example, this time from *Roughing It,* deserves attention since it provides an interesting parallel to both Twain's description of Versailles and Jarves's reverie on the mountains of Kauai. While riding horseback on the island of Oahu, Twain comments aloud on the landscape spread out before his eyes. Giving "voice to his thoughts," he holds forth dramatically in a monologue:

> "What a picture is here slumbering in the solemn glory of the moon! How strong the rugged outlines of the dead volcano stand out against the clear sky! What a snowy fringe marks the bursting of the surf over the long, curved reef! How calmly the dim city sleeps yonder in the plain! How soft the shadows lie upon the stately mountains that border the dream-haunted Mauoa Valley! What a grand pyramid of billowy clouds towers above the storied Pari! How the grim warriors of the past seem flocking in ghostly squadrons to their ancient battlefield again— how the wails of the dying well up from the—" (467)

Twain stops himself midsentence as his horse sits down—"to listen, I suppose." In essence, this passage parallels the reverie at Versailles, but the degree to which this passage uses high-flown rhetoric carries it over the edge of reverie and plunges it down into sappy sentimentalism according to Twain. Clearly a conscious choice for Twain here, the self-mockery is evidenced by the exclamation points that end each declaration as well as the abrupt rejection of the reverie by none other than his horse. In addition, by using the horse as a respondent to his rhapsodizing, Twain installs himself, posed as the romantic traveler, as the object of the parody. It would seem that for Twain a fine—but vital—line separates legitimate reveries from illegitimate ones.

In a tour of nineteenth-century travel books, we could find in abundance other types of distinctive entertainment beyond the romantic reveries. Travel writers also tried to move their readers emotionally by capitalizing on the public's seemingly insatiable curiosity for the exotic and the sensational. The passion for "strange" peoples and customs, always common fare in travel writing, easily translated into a fascination with the morbid, and travel writers readily supplied content to meet this demand. We could certainly expect in our tour to be shocked and titillated. Specifically, a preoccupation with death and violence is prevalent in tours to Europe as many writers stretched Irving's interests in the "shadowy grandeurs of the past" to macabre lengths.[26] For example, John Ross Browne, in *An American Family in Germany* (1866), takes us through a lesson in medieval torture practices:

> When the accused was convicted, which was nearly always the case, he was fastened to a strong wooden frame. A collar of iron was screwed around his head, which was dragged back by other screws. In this position, unable to move the eighth of an inch, a piece of hollow iron with closed claws was inserted in his mouth. A spring was touched. The claws sprang open and forced his jaws wide apart. A pair of pincers, with sharp teeth on the end, was then thrust into the tube, his tongue gripped by the roots and torn out, a maimed and bleeding mass. (86–87)

Such a graphic description, protected from censure due to its presentation in the guise of instruction, would shock even the most worldly of readers in the nineteenth century. Its horror could both appease reader interest in the morbid and appeal to a well-established assumption in American popular culture that European history was rife with such atrocities. As readers toured scenes of unspeakable carnage, they could also reassure themselves that such things could not occur in the United States (the delusory nature of such assumptions is beyond the scope of this discussion). Browne continues this particular lesson for five pages, carefully detailing all the instruments of torture (in a similar fashion to his cataloging of whaling implements in *Etchings of a Whaling Cruise* discussed above).

Browne was by no means alone in his penchant for the morbid. In *Pencillings by the Way* (1836), Nathaniel Parker Willis visits the public burial ground in Naples and shares the experience: "I could see all the horrors of the scene but too distinctly. Eight corpses, all of grown persons, lay in a confused heap together, as they had been thrown in one after another in the course of the day. The last was a powerfully made, gray old man, who had fallen flat on his back, with his right hand lying across and half covering the face of a woman" (96). Graveyards and catacombs became highly popular tourist sights for Americans touring Europe, and their wide if morbid appeal, however grisly, is evidenced by the copious records of visits to them within narratives. For readers new to nineteenth-century travel books to the Old World, the prevalence of this type of material is striking. Oddly, writers often couched their gothic tours within a moral framework, perhaps to shield themselves from charges of making gratuitous forays into violence and mayhem. In his tours of open graves, catacombs, and lunatic asylums in Palermo and Constantinople, Willis usually follows their descriptions with long-winded moral discourses on the miseries of death and the cruelties initiated by corrupt European culture. In so doing, he and others helped to solidify their moral superiority while also feeding their prurient interests. Writers were able to create a comfortable perspective from which to view the unsavory, though compelling, behaviors of other cultures, and by disingenuously placing such material in instructive contexts (as opposed to the more accurate vulgar contexts) they could protect themselves and readers from admitting their complicity.

One of the most famous sights was the Paris Morgue, visited by countless American tourists. In *Parisian Sights,* Jarves offers us a glimpse inside: "It was THE MORGUE, a name which, like that of Judas, stands by itself, the sole representative of its genus, species, and kind throughout the world. . . . I entered, and saw three corpses, behind a glass partition, naked, with the exception of waist cloths, and laid out upon inclined slabs, something like butcher's blocks. Tiny streams of water were directed over them to keep them fresh" (49–50). Jarves follows this passage by denouncing the indecency of Parisian officials for allowing the public to view such a morbid scene because it made a "public spectacle of the naked bodies." Despite his protestations and apparently unaware of the irony, Jarves was fully willing to add to this "spectacle" by sharing it with his readers and even conjuring up the horrific image of the bodies lying on "butcher's blocks." Like many other writers, he denounces customs while helping to perpetuate them. He adds to the picture by listing statistics for 1851, during which the Morgue displayed "three hundred and seventy-one bodies . . . and seven fragments of limbs" (50). Jarves also addresses prostitution in Paris with the same clinical detail, and lascivious interest. Armed with data tables, he shares a wealth of information, including the number of registered prostitutes each year (3,588 in 1832), their reasons for choosing the profession (poverty, abandonment), their ages (from ten to sixty), and their educational levels. He closes the section by discussing sententiously the importance of female virtue.

The urge to delve into the sensational for its intrinsic entertainment value is one of the few conventions of travel writing that Twain did not expressly satirize, which makes it conspicuous. Like so many tourists before him, Twain visited the macabre sights that had become staples for tourists and travelogues, of which the Paris Morgue and the Capuchin catacombs in Sicily were paramount. In *The Innocents Abroad,* his description of the Morgue provides a nice parallel to Jarves's and helps to illustrate the conventionality of such tours:

Next we went to visit the Morgue, that horrible receptacle for the dead who die mysteriously and leave the manner of their taking off a dismal secret. We stood before a grating and looked through into a room which was hung all about with the clothing of dead men; coarse blouses, water-soaked; the delicate garments of women and children; patrician vestments, hacked and stabbed and stained with red; a hat that was crushed and bloody. On a slanting stone lay a drowned man, naked, swollen, purple; clasping the fragment of a broken bush with a grip which death had so petrified that human strength could not unloose it— mute witness of the last despairing effort to save the life that was doomed beyond all help. A stream of water trickled ceaselessly over the hideous face. (132–33)

With evocative detail ("delicate garments of women and children" and "doomed beyond all help") and sensational language ("hacked and stabbed and stained with red"), Twain creates a compelling and tragic picture, a spectacle. Again, like Jarves and others before (and after) him, Twain offers a commentary on the sight's moral incongruity, implying that it was inappropriate to make the misfortune of others a subject of entertainment. He closes the tour with an indictment:

> Men and women came, and some looked eagerly in, and pressed their faces against the bars; others glanced carelessly at the body, and turned away with a disappointed look—people, I thought, who live upon strong excitements, and who attend the exhibitions of the Morgue regularly, just as other people go to see theatrical spectacles every night. When one of these looked in and passed on, I could not help thinking—"Now this don't afford you any satisfaction—a party with his head shot off is what *you* need." (133)

Twain's indignation at the coldness with which some tourists view the horrors of the Morgue aside, he shares the spectacle with his readers, who are glancing likewise into a theatrical production, but this one of his creation. One of several tours into the macabre, this passage, along with others, allows Twain's readers to peek into the dark underbelly of Europe to satisfy their curiosity and reaffirm their convictions that Europe was, all in all, a society permeated with decay and death.[27]

Comforting Readers

The ability of travel writers to instruct and entertain largely determined their success within the genre, but underlying those two explicit purposes was another requirement equally crucial in establishing and maintaining a close rapport between touring partners: a tour should be comfortable. Travel, with all its promises of encountering the excitements of the new, exotic, and strange, can also initiate a fear of those encounters. As tourists roam the world, they must inevitably face behaviors and beliefs that challenge or even offend their own. The subsequent discomfort may undermine the search for a pleasurable and self-serving touristic experience. Accordingly, most writers developed coping mechanisms to pad the emotional bumps that often interrupted their tours.

In overwhelming numbers, American travel writers tapped into a sense of national identity as a device to defray or counterbalance awkward, challenging moments. Narratives are filled with overt and veiled references assuring readers that the United States was, after all, the best country in the world in which to live.[28] They could easily rely on appeals to a shared nostalgia for home—its values, natural wonders, and customs—and on common prejudices toward other peoples and cultures. The key to comfort in any tour is for the tour guide (the narrator) to transport tourists to the fascinations of faraway lands without challenging their complacency and confidence. Yes, readers yearned to learn through travel and to be entertained along the way, but they also wanted to avoid being discommoded or losing confidence in the goodness and righteousness of their particular home.

The ideals of the travel book supposedly ask for objectivity; in practice, however, writers, like their readers, are far from impartial. The simplest and most powerful strategy for comforting readers was to compare the foreign with the familiar. There is a practical reason for making direct or indirect comparisons between tourist sights and home sights, of course. By juxtaposing the known with the unknown, writers could provide a clear, common point of reference, but such narrative tools also could produce other, less obvious benefits. Comparisons helped to delineate invidious distinctions between "us" and "them."[29] Comparisons to home could come in a multitude of forms, but three types deserve special attention: natural landscape, politics, and religion. It should come as no surprise that most often in any direct comparison, America's natural beauty, its democracy, and its dominant Protestantism fared well.

Let us start by returning to Irving's *The Sketch-Book,* in "The Author's Account of Himself," wherein Irving captures a prevailing sentiment of nineteenth-century American tourists in relation to the American natural landscape. He writes that "on no country have the charms of nature been more prodigally lavished" and goes on to expound the virtues of those "charms":

> Her mighty lakes, like oceans of liquid silver; her mountains, with their bright aerial tints; her valleys, teeming with wild fertility; her tremendous cataracts, thundering in their solitudes; her boundless plains, waving with spontaneous verdure; her broad deep rivers, rolling in solemn silence to the ocean; her

trackless forests, where vegetation puts forth all its magnificence; her skies, kindling with the magic of summer clouds and glorious sunshine;—no, never need an American look beyond his own country for the sublime and beautiful of natural scenery. (10)

The energy present in this passage serves as a striking contrast with the "shadowy grandeurs of the past" that dominate Irving's romantic musings on Europe. In his description of the natural beauty of America, he highlights the vitality of life—"teeming with wild fertility" and "spontaneous verdure." If American tourists went out into the rest of the world, especially Europe, with insecurities about their cultural and intellectual status, they could at least be highly confident in the potential of the land itself, so when opportunities afforded themselves to showcase a point of national pride, travel writers often took them. An example from Bayard Taylor should help affirm this point. In *Views A-Foot* (1846), he describes the Odenwald, a heralded portion of Germany's Black Forest: "It reminded me of our forest scenery at home. The principal difference is, that our trees are two or three times the size of theirs" (69). Freudian implications aside, we can recognize that Taylor takes a quick opportunity under the guise of instructive clarification to celebrate American forests; does he mean forests in the Carolinas, upstate New York, or the redwoods of California? It does not matter. "Home" is the key word, and the pleasure this comparison may bring to readers does not require detail; during our tour of Germany (along with Taylor and his contemporary readers), all we need to know is that "our" trees are bigger.

Twain made extensive use of natural comparisons, and like other writers, he capitalized on their implicit potential to stroke the pride of his touring partners. We can consider one of his most effective comparisons from *The Innocents Abroad* as he tours Lake Como in Italy and uses Lake Tahoe in Nevada as his American reference point. For Twain, the waters of Como are "clearer than a great many lakes, but how dull its waters are compared with the wonderful transparence of Lake Tahoe!" Although he continues at length with a humorous exercise in self-conscious hyperbole, the larger cultural point of the comparison remains intact. He concludes, noting that "Como would only seem a bedizened little courtier in that august presence" (204). Thus, according to Taylor and Twain, Europe's natural landscape is attractive only if one prefers smaller trees and duller lakes than those representative of America. Europe is not the only region that suffers by such comparisons. Later, in his tour of the Holy Land, Twain brings up Tahoe again in reference to the Sea of Galilee, writing that the latter "is not so large a sea as Lake Tahoe by a good deal—it is just about two-thirds as large. And when we come to speak of beauty, this sea is no more to be compared to Tahoe than a meridian of longitude is to a rainbow" (507). Although it actually provides little informative value for readers trying to picture the Sea of Galilee, Twain's unequivocal assessment allows for a sense of pride and re-asserts, over forty years later, Irving's unbridled confidence. In other words, if anyone prefers to see nature at its most wondrous, he or she need only step out, metaphorically, into the backyards of America. It is a comforting notion.

Next to natural beauty, no other point of comparison encouraged more hubris than democracy, and writers took ample opportunities to tout their republicanism. All American writers in Europe professed to be aware of what they perceived as the political corruption and injustice of Europe. Caroline Kirkland, in her *Holidays Abroad* (1849), after commenting on the grace and opulence of London, pauses to observe:

> I was ever conscious of the truth, that much of this splendor is the result of an unjust and oppressive inequality of condition, in this land, so favored of Heaven. I felt all this; but the scene as it was made an indelible impression, and I shall ever think of it as a model of what may be done, and, in our own country at least, without any of the attendant evils which seem but too pertinaciously to dog the steps of whatever is best and most glorious in England, and especially London. (103)

The inequalities created by European monarchies became emblematic of the ruin and failure of Old World society as a whole, and American travel writers could not share with readers the glory of European accomplishments without making asides on the injustice that made them possible. The Kirkland passage also indicates the absolute confidence many Americans had in the potential of their own political system, a sensibility that pervaded narratives throughout the century. Although Kirkland's tone is sad and reflective, most often travel writers were belligerent and even aggressive. "Tyranny" is a word repeated often, and much of the analytical commentary on political and social issues invokes passionate, righteous indignation. Like the romantic reveries we have already discussed, these appeals to emotion could arouse the reader's reactions. Taylor, again from *Views A-Foot,* tries to provoke similar feelings in his touring partners. In noting a group of miners protesting in the London streets, he comments: "It made my blood boil to hear those tones, wrung from the heart of poverty by the hand of tyranny" (36). In ostensibly reporting a street protest, Taylor inserts himself into the scene and speaks out the assumed attitude of his American readers. As a result, the crux of the narrative moment is his outrage—his boiling blood—not the impoverished "tones" of the miners. Willis, in *Pencillings by the Way,* upon observing the sufferings of the working classes in France, states: "We *apprehend* oppressive measures in our country with sufficient indignation and outcry; but to see the result upon those who bear their burdens till they are galled into the bone, is enough to fire the most unwilling blood to resentment. . . . Thank God! Our own country is yet free from the scourges of Europe" (9). By eliciting pity and anger for the oppressed citizens of France, Willis both establishes the superiority of his and his readers' moral grounding and celebrates America's democratic freedom. As readers made their tour by armchair, they could find comfort in his observations and quietly rejoice in their own political good fortune.

Twain, likewise, carefully keeps in touch emotionally with his touring partners at home with prideful Americanisms. Early in *The Innocents Abroad,* as the *Quaker City* approaches Gibraltar, the tourists are distracted by the sight of a "stately ship":

Africa and Spain were forgotten. All homage was for the beautiful stranger. While every body gazed, she swept superbly by and flung the Stars and Stripes to the breeze! Quicker than thought, hats and handkerchiefs flashed in the air, and a cheer went up! She was beautiful before—she was radiant now. Many a one on our decks knew then for the first time how tame a sight his country's flag is at home compared to what it is in a foreign land. To see it is to see a vision of home itself and all its idols, and feel a thrill that would stir a very river of sluggish blood! (64)

Just as he is about to bring readers to one of the most renowned geo-graphical oddities in the world, the first sight of the Old World, he pauses for a substantive, purely American celebration. Rarely is Twain so effusive, and many writers engaged in foreign travel introduce this particular type of patriotic description as they embrace (or create) the opportunity to spread over readers a security blanket of red, white, and blue. Just as these American tourists are gaining their first sight of continental Europe, they exhibit the greatest joy at seeing a glorious reminder of home; in their salute to the flag, the Old World can only be "forgotten." Although the ship passes and the tourists continue their journey, the powerful symbol of this "vision of home and all its idols" lingers, always symbolically at their sides.

Allied to political smugness was another common point of com-parison: religion. The overwhelming majority of American tourists were Protestants, and in an age of ignorance and distrust, attacks upon Catholicism run rampant in their narratives. These comparisons of religious practices and rituals served the same purpose as those of natural beauty and political systems. Despite their specific relevance, they engendered pride in Protestant readers and reasserted commonly held beliefs in the moral and theological degradation of Roman Ca-tholicism.[30] Willis provides a representative passage as he describes a mass performed by the pope: "[He] entered by a door at the side of the altar. With him came a host of dignitaries and church servants, and, as he tottered round in front of the altar, to kneel, his cap was taken off and put on, his flowing robes lifted and spread, and he was treated in all respects, as if he were the Deity himself. In fact, the whole service was the worship, not of God, but of the pope" (64). Willis's description, especially words like "dignitaries" and "ser-vants," parallels those directed toward monarchies, an implicit con-nection that intensified Protestant disdain. His bias against the pope who "tottered round" perhaps comforted like-minded readers by jus-tifying long-held prejudices. In short, this passage offers not an objec-tive description of a Catholic mass but a reinforcement of Protestant American stereotypes.

Although the ostensible purpose of travel is to learn of new and different ideas and customs, more often it permits tourists simply to substantiate their own. In the context of perpetuating religious stereotyping, writers employed a variety of images. In an especially popular trope, anti-Catholic writers would carefully counter the ornate riches of cathedrals with the wretched conditions of the peasantry who worshiped there. "There can be no greater contrast," Willis writes, "than that seen in catholic churches, between the splendor of architecture, renowned pictures, statues and ornaments of silver and gold, and the crowd of tattered, famished, misery-marked, worshipers that throng them. I wonder it never occurs to them, that the costly pavement upon which they kneel might feed and clothe them" (72). Such a juxtaposition was a ready-made symbol not only for devout Protestantism but for republicanism as well, since the Catholic Church was often closely allied with class-ridden political institutions, and many American tourists viewed them with equal distrust and contempt.[31] Thirty years after Willis's remarks, Twain would rework the same image in *The Innocents Abroad*. Upon entering a cathedral in Venice, Twain writes,

> All about that church wretchedness and poverty abound. At its door a dozen hats and bonnets were doffed to us, as many heads were humbly bowed, and as many hands extended, appealing for pennies—appealing with foreign words we could not understand, but appealing mutely, with sad eyes, and sunken cheeks, and ragged raiment, that no words were needed to translate. Then we passed within the great doors, and it seemed that the riches of the world were before us! (257)

Of course, one reason so many writers in the nineteenth century commented on such a striking and pathetic contrast is that it was often evident. There is no doubt that poverty plagued European city streets and that many churches displayed staggering wealth, yet the carefully constructed language that captures these scenes reflects the expectations of Protestant American tourists in Catholic Europe. Twain provides a good test case. This passage, in particular, represents Twain at his most melodramatic, and the emotionalism of his language mimics that of other sentimental writers, such as William Prime. Consciously trying to elicit pity and outrage in his readers, Twain constructs the picture with stock pathos as the poor approach him (and his readers) with "heads humbly bowed," "sad eyes," and "sunken cheeks." The beggars' needs are so painfully clear in this scene as to render language barriers no longer pertinent, since "no words were needed to translate." He follows with the cinching picture of "the riches of the world" within the cathedral, and thus within Catholicism on the whole. Indeed, throughout much of *The Innocents Abroad,* Twain finds beggars thoroughly annoying and worthy of little sympathy or sentiment. Here, however, the potential of the pathetic image to cater to audience expectations proved too great to resist. In this context, his melodrama is less an example of his hypocrisy than of his willingness to capitalize on a prevalent convention to comfort readers. Twain continues, noting that, because of the Catholic Church's desire to build magnificent cathedrals, Italy is "one vast museum of magnificence and misery" (258). He closes with a carefully constructed comparison: "All the churches in an ordinary American city put together could hardly buy the jeweled frippery in one of her hundred cathedrals. And for every beggar in America, Italy can show a hundred—and rags and vermin to match" (258). No matter the beauty of cathedrals to which tourists flocked in vast numbers; the edifices could be viewed as perversions of Christian ideals because their "jeweled frippery" came at the expense of charity. Later, after several attacks on monks and priests in general, Twain makes his most obvious connection to the assumed religious fervor of his readers. In recognizing the good works of Dominican friars, he points out that their unselfishness would certainly "save their souls though they were bankrupt in the true religion—which is ours" (261). Given the context of the surrounding material that prompts this assertion, it is hard to believe that he is being ironic here. Moreover, this passage appears long before Twain exploits himself at length in his role as a "sinner" opposed to the "pilgrims" as the tour makes its way through the Holy Land. Although he meticulously emphasizes his Protestantism in Europe, he later separates himself from its most obvious practitioners in the Holy Land. While his target is ostensibly the hypocrisy that derives from their "true religion," we should note that Catholicism outside of Europe is no longer a conventional target for American tourists; Twain, in moving to a different cultural context, has simply switched literary objectives. As such, this is a potentially troubling passage for modern readers; although Twain (Clemens) was never an especially religious man, Twain (tourist) aligns himself with his Protestant readers and their "true religion," emphasizing the point with a dash to highlight the connection and celebrate Protestant self-righteousness—"ours." In the touring process, then, Protestant readers could reaffirm their perceptions of the democratic benevolence of their own religion and rest easy in their piety, and, moreover, feel confident that their narrating partner agreed with them. Twain was simply one of many to capitalize on such authorial expediency.

In tours of non-European countries, anti-Catholicism is much less common; however, another convention of comfort manifests itself in travels westward into the New World and deserves attention. If we embark upon any of numerous tours looking westward, we encounter more racial prejudices, especially in terms of "savagery" and its antithetical term, "civilization." American travelers to Europe, no matter how irreverent they were about contemporary conditions, were nonetheless confident that European culture at its highest represented the most formidable civilization the world had ever known. In turn, many confidently believed that the United States was its heir designate. A combination of European achievements and American improvements—natural landscape, democracy, and Protestantism— would inevitably produce an even higher civilization in the New World. This manifest confidence, however, often put tourists at odds with native peoples and customs, especially as more and more tourists and settlers moved westward in North America and into the South Seas. The most common paradigm for travel books in this context was to counter the implied "civilized" world of Euro-Americans with the supposed "savagery" (or "barbarism") of native populations. It is important to note that for most nineteenth-century tourists, "civilization" was synonymous with "white," and the level of advancement granted to any part of the world was in direct proportion to the amount of white influence—the more white, the more civilized. Travel books touring westward are rife with such observations. For example, Francis Parkman, in *The California and Oregon Trail* (1849), defines the natives of an "Ogillallah" village as "thorough savages" and notes that "neither their manners nor their ideas were in the slightest degree modified by contact with civilization" (176). Parkman, an early traveler west, reveals an attitude central to popular perceptions about native American peoples on the whole, an attitude easily extended to South Sea Island cultures. James Jackson Jarves, in *Scenes and Scenery in the Sandwich Islands,* draws from another common synonym for civilization, "Christianity," to symbolize beneficial Euro-American influence on native populations. In attempting to characterize Hawaiians, Jarves provides an overview of their Malaysian ancestry, claiming they were "sensual beyond description; lying and treacherous to friend and foe; a warm, excitable imagination, and docile to instruction; by turns a child or adult in pleasures and passions—weeping the one moment, the other reveling with boisterous mirth; in short, a creature of base sentiments, more like a man who, under the influence of intoxicating gas, acts out that which is uppermost in his nature, than a human being endowed with moral feelings" (182–83). As offensive as his patronizing definition of Malaysian-Hawaiian characteristics is, Jarves's racist assumptions were nonetheless common. To clarify his conclusions about natives, he makes a direct comparison between Malaysian heritage and that of the Anglo-Saxon: "Our forefathers [were] off-shoots of the noblest race, the Caucasian; cruel heathens but bold, free, and intelligent; sacrificing human victims in obedience to their priests, but, in domestic relations, chaste and affectionate. If their animal passions were strong and conspicuous, their virtues also shone out brightly, and they proved themselves a thinking race" (183). Such a comparison would be laughable and easily dismissed if it were not representative of such a common feature of nineteenth-century travel writing. Although such pernicious racism was rarely so clearly laid out on one page, this attitude was no less pervasive. As with the anti-Catholicism of narratives to Europe, such comparisons reaffirm prejudices and encourage complacency. Jarves tempers any potentially negative traits of Anglo-Saxon forebears with a positive spin: "cruel heathens" but "bold, free, and intelligent." And if they performed human sacrifices, they did so only because their "priests" made them do it (see anti-Catholicism above). Jarves closes out his dissertation by warning Christian missionaries not to expect too much progress from the Hawaiians. In the end, although he acknowledges the difficulties Euro-Americans face in bringing civilization to the South Seas, he hopes that with earnest efforts someday the "remaining dark spots may be washed white" (190).

John Ross Browne, on the other hand, provides a refreshing escape from the normal racist assumptions. In his *Adventures in Apache Country* (1868) he mocks the popular notions of his contemporaries and predecessors, undermining their use of the term "civilization." In this instance, Browne describes his feelings after being cheated in a trade by a group of Pimo Indians: "It was gratifying at all events to know that the Pimos were rapidly becoming a civilized people. Under these circumstances we thought it advisable to pursue our journey without further waste of time" (128). Instead of following typical patterns, Browne humorously demonstrates that "civilization" promotes dishonesty; the Pimos, in this case, in becoming more advanced, were also becoming more treacherous and better cheaters. He continues this point later in the tour by speculating how a South Sea Islander might react to life in Nevada. Using this reversed point of view, he writes: "Why do [whites] send missionaries to the Fejee islands and leave their own country in such a dreadful state of neglect? The Fejeeans devour their enemies occasionally as a war measure; the white man swallows his enemy all the time without regard to measure" (362).[32] Twain, as we should have come to expect in our tour of conventions, both follows popular racial assumptions in regard to "civilization" and "savagery" and also manipulates them. Although his condescension is not placed universally upon all native Americans, Twain, in *Roughing It*, often uses negative descriptions, especially for a tribe he calls the "Goshoots" (actually the Gosiute).[33] The violence implicit in his term (*go shoot* Indians) is unnerving. He notes that they lived "far from any habitation of white men" and were subsequently "the wretchedest type of mankind" he had ever seen (146). Although no other such examples match Twain's disdain here, other disparaging remarks are scattered throughout the narrative. Twain, like Browne, however, recognizes that the attempt to civilize nonwhite populations was not an inherently noble endeavor. For example, while discussing the possible future for the Hawaiians, Twain states that "contact with civilization and the whites has reduced the native population from *four hundred thousand* (Captain Cook's estimate) to *fifty-five thousand* in something over eighty years!" (424). For the Hawaiians, white civilization and its Christianity mainly offered death. He makes a similar point in *Following the Equator* twenty-five years later, observing that white civilization has developed superior skills at limiting the numbers of dark-skinned peoples: "The white man knew ways of reducing the native population 80 per cent in 20 years. The native had never seen anything as fine as that before" (208). Twain's sarcastic inversion of the "fine" population-control methods of disease and war represents a more caustic tone but not a new idea. He closes this discussion of the disastrous effects of white presence among aboriginal peoples in Australia by redressing the long-held assumptions of Euro-American "civilization": "There are many humorous things in the world; among them the white man's notion that he is less savage than the other savages" (213). Although Twain in his narratives capitalized on the prejudices of his companions at home by viewing many nonwhite cultures with derision and condescension, his adherence to this popular convention was by no means absolute. He was equally capable of questioning and mocking racist assumptions, and in so doing he could presumably unsettle readers' complacency in their superiority.

American readers of the nineteenth century had a powerful need to define their place and identity in relation to—or, more frequently, in opposition to—the rest of the world. Travel books recorded and shared touring experiences that reflect this desire. In reference to the Old World, many Americans felt a contradiction between wanting to respect the accomplishments of its cultures and wanting to debunk them, and travel writers often accomplished a balancing act of these impulses. Writers could not denigrate all that they saw and thereby risk losing the perception of objectivity. Likewise, they could not seem overly impressed with European grandeur, appearing subservient. Their focus, then, most often became Europe's past with an inherent confidence that the United States represented a more idyllic present and future. In looking toward the other horizon, travel books focusing on the New World and, by extension, the South Seas most often sought to define themselves by dismissing the accomplishments and integrity of native cultures, or, in a more benign condescension, viewing them as simplistic and romantically alluring as a new Eden. As self-appointed messengers of a new world order, nineteenth-century Euro-American tourists typically patronized the peoples they encountered, and as representatives of what they saw as a beneficent civilization on the rise they provided a strong cultural framework for the aggressive late-nineteenth-century political imperialism.

Twain was remarkably adept at keeping his armchair touring counterparts safe among foreigners. He carefully allowed readers to feel at home in strange lands by reassuring them of their innate superiority as Americans, both by virtue of the natural beauty of their homeland and by the righteousness of their white-Protestant-democratic society. But he did not always remain wholly true to formula. Although he was clearly desirous of meeting his audience's expectations, he was also willing to challenge conventional perceptions to enhance his humor and satire. In so doing, Twain was often able to nudge his readers' assumptions under the veil of laughter.

By allowing people to travel the world safe in their existing world-view, writers proved the correctness of Ralph Waldo Emerson's assessment in "Self-Reliance" that "traveling is a fool's paradise." The comforts provided by vicarious tourism, combined with its instructive and entertaining features, helped to ensure the genre's success throughout the century even as growing numbers of Americans made actual tours. Travel writers and their readers back home reorganized the world and defined it on thoroughly American terms.

Coming Home

As readers reached the end of any narrative tour, they would expect a friendly and assuring farewell from their expedition leader, an epilogue of sorts closing out the tour and welcoming them back home. Like the prefatory greetings discussed earlier, the closing paragraphs of travel books were highly formulaic. Of course, structurally and symbolically, the last chapter (or paragraphs or epilogue proper) needed to finish the trip itself and provide concluding remarks based on the just-completed experience. Often the closings reiterated intentions set out in the introductory remarks, and writers consciously reassumed their humble, honest, and friendly demeanor. For example, in *Parisian Sights,* Jarves closes in the same manner as he begins, with a quiet bow to his readers: "If I have succeeded in making a single one of my fellow citizens at once more patriotic and more charitable, with a juster appreciation of the causes which make nations differ, I shall feel that my experience has not been without its reward" (264). He thus makes overt the implicit purpose of travel books in the nineteenth century, although it might appear antithetical to the explicit purposes of travel and travel writing: to increase one's appreciation not of the world but of *home.* For Jarves and so many others, patriotism was the primary goal of travel. Taylor offers a similar sentiment, although he is more subtle. In winding up *At Home and Abroad* (first series), he writes: "As I look up from this page, and see, through the open window, *my own trees* tossing the silver lining of their leaves to the summer wind, and the peaceful beauty of the vales and blue hills stretching beyond, I know that no tropic island, no place on a Mediterranean shore, no advantage of wealth and position in the great capitals of Europe, could ever tempt me to give up the name, the rights, and the immunities of an American Citizen" (500). Taylor learned foremost that he belongs at home, the message his touring partners in their armchairs presumably always wanted to receive. As exciting as world tourism may be, writers insisted that they were nonetheless consistently happy to be home, which was, as noted by Adelaide Hall in *Two Travelers in Europe* (1898), "the most precious spot on earth, after all!" (510).

Twain mastered this "no place like home" closing. *The Innocents Abroad* has essentially two concluding chapters, beginning with chapter 61 and his article for the *New York Herald*,[34] which serves as an overview (an "obituary" and "exhaustive summing up") of the *Quaker City* excursion, and ending with the conclusion proper, a more introspective reminiscence of the tour. In evaluating the behavior of the tourists abroad, Twain notes: "We always took care to make it understood that we were Americans—Americans!" (645). He illustrates both his understanding of American obnoxious conceit and the implicit need for strong home identity, and although he laughs at the tourists' pomposity he is by no means wholly dismissive. If humorous, such self-indulgence is no less natural, and for the new Tourist Age, it becomes in the end a sign of ascendancy. Like so many other travel writers, he reiterates this sentiment in the closing pages: "We did not care any thing about any place at all. We wanted to go home" (647). In the final paragraph of *A Tramp Abroad* he offers his most expressive opinion of travel abroad: "I think that short visits to Europe are better for us than long ones. The former preserve us from becoming Europeanized; they keep our pride of country intact, and at the same time they intensify our affection for our country and our people" (580). Again, the main goal of the narrative tour is to heighten one's love for home. All in all, perhaps *Roughing It* best captures the overarching moral for tourists in general: "If you are of any account, stay at home" (570).

Forms and conventions prevalent in nineteenth-century travel books reveal much about the expectations of readers and the methods by which writers fulfilled them. If the highly formulaic structure and tone of the travel book appeared trite at times, dissatisfaction did not result in a lack of support for the genre as a whole; the market never reached saturation. Many conventions probably derived from lack of imagination; others arose from practicality as well as the psychological and sociological needs of the reading public. In any case, travel readers booked their vicarious tours with expectations duly informed by the cultural and literary patterns of their time.

Twain was in many ways an effective conventional writer; he incorporated established formulas into his narrative tours, and he dutifully fulfilled the standard obligations facing travel writers on the whole by offering instruction, entertainment, and comfort to his partners reading at home. Such adherence is by no means a lack of skill; rather, it reveals a successful writer at work. William Dean Howells, in a review of *A Tramp Abroad,* captures the essence of Twain's effective use of convention:

> Every account of European travel, or European life, by a writer who is worth reading for any reason, is something for our reflection and possible instruction; and in this delightful work of a man of most original and characteristic genius "the average American" will find much to enlighten as well as amuse him, much to comfort and stay him in such Americanism as is worth having, and nothing to flatter him in a mistaken national vanity or stupid national prejudice. (688)

Although Howells ignores Twain's ability to "flatter" readers' national complacency, he correctly recognizes his craft, his remarkable balance, and his ability to fulfill the reading expectations of "the average American." The travel book is a specific genre that generated expectations among its readers, for whom conventions were both necessary and commendable. This is not to say, however, that these same readers could not respond favorably to fresh approaches. Twain developed the best of both features by carefully following certain patterns while also manipulating them to suit his humorous and critical inclinations. In so doing, he offered his contemporary readers familiar yet often innovative approaches on the art form, and his five travel books represent the work of not only a master travel writer but also an intuitive tourist who fully understood the new Tourist Age.

3
Touring the Old World

Faith and Leisure in *The Innocents Abroad* and *A Tramp Abroad*

Touring eastward in *The Innocents Abroad* and *A Tramp Abroad,* Mark Twain repeatedly snubs the grandiose pretensions of the cultures he encounters.[1] He shows readers that the Old World, especially Europe, if viewed honestly through definitively American eyes, falls far short of common, overblown expectations. Although such a reading of Twain's Old World tours helps us understand a pervasive theme—that of high anticipation meeting with deep disappointment—we should also consider that his reactions are tied more to touristic expectations than to any national braggadocio or stubborn Yankee self-reliance. Both *The Innocents Abroad* and *A Tramp Abroad,* then, are records not simply of the failure of the Old World civilizations he encounters but of the failure of touring itself, which becomes the real object of Twain's satire and cultural criticism. The Old World has a few shams, but tourism is rife with them. All the same, as his narratives indicate, Twain adapts well to the demands of tourism. His two best-selling travel books, in turn, masterfully illustrate how the new American, the tourist, should function in the new age.

Because the Old World, especially Europe, proved to be the most compelling draw for nineteenth-century American tourists, it also provided the best context for Twain's narrative examination of the "great popular movement." *The Innocents Abroad* and *A Tramp Abroad* make ideal travel-book companions,[2] both books capturing the vagaries of the Tourist Age—at its beginning with *The Innocents Abroad* and in full stride in *A Tramp Abroad.* These two literary texts are also well-crafted cultural documents that showcase, first, a new way of seeing the world, and second, a new way of participating in that world as the tide of tourism enveloped the globe.

Although in the preface to *The Innocents Abroad* Twain offers "no apologies for any departures from the usual style of travel-writing" (5), implying that his narrative does indeed take its own course, his implicit claim itself bows to convention. However, despite this innocuous wordplay, *The Innocents Abroad* does serve as a watershed in the history of American travel writing, but for different reasons. As a "record of a pleasure excursion," the first transatlantic cruise, it marks the beginning of a new Tourist Age, and neither Twain nor American tourism at large would be the same afterward. The actual tour, of course, changed Samuel Clemens forever, giving to him an opportunity that led to financial and literary status he could never have obtained as a roving journalist or newspaper editor, and the narrative tour in *The Innocents Abroad* launched Mark Twain as a consummate travel writer and tourist who would define the new Tourist Age as an elaborate "picnic on a gigantic scale."

A natural and logical theme of any travel book centers around the inevitable differences between expectations and realities, and Twain employs the subsequent disappointment caused by those variances as a touchstone throughout the tour. Yet there is more to this theme than the unfulfilled wishes of an American innocent abroad for the first time; it is also the record of the too-soon failures of the Tourist Age as a whole. Twain's dilemma—balancing the needs of his skepticism and honesty in his role as a travel writer with his needs for authenticity as a tourist—becomes evident as he juxtaposes attacks on the humbugs of previous romantic travel writers (and the disingenuous reactions of other tourists) against his own willingness to imagine and then create a more favorable touristic experience.

Chapter 1 helps to clarify Twain's purpose and his early intuitive assessment of the *Quaker City* pleasure excursion and its social import. Perhaps the opening chapter, with its enthusiasm and its seeming overstatement, is not as ironic as it might appear on an initial reading. In the first paragraph, Twain explains the significance of the new undertaking and, while extolling its grand scale, implies that other expeditions will follow. The idea of the "picnic" changes considerably as a result. The first wave of participants in this gigantic outing, these *Quaker City* excursionists would be a new breed of tourists. They would not simply paddle up an "obscure creek" for a "long summer day's laborious frolicking"; they would be embarking instead on a "royal holiday beyond the broad ocean, in many a strange clime and in many a land renowned in history!" (19). The largeness of the enterprise was fit for hyperbole—even the ship's ballroom stretches "from horizon to horizon." Once he sets the stage, Twain includes the program for the tour in its entirety, saying that it will serve as a "map" and "text" for the narrative tour. In turn, *The Innocents Abroad* becomes a map and text for the touristic experience at large. As a text for this "brave conception" called "the *Quaker City* pleasure excursion," *The Innocents Abroad* records both the first great touring experiment conducted by Americans and Twain's struggle with its essential and inevitable failures.

As we have seen, all efforts of tourists to seek truly authentic experiences are by their very nature destined to fail. When we engage in any sightseeing activity, we participate in a staged production not unlike that of the theater; there are eager performers (guides, advertisers, shop owners, etc.) and attentive audience members (tourists). In recognition of the play, tourists allow for "a willing suspension of disbelief," to adapt Samuel Taylor Coleridge's well-known description of poetic faith (6).[3] For my purposes here, this obliging participation in the illusion can be called "touristic faith." As tourists move in and out of theatrical productions ("sights")—Versailles, the Colosseum in Rome, the Holy Sepulcher in Jerusalem, the Great Sphinx in Egypt—they seek varying levels of instruction, entertainment, and comfort. As audience members for a staged production, nonetheless, they demand authenticity on some level. Herein is a basic inner conflict for the tourist: how to obtain the authentic in a world of prefabricated make-believe. As both a tourist and a travel writer, Twain faced the same problem, and his narrative records the struggles that abound during the education of a novice tourist. As such, the narrative also illustrates how Twain overcomes the inherent perils of tourism within his own production called *The Innocents Abroad*.

How do Twain's palpable expectations meet with the reality of the tour itself? Twain's short side excursion to Tangier is the symbolic and definitive first contact with what he believes to be wholly "foreign" on the cruise, and it is therefore a crucial moment for establishing a point of reference and for examining touristic behavior. His reaction to the sights parallels the unbridled enthusiasm established in the opening chapter:

Tangier is the spot we have been longing for all the time. Else-where we have found foreign-looking things and foreign-looking people, but always with things and people intermixed that we were familiar with before, and so the novelty of the situation lost a deal of its force. We wanted something thoroughly and un-compromisingly foreign—foreign from top to bottom—foreign from centre to circumference—foreign inside and outside and all around—nothing any where about it to dilute its foreignness —nothing to remind us of any other people or any other land under the sun. And lo! in Tangier we have found it. (76)

Rhetorically, Twain's conspicuous repetition of "foreign" highlights the readiness of the tourist abroad to see sights wholly different from those available at home; symbolically, this passage also confirms how completely tourists see the world as "other."[4] Twain and his fellow tourists are, in actuality, the foreigners in Tangier. Moreover, it is im-portant to note that Twain witnesses people simply going about their normal daily lives (which for many meant catering to the whims and interests of tourists), yet Twain, as a tourist, defines it as a spectacle to be viewed, a production to be savored. Twain goes on to provide read-ers with a long list of descriptive details to clarify Tangier's "foreign-ness," and in one of the few direct addresses to his readers, he closes with a powerful suggestion: "Isn't it an oriental picture?"

Tourists can identify the "foreign" by its difference from home, but to define it they need a preconceived image, a picture. In the case of Tangier, it is an "oriental picture." Twain's reactions, then, must be based on what he expects to see. Although he has never been to Tan-gier, he has an *idea* of its appearance based on the "oriental pictures" in his mind, and it is these pictures to which Twain responds raptur-ously. The reality of the scene thus gains value by matching his ex-pectations for the strange, the exotic, the "foreign." Meanwhile, the people on the street are going about their typical daily activities, un-aware of the frame within which they exist in *The Innocents Abroad* and in Twain's mind, and in ours. Twain notes that he has previously "mistrusted" pictures of the Orient because of their seeming exag-geration. Presently, witnessing street life in Tangier, he acknowledges that the pictures he held previous to the tour inadequately match the strangeness of the reality. Unable to escape from the essential quality of the tourist experience despite his excitement, however, he still frames the visual experience as an "oriental picture." He carries a literary equivalent to the Claude Glass (named for French painter Claude Lorrain), a tinted or mirrored gilt frame through which a nineteenth-century tourist could view landscapes as if they were paintings. A viewer would stand on a hillside, for instance, hold the frame at arm's length toward the valley, and look at the landscape through the ornate frame. The Claude Glass orders the natural landscape into a gilded rectangle and transforms it into "art," a commodity. For the travel writer, such framing via narrative devices serves two purposes: first, like the Claude Glass, it effectively focuses the eyes on a particular part of the whole; and second, it provides a point of comparison between the actual and the preconceived tourist expectations, between the street life Twain saw in Tangier and the "oriental picture" he brought with him from home. Tourists inevitably think about, preview, and see the world initially in pictures. The same is the case for travel readers, though their pictures derive primarily from an author's language (and the illustrations that often accompany travel books). Both frames help make touristic experiences manageable, structured, and more convenient for the tourist.

For a helpful parallel, let us take a look at another "oriental picture" in *The Innocents Abroad*. Much later in the tour, Twain encounters Constantinople and witnesses a street scene strikingly similar to that in Tangier, yet the "oriental picture" he frames in this instance differs significantly from the earlier experience:

> Ashore, it was—well, it was an eternal circus. People were thicker than bees, in those narrow streets, and the men were dressed in all the outrageous, outlandish, idolatrous, extravagant, thunder-and-lightning costumes that ever a tailor with the delirium tremens and seven devils could conceive of. There was no freak in dress too crazy to be indulged in; no absurdity too absurd to be tolerated; no frenzy in ragged diabolism too fantastic to be attempted. No two men were dressed alike. It was a wild masquerade of all imaginable costumes—every struggling throng in every street was a dissolving view of stunning contrasts. Some patriarchs wore awful turbans, but the grand mass of the infidel horde wore the fiery red skull-cap they call a fez. All the remainder of the raiment they indulged in was utterly indescribable. (358–59)

The "stunning contrasts" of this subsequent "oriental picture" no longer thrill the tourist in Twain as they did in Tangier, so the picture he provides for his readers back home exudes a comic tone rife with negative overtones; a mirthful exuberance is replaced by annoyance and disdain. The variety in dress so compelling if "weird" in Tangier is now so "outrageous" and "outlandish" that there is "no freak in dress too crazy." Several factors contribute to the altered response. First, having little respect for the Ottoman Empire (see, for example, his description of Abdul Aziz in chapter 13), Twain enters Constantinople with an unprepossessing "picture" already in the forefront of his expectations. Second, he is beginning to show signs of what could be called tourist fatigue. As the days, weeks, and months pass, the tour inevitably taxes the energy (and thus enthusiasm) of any tourist, and the "foreignness" so charming and enticing at the beginning soon becomes tiresome indeed. Specifically, as the *Quaker City* moves steadily around the Mediterranean, Twain's most pleasant moments coincide with a return to the ship, especially in the Holy Land and Egypt: "It was worth a kingdom to be at sea again" (609). Third, and perhaps most important to the touristic experience, once the tourist sees the "oriental picture" and adds it to his or her basket of memories, there is little interest in seeing a similar scene again. The novelty, the "foreignness," is gone. After framing the street scene in Constantinople, Twain writes that it is "a picture which one ought to see once—not oftener" (359).

Twain does, however, see other "oriental pictures" as he continues his tour of the eastern Mediterranean. In Smyrna, in effect, he re-creates a picture similar to that of Tangier, but unlike the Constantinople version, he allows for a more positive coloring. Although the scene parallels the others, one feature is indeed new to his experience: camels. The novel sight of these beasts "laden with spices of Arabia and the rare fabrics of Persia" marching through the crowded streets recaptures Twain's imagination, and he dreams of *Arabian Nights*—the oriental pictures he remembers from childhood—as he did earlier in Tangier. He concludes contentedly, "The picture lacks nothing" (411).

Ultimately, this struggle between local reality and touristic imagining convinces Twain to make a simple judgment: reality is usually disappointing. Still traveling in Syria, he describes yet another "oriental picture" as the tourists stop at a well which was "walled three feet above ground with squared and heavy blocks of stone, after the manner of Bible pictures" (543). Significantly, the well's characteristics match pictures from the Bible, not vice versa. In assessing the crowd of people and animals surrounding the well, Twain notes:

> Here was a grand Oriental picture which I had worshiped a thousand times in soft, rich steel engravings! But in the engraving there was no desolation; no dirt; no rags; no fleas; no ugly features; no sore eyes; no feasting flies; no besotted ignorance in the countenances; no raw places on the donkeys' backs; no disagreeable jabbering in unknown tongues; no stench of camels; no suggestion that a couple of tons of powder placed under the party and touched off would heighten the effect and give to the scene a genuine interest and a charm which it would always be pleasant to recall, even though a man lived a thousand years. (543–44)

The distinction typifies Twain's struggle in the Holy Land between imagination and reality as the tangible conflict between that reality and touristic expectations presents a potentially overwhelming crisis. Twain must juxtapose the actual well scene, which includes a preponderance of unpleasant characteristics (desolation, dirt, rags, ugly features, sore eyes, feasting flies, etc.), against his more pleasing pictures derived from the Bible. Trying to define the experience, the tourist and travel writer both face a formidable challenge. Twain, confronted with the disparity, has only two options: reconcile the striking differences between the pictures, altering each, or reject one of the pictures outright. Twain ultimately chooses the latter, as do most tourists. He symbolically destroys the actual picture by wishing for its annihilation via "a couple of tons of powder." With the ugliness of the actual picture removed, Twain as tourist can return to the beloved oriental pictures he has carried with him from home. He thereby demonstrates one of the basic truths of tourism: "Oriental scenes look best in steel engravings" (544). Twain had promised in his preface to look at the Old World through his own eyes, a noble if conventional declaration. This proposition endeavors to remove from our perceptions the falsities of our imagined pictures as given to us by earlier travel writers, but Twain cannot escape such images so easily. This is especially troubling when the tourist faces the actual scenes. The "oriental pictures," in this case, are deeply interwoven with the tourist's aesthetic sensibilities, and if Twain cannot dismiss the actual pictures entirely, he can at least fantasize about their destruction.

The Old World provides more than a convenient cultural target for his Americanism; it also represents the essence of the touristic experience. Twain marvels in his first exposure to the foreign, but his enthusiasm quickly wanes and his subsequent struggles between the beauty of his expectations and the too-often dismal reality mimic the struggle of tourists at large to reconcile the contrasts between the "authentic" pictures in front of them and the delicately crafted images in their minds. Twain's method of picturing is not a rhetorical accident. His early use of the phrase "oriental picture" reflects a more general narrative strategy through which he transfers to his readers not simply a pictorial tour of the Old World, but more importantly, an overview of touristic experience itself.

In Paris, Twain delights in "recognizing certain names and places with which books had long ago made us familiar," and he continues, "we knew the genuine vast palace of the Louvre as well as we knew its picture" (112). Twain as a tourist feels "familiar" with the museum because he knows what it looks like from pictures firmly entrenched in his memory, so when the actual building matches the image, there is no need for much commentary or conflict—there are no surprises. Likewise, at Notre Dame, he writes, "We recognized the brown old Gothic pile in a moment; it was like the pictures" (130). In both instances the emphasis is on how well the actual landmark coincides with his expectations, and what seems to be important is the knowledge base of the tourists, a source of pride as they come to Paris *knowing* it. So far the tour is moving along smoothly. The actual pictures are meeting the qualities of the imagined ones except for small annoyances like the absence of soap or the dangers of a Parisian shave.

As the tour progresses, however, the frustration with failed expectations grows, and Twain faces the prototypical touristic dilemma: how to salvage a treasured picture of the Old World in the face of dissenting realities. One such threat occurs in Venice. Twain fears that his charming image of the city is teetering in the balance as he is assailed by a gondolier who sings terribly. Allowing for the humor of such a scene, the encounter also reiterates the primary goal of the tourist to reaffirm his images. In protest to the "caterwauling," Twain complains that his "cherished dreams of Venice have been blighted forever as to the romantic gondola and the gorgeous gondolier" (218). Fortunately for Twain the tourist, the gondola soon moves into the Grand Canal, and "under the mellow moonlight the Venice of poetry and romance stood revealed" (218). Twain has traveled to see the "poetry and romance," the Venice of his dreams, and only when he can match the actual scene with his expectations is he satisfied. Once this willing deception is accomplished, "Venice was complete" (219). Of course, it is his picture of Venice that is complete. When the stark realities of a city, however, conspire to challenge the image, darkness can soften the glare of the sun, and Venice, it seems, is supposed to be "dreamy." Its actual appearance, therefore, needs the softening glow of moonlight to capture the qualities of the Venice which Twain and other American tourists know, the Venice they travel to see.

Nathaniel Hawthorne's preface to *The House of Seven Gables* (1851) provides a corollary here. Hawthorne insists that a writer of romance may claim a "certain latitude" to restructure scenes regardless of probability in real life, as long as the writer does not "swerve aside from the truth of the human heart." The writer, Hawthorne continues, may "present that truth under circumstances . . . of the writer's own choosing or creation," and moreover, he or she may "bring out or mellow the lights, and deepen and enrich the shadows, of the picture" (1). Although Hawthorne is not referring to travel writers, his observations nonetheless apply to the genre. Because the truth of the tourist's heart is not necessarily in the actual picture but rather the imagined one, the travel writer often chooses to "mellow" the lights or "deepen" the shadows of the actual in order to preserve the aesthetic superiority of the imagined picture. Twain, in similar fashion to Hawthorne's romance author, captures the perfect touristic Venice by dimming lights and manipulating shadows: "It was a beautiful picture—very soft and dreamy and beautiful" (219). Twain affirms one of the most compelling desires of the American in Europe—to find the "shadowy grandeurs of the past," in the words of Washington Irving from *The Sketch-Book* (1819–20).[5] Twain is echoing Irving when he writes that touring Venice has seemed like "drifting back, back, back, into the solemn past, and looking upon the scenes and mingling with the peoples of a remote antiquity." Twain continues: "We have been in a half-waking sort of dream all the time. I do not know how else to describe the feeling. A part of our being has remained still in the nineteenth century, while another part of it has seemed in some unaccountable way walking among the phantoms of the tenth" (236).

Athens provides another opportunity for Twain to confront his dreamy expectations for shadowy grandeur. Unlike the jarring incompatibility of the initial visions of the actual Venice and his image, the problem in Athens is that the *Quaker City* is quarantined in the harbor and the tourists are not allowed to disembark. Although this disappointment is an unmitigated disaster for most of the excursionists, for Twain—willing and able to run the blockade, as it were—it is a fortunate break because it gives him and his comrades (and his readers) the chance to see Athens under cover of night. Walking among the fallen statues on the Acropolis at night, Twain can ignore any possible flaws in the actual picture and more easily match it to his own image. The opportunity allows him to create another touristic dream:

> The full moon was riding high in the cloudless heavens, now. We sauntered carelessly and unthinkingly to the edge of the lofty battlements of the citadel, and looked down—a vision! And such a vision! Athens by moonlight! The prophet that thought the splendors of the New Jerusalem were revealed to him, surely saw this instead! It lay in the level plain right under our feet—all spread abroad like a picture—and we looked down upon it as we might have looked from a balloon. We saw no semblance of a street, but every house, every window, every clinging vine, every projection, was as distinct and sharply marked as if the time were noon-day; and yet there was no glare, no glitter, nothing harsh or repulsive—the noiseless city was flooded with the mellowest light that ever streamed from the moon, and seemed like some living creature wrapped in peaceful slumber. (347–48)

This romantic evocation of a "vision!" is similar to Twain's ecstatic reaction to Versailles, but it is more closely aligned with his description of Venice in the way he frames the picture. He situates himself and his readers in a comfortable perspective from which to verify a popular image of Athens, a frame that has carefully removed all evidence of modern daily life. There is no present within a frame defined solely by the past. To gain the ideal picture of Athens, Twain brushes the canvas with strokes of darkness and touristic wish fulfillment. Again, like in Venice, the picture, steeped in a romantic reverence for the past, is presented in all its shadowy grandeur. Twain celebrates not Athens but his image of Athens, a vision of "Athens by moonlight." The picture is perfect, with all its detail miraculously "distinct and sharply marked" but without a corresponding "glare." As travel writer and as tourist, Twain, by the light of the silvery moon, sees nothing "harsh" or "repulsive." He closes out the Acropolis meanderings with a carefully constructed image wherein he and his readers gain the Athens they could only have hoped to see: "Overhead the stately columns, majestic still in their ruin—under foot the dreaming city—in the distance the silver sea—not on the broad earth is there another picture half so beautiful!" (348). Twain, author of travel romance, dreams an ideal moment for the tourist. Isn't it a Grecian picture?

Touristic ways of seeing become even more pronounced as Twain enters the Holy Land. The region's most renowned body of water, the Sea of Galilee, offers Twain another opportunity to confront the issue of expectations and reality. The first picture he shares is under the harsh light of day, and it is a forthright one. According to Twain, the Sea of Galilee, no matter its marvelous associations, is a dismal, barren body of water. Again he writes in terms of pictures, noting that the sea and its environs "never, never, never do shake the glare from their harsh outlines, and fade and faint into vague perspective" (508). Twain as tourist and travel writer faces a dilemma, for his preconceived images of the Sea of Galilee contrast sharply with the actual landscape. In this reaction, Twain fulfills his promise set out in the preface—that he will see (and report) with his own eyes rather than with those of tourists who preceded him. Frustrated, he lashes out at those who have deceived him, other travel writers. Citing several lengthy passages from "Wm. C. Grimes" and "C. W. E.," Twain deconstructs their pictures and proceeds to set the record straight. Rejecting other writers' efforts to perpetuate deceptions, Twain argues that "no ingenuity could make such a picture beautiful—to one's actual vision" (509). He ignores, for the moment, his own narrative ingenuity. Since Twain's primary concern is not the tourist's "*actual* vision" but the dream vision of expectancy, he has learned a method for reshaping a scene by simply recasting the context for his "actual vision." Using the method learned in Venice and perfected in Athens, he writes under the softening cover of night and produces a poetic and evocative picture the tourist wants to see:

> Night is the time to see Galilee. Genessaret under these lustrous stars has nothing repulsive about it. Genessaret with the glittering reflections of the constellations flecking its surface, almost makes me regret that I ever saw the rude glare of the day upon it. Its history and its associations are its chiefest charm, in any eyes, and the spells they weave are feeble in the searching light of the sun. *Then,* we scarcely feel the fetters. Our thoughts wander constantly to the practical concerns of life, and refuse to dwell upon things that seem vague and unreal. But when the day is done, even the most unimpressible must yield to the dreamy influences of this tranquil starlight. The old traditions of the place steal upon his memory and haunt his reveries, and then his fancy clothes all sights and sounds with the supernatural. In the lapping of the waves upon the beach, he hears the dip of ghostly oars; in the secret noises of the night he hears spirit voices; in the soft sweep of the breeze, the rush of invisible wings. Phantom ships are on the sea, the dead of twenty centuries come forth from the tombs, and in the dirges of the night wind the songs of old forgotten ages find utterance again. (512–13)

This rich passage recaptures the dreamlike allure of the Sea of Galilee and the romantic image that the severe light of day had so tarnished. The imaginative picture, for Twain and thus his readers, materializes only after sunset as the moonlight and the solitude give Twain the chance to restructure his Sea of Galilee picture, invoking the powers of biblical association, the "chiefest charm" for the tourist in the Holy Land. He appears sincere in wishing he had not seen the picture during the daylight, but the unpleasant experience is not fatal to the image he wants to maintain. Twain's nighttime reverie by the sea—a touristic revision—in effect paints over the unpleasant picture created in the "rude glare of day," thereby preserving beloved images of the revered setting.

The night can offer only so much protection for the hopeful tourist, however. Another way of seeing for the tourist takes its advantage from distance. On several occasions Twain plays with the notion of distant viewing in reference to the expectation-versus-reality theme. Damascus is one such example.[6] Twain refers to the story of Mahomet's view from the mountain overlooking the city. According to legend, Mahomet claimed that "man could enter only one paradise; he preferred to go to the one above. So he sat down there and feasted his eyes upon the earthly paradise of Damascus, and then went away without entering its gates" (455). Twain sits in the same spot and views the city below, a broad, panoramic picture, and declares, "Damascus *is* beautiful from the mountain" (455). He goes on to emphasize, however, that Damascus probably seems a paradise because of the utter desolation of all that surrounds it. The city benefits by comparison with the ugliness outside its gates. Noting that the city is nestled in a "billowy expanse of green foliage," he continues: "This is the picture you see spread far below you, with distance to soften it, the sun to glorify it, strong contrasts to heighten the effects, and over it and about it a drowsing air of repose to spiritualize it and make it seem rather a beautiful estray from the mysterious worlds we visit in dreams than a substantial tenant of our coarse, dull globe" (456). Again, Twain uses dream imagery to capture an evocative picture for his readers, placing them in an ideal perspective, the mountaintop. Mahomet was wise, according to Twain, for he saved himself from facing the dreariness that is Damascus when seen from close up. Once inside the city, Twain loses the favorable and pleasant picture, and "paradise is become a very sink of pollution and uncomeliness" (456). Not even the most aggressive imagination can undo the harshness of reality and the damage it causes the preconceived image. Twain concludes that Mahomet unwittingly made the right choice aesthetically, and the tourist in Twain can only wish he had done the same and thereby avoided the unfortunate challenge to his comfortable image acquired from a distance.

The tourist to the Holy Land travels to touch the landmarks (tourist sights) authenticated by the Bible. For them, the present is largely irrelevant and, moreover, a nuisance, but it still remains as an obstacle between the tourists and what they seek. If Twain honestly points out the harshness of the actual pictures he sees, he also carefully reaffirms the imagined pictures he and his readers share. The touristic way of seeing is predisposed to the familiar, to what the tourist already *knows*. There are two essential components to that touristic knowledge: imagination and faith.

To sit at home in America and read about the Holy Land in the Bible and in works of travel requires an active, fully engaged imagination. The tourists who make pilgrimages to the places illuminated by such texts must be equally imaginative because their journey bears no connection to any realities of their present. Within his narrative tour, Twain seems to understand the two often opposing pictures of the Holy Land, and he struggles for some pleasing balance. He often shows us multiple views of the Holy Land, pictures tempered by both sharp and mellow lighting, by caustic wit as well as romantic wishfulness. As his preface indicates, Twain does see with "his own eyes," but he fails to note that those eyes see pictures both real and imagined, both skeptical and faithful. He does, however, in the end favor the power of the imagination to render the Holy Land acceptable for the Tourist Age. In short, despite his self-image as the "sinner," he keeps the Holy Land holy. Accomplishing this task, though, requires substantive imaginative leaps and a will to see—despite the prevalence of contrary images—what he came to see. We have already examined how he revises the Sea of Galilee to maintain its poetic associations. He faces a similar conflict in Nazareth as he tours the Grotto of the Annunciation:

> The very scene of the Annunciation—an event which has been commemorated by splendid shrines and august temples all over the civilized world, and one which the princes of art have made it their loftiest ambition to picture worthily on their canvas; a spot whose history is familiar to the very children of every house, and city, and obscure hamlet of the furthest lands of Christendom; a spot which myriads of men would toil across the breadth of a world to see, would consider it a priceless privilege to look upon. It was easy to think these thoughts. But it was not easy to bring myself up to the magnitude of the situation. (527)

The grotto itself proves to be simply too small to accommodate the weighty associations that define it as a holy sight. Twain acknowledges his obligation to *feel* something remarkable, yet he confesses that he can only provide an intellectual reaction; he can only "think these thoughts." Like the "princes of art" who preceded him, Twain endeavors to place the spot on his literary canvas. He stands before it overwhelmed by its associative power but also undeniably under-whelmed by its physical smallness (dullness). He continues:

> I could sit off several thousand miles and imagine the angel ap-pearing, with shadowy wings and lustrous countenance, and note the glory that streamed downward upon the Virgin's head while the message from the Throne of God fell upon her ears—any one can do that, beyond the ocean, but few can do it here. I saw the little recess from which the angel stepped, but could not fill its void. The angels that I know are creatures of unstable fancy—they will not fit in niches of substantial stone. Imagina-tion labors best in distant fields. (527)

The conflict arises from the fact that the imagined "Grotto of the Annunciation" is larger, more powerful, more "shadowy" and "lus-trous" than the simple stone cave in which Twain stands. The two pictures clash with one another. But once Twain removes himself metaphorically and revises the grotto by divorcing the imaginary from the actual, he recaptures the emotional context and pictures the "glory that streamed downward" so long ago. Twain closes the reverie by doubting whether anyone could stand in the actual grotto and in-corporate the "phantom images of his mind" into the "too tangible walls of stone" (527). His dilemma in the grotto is that of any tourist who seeks a sight with strong historical associations. The conflict is especially sharp when that tourist is a pilgrim, who most often fills expectations with images more closely aligned with the "Throne of God" than with stone abodes in Palestine. Twain goes on to ques-tion the authenticity of the actual grotto and points out that such sights are fabrications formed by Catholic monks. Whereas he recoils at such impostures throughout his tour, he supports the deception in this case. His reasoning is simple and directly related to touris-tic imagination: the value of the tourist sight—especially the holy sight—lies not in its specific authenticity but in its evocative power. Whether or not the actual grotto in which he stands is the grotto wherein the Annunciation took place is irrelevant; it signifies, none-theless, the "Grotto of the Annunciation" venerated (and thus authen-ticated) by thousands of tourists. The monks who originated the de-ception, according to Twain, have provided a service by creating "a particular spot to chain your eye, rivet your interest, and make you think" (529). Of course, seeing the actual "spot" is basically a matter of convenience for the tourist and expedience for the pilgrim. In any case, its existence helps to "drive a stake through a pleasant tradition that will hold it to its place forever" (529). The touristic imagination, then, can always infuse the "too tangible walls of stone" with "phantom images" and thus move Twain toward faith. Still, Twain needs the peace, serenity, and imaginative perspective allowed by "distant fields." His struggle, though, is not resolved. He takes his final step to touristic faith in the Church of the Holy Sepulcher.

Twain's picture of Jerusalem is the most crucial for the tourist, and it is within the walls of this ancient city that he fully reconciles the conflict between the actual and the imagined. Throughout the *Quaker City* excursion, Twain has struggled with competing impulses, one to view the Old World with skeptical eyes, the other to see with the imaginative eyes of the tourist. In Jerusalem, however, Twain fully embraces touristic faith, and in so doing he salvages his imaginative pictures of Palestine, the pictures that make the land holy. Twain's first picture of Jerusalem is typical; it offers a distant, carefully framed image so popular in travel books to the Holy Land, the same perspective used by "Grimes" (William Prime). He writes: "Perched on its eternal hills, white and domed and solid, massed together and hooped with high gray walls, the venerable city gleamed in the sun" (556). Once he establishes the image, he fills the frame with notable details: "We dismounted and looked, without speaking a dozen sentences, across the wide intervening valley for an hour or more; and noted those prominent features of the city that pictures make familiar to all men from their school days till their death. We could recognize the Tower of Hippicus, the Mosque of Omar, the Damascus Gate, the Mount of Olives, the Valley of Jehoshaphat, the Tower of David, and the Garden of Gethsemane" (556). Twain and his fellow tourists "recognize" Jerusalem. Of course, they have never been there physically, yet due to their lifetime education from the Bible and travel writing, they react through their imaginations as if they have seen it before. They have come to verify those pictures they derived directly from Scripture. Twain writes: "I think there was no individual in the party whose brain was not teeming with thoughts and images and memories invoked by the grand history of the venerable city that lay before us" (557). Although Twain methodically differentiates himself from Prime and writers like him, he does, nonetheless, have similar touristic impulses. The difference is that Twain is a far better writer, though not necessarily a better tourist. Like Prime, Twain seeks the past, the poetical associations for which he has traveled, the pictures he can "recognize" from memory, not experience.

Still, Twain's aggravation with Prime's overt emotionalism indicates some discomfort with the imaginative picture of Jerusalem that wholly ignores the pragmatic, actual one. In the Church of the Holy Sepulcher, Twain fully integrates the two ways of seeing in a manner that, like Prime, privileges the imagination and its prefigured pictures of the Holy Land. As in the case of the Grotto of the Annunciation, Twain doubts the authenticity of the actual pictures within the Holy Sepulcher, and he struggles with his conflicting impulses: "One is grave and thoughtful when he stands in the little Tomb of the Saviour —he could not well be otherwise in such a place—but he has not the slightest possible belief that ever the Lord lay there, and so the interest he feels in the spot is very, very greatly marred by that reflection" (570). He goes on to claim that he feels the same way at each of the "spots" within the church, that "there is nothing genuine about them, and that they are imaginary holy places created by the monks." Twain is experiencing a crisis in touristic faith as he momentarily denies the importance and validity—within the tourist context—of "imaginary holy places," a validity he has already affirmed in the Grotto of the Annunciation. Describing his feelings using the third person (and thus emphasizing the plight of tourists on the whole), Twain claims that the "place of the Crucifixion affects him differently," and "he fully believes" in the authenticity of the "spot" (570). Twain justifies his belief by working through a logical, practical argument, one that could just as well apply to the other "spots." He notes that such a crucial location certainly would have been duly noted by Christ's contemporaries with a precision that matched the importance of the event, and the exact location would, then, have been passed down through the generations with accuracy and reverence. In perhaps one of the most interesting and ironic moments in *The Innocents Abroad,* Twain credits, of all people, William Prime for the logical gamesmanship by which Twain testifies his touristic faith (he adds a footnote using Prime's actual name, not "Grimes"). Prime does more than simply provide Twain with a helpful, if flawed, logic; he also leads Twain beyond his skepticism and to touristic faith. Although the argument is presented as intellectual reasoning—as one would expect from a skeptic—it derives from the needs of the tourist to preserve the pictures of the romantic imagination. Twain effectively salvages the imaginary Church of the Holy Sepulcher for himself and his readers, despite acknowledging its "clap-trap side-shows and unseemly impostures of every kind" (573). The holy church's "tremendous associations" remain intact, its pictures safe.

Twain does not abandon his skepticism by any means, nor does he wholly dismiss the harshness of the actual Old World after his conversion in the Church of the Holy Sepulcher. However, the touristic faith embodied within the narrative encounter inside the church solidifies a desire he reveals throughout *The Innocents Abroad*. Twain, as tourist and as travel writer, wants to preserve his and his readers' pictures of the Old World, especially when such pictures are deeply rooted and spiritual. When his other motive—to identify impostures—comes in conflict with his primary goal, he holds on to his imagined pictures; he chooses faith.

If imagination is the key to maintaining preconceived pictures in the face of reality, memory is the key to redefining touristic experience in perpetuity. In this sense, as Twain observes, memory is an active process of creation and a further defense mechanism for the tourist. Following the visit to the Church of the Holy Sepulcher, the dominant theme of *The Innocents Abroad* becomes the comforting assurances of memory. Approaching the end of the Holy Land portion of the tour, Twain writes:

> We have full comfort in one reflection, however. Our experiences in Europe have taught us that in time this fatigue will be forgotten; the heat will be forgotten; the thirst, the tiresome volubility of the guide, the persecutions of the beggars—and then, all that will be left will be pleasant memories of Jerusalem, memories we shall call up with always increasing interest as the years go by, memories which some day will become all beautiful when the last annoyance that incumbers them shall have faded out of our minds never again to return. (585)

Memory is a tool on which the tourist can rely to reshape any experience, no matter how unpalatable. The ability of touristic memory in conjunction with imagination to erase the unpleasant details of a journey, to mellow the lights and soften the rough edges, allows for any experience to be salvaged and repackaged. Whatever skepticism he maintains in the moment of viewing the actual "spots" will, according to Twain (and to his great relief), fade in the coming days, months, and years until they happily disappear altogether. In this touristic dream, Twain can always visit the Holy Land and Europe and "in fancy . . . revisit alone, the solemn monuments of the past, and summon the phantom pageants of an age that has passed away" (603). Twain reiterates this wish in the remainder of his tour, and as he leaves the Holy Land for good physically, he sums up its essential value for the tourist: "It is dream-land" (608).[7]

The imagination holds the promise of altering the actual to preserve on some level a place defined by touristic expectations, and memory completes the picture for the long term, a willful editing of experience to remove all unpleasantness. If *The Innocents Abroad* is a record of an innocent's struggle with touristic faith, then the Holy Land portions of the narrative contain absolution for Twain as he reconciles the skeptic with the dreamer. Twain recognizes the implicit failure of tourism to offer authentic experiences, but during the excursion he learns also how to temper that inherent failure and to redefine the world with the grace allowed by touristic faith and the redemption offered by touristic memory. Tourists are dreamers, and ultimately Twain's eyes are not simply those of the young American skeptic but those of the tourist.

Twain recognizes the difficulty of maintaining his pictures of the Old World, and as we have seen, he struggles with balancing his expectations with the reality he encounters throughout the *Quaker City* tour—in Tangier, Paris, Venice, Constantinople, and the Holy Land. He sees as the tourist sees, and the world is therefore a series of pictures, images he hopes to "recognize" and keep with him forever. He travels, then, to affirm them. Travel is rarely fatal to prejudice, despite his claim otherwise in the last chapter; it is, however, always potentially fatal to touristic expectations. As the imagined pictures collide with actual ones, tourists must adapt, and Twain is no exception. The conclusion is the benediction for Twain's redemption, and its rhetorical structure carefully reiterates his discovery of touristic faith in Europe and the Holy Land. The repetition in the closing paragraphs provides a hypnotic resonance of memory and imagination as the tourists define their experiences. Although the tour is over, memory remains, and it exists, like the tour itself, in the form of pictures: "Yet our holyday flight has not been in vain—for above the confusion of vague recollections, certain of its best prized pictures lift themselves and will still continue perfect in tint and outline after their surroundings shall have faded away" (650). The last three paragraphs then summarize the five-month excursion as a series of actively constructed and edited remembrances. Twain moves us again through the entire tour and (with no hint of skepticism) highlights the most special and endearing moments—"pleasant France," "majestic Gibraltar," "the delicious atmosphere of Greece," and "venerable Rome." He describes St. Peter's in Rome as standing "full of dignity and grace, strongly outlined as a mountain" (651). This passage can apply to all of the moments he recounts. Using these mellowed descriptions together with the soft repetition of "we shall remember" helps to lull Twain and his readers into the realm of dream, a somnambulant journey of pleasing images, all "perfect in tint" with their blemishes wonderfully "faded away." It is the dream of the Tourist Age.

A Tramp Abroad and Adventures in Leisure

A Tramp Abroad is a natural extension of The Innocents Abroad as a travel narrative, a return to the Old World. As a cultural document, it is also a natural continuation of the great popular movement of tourism, wherein the "innocent" becomes a "tramp." The energy of the first swell of the tide captured in The Innocents Abroad has settled into the comfortable inertia of leisure, of tourism at high tide, eleven years later in A Tramp Abroad. Twain, having fully accepted the possibilities of manipulating experience in his first tour, is free to push further in his second. No longer caught in the first wave of the Tourist Age, Twain enjoys in his second narrative tour of the Old World the benefits of both his social stature and the changing face of tourism. In A Tramp Abroad he truly drifts with the tide, or, perhaps more accurately, he floats.

A Tramp Abroad, unlike its predecessor, has no distinct itinerary, no grand program. Although for some readers the narrative suffers as a result of such floating, the rambling structure accurately captures the changing emphasis for American tourists at large, a move away from seeing the world as a set of pictures to being in the pictures themselves —more settled, more affluent, more experienced, more self-absorbed. In 1878, Twain the tourist mirrors this cultural change, and he returns to Europe with his own entourage traveling the continent at will and always in comfort, a comfort paid for from his own pockets rather than those of the *Alta California*. Not surprisingly, the theme of expectation versus reality, so prominent in *The Innocents Abroad,* is practically nonexistent in its sequel; the narrative focuses more often on Twain himself, the leisured tourist—artist, German-language student, mountain-climbing adventurer. The satire and parody within the narrative, then, depend not on what he sees but on what he does. With the security of resting comfortably on a high tide, Twain the leisure tourist does nothing at all.

If in *The Innocents Abroad* Twain struggles to hold on to his pictures of the imaginary touristic Old World, *A Tramp Abroad* shows that such struggles are the work of an innocent; the high-tide tourist has apprehended that *all* is irrelevant. The innocent learns to manipulate pictures to suit his expectations and memory; the tramp learns to alter his sense of self to match any place, any occasion. Whereas the place for an innocent tourist becomes negotiable as he learns the vagaries of tourism, for the tramp tourist the self is fungible and the place is simply immaterial. *The Innocents Abroad* blurs the distinctions between the imaginary and the actual in touristic experience and ultimately privileges the dream of the imaginary. In *A Tramp Abroad* there are no distinctions at all—"actual" and "imaginary" are simply words that have little connection to experience. The novice tourist of the first tour confronts the basic failure of tourism to provide authentic experiences. The veteran tourist of the second tour simply does not care. By the close of *The Innocents Abroad,* the tourist comes to grips with his conflicting impulses and ultimately celebrates the impostures of tourism by embracing touristic faith and immersing himself in imagination and memory. So this conflict between expectation and reality is settled. In *A Tramp Abroad,* however, Twain takes the next logical step apropos to the swelling tide: he embraces leisure. For the leisure tourist, the primary goal is not to see the world but to be the center of it.

There is little room for disappointment in such self-indulgence. Thorstein Veblen, in his seminal study of the late-nineteenth-century gilded culture, *The Theory of the Leisure Class* (1899), provides a helpful context for touristic behavior.[8] Noting that leisure is "nonproductive consumption of time," Veblen argues that this time consumption occurs because the leisure class regards productive work as

undesirable and below the dignity of the privileged and that therefore it serves as the underpinning for their desire to show a "pecuni-
ary ability to afford a life of idleness" (46). There is a catch, however,
according to Veblen. Although they endeavor to be nonproductive in
the more mundane considerations, people of leisure are obligated socially to show some evidence of intellectual work, what he calls "immaterial evidences," such as "quasi-scholarly or quasi-artistic accomplishments" (46). The leisured gentleman or lady may also tackle
physical challenges, as long as such challenges are conspicuous and
therefore afford some distinguished notoriety. Although Veblen does
not focus on tourism specifically (only as a behavior associated with
the leisure class), his study is relevant to the social imperatives that
helped to form Twain's own notions of touristic behavior in all of his
travel narratives. This context is especially applicable to *A Tramp
Abroad,* which contains in a sense Twain's own informal theory of the
leisure class. Twain, of course, did not have the benefit of Veblen's
study, but he had his own experience as leisured tourist to draw from,
and as his premise for *A Tramp Abroad* indicates, Twain the travel
writer understood well the potential that a "life of idleness" may have
as a literary theme. His narrative strategy, then, offers readers a life of
idleness via their beloved "innocent" who has transformed into a
gentleman of leisure, a rich "tramp." The result is a record of a tourist's "non-productive consumption of time," and as such *A Tramp
Abroad* is also an extended parody of life in the leisure class.

Within this self-focused tour of Europe, Twain sets up his hopeful
goals right away. To show the "immaterial evidences" of his idleness,
he plans to learn German and become an artist. His primary justification for the tour, however, is his proposed physical goal, to walk
across Europe. Twain uses these three quasi-respectable versions of the
modern tourist to provide a coherence to *A Tramp Abroad:* the artist,
the student (of German), and the adventurer. Although the narrative
is peppered with references and jokes based on Twain's seemingly infinite capacity for ignorance of both art and German linguistics, the
primary structural tool of the narrative is his manipulation of his
quasi-adventurer self. It is within this parody that Twain fully recognizes the absurdities of touristic idleness.

One of the most effective narrative personae in nineteenth-
century travel books was that of the "adventurer," and the most successful purveyor of that pose was Bayard Taylor, the "Great American

Traveler" (Beatty 146). Taylor, the most prolific and best-known travel writer of his era, published eleven full-length travel books, most of which earned a vast popularity and were reprinted often.[9] Although virtually unknown to twentieth-century readers, Taylor garnered widespread respect and admiration from his contemporaries. His death on 19 December 1878 prompted laudatory responses in newspapers around the world. The *New York Times* ran his obituary on the front page and called him "a great traveler, both on land and paper."[10] Much of Taylor's appeal came from his ability to create an exciting narrative persona that dominates all his travel books, an American heroic ideal—the adventurer, the essence of the rugged individualist in the American popular imagination.

Views A-Foot (1846) marks the beginning of Bayard Taylor the adventurer, establishing perhaps accidentally the identity that would serve him throughout his career. The very method of his travels showcases the narrator's adventurous spirit, recording an intimidating, often risky two-year journey on foot ("with knapsack and staff") through Europe. The novelty and scope of the idea in the mid-nineteenth century added to its charm. As indicated clearly by his voluminous sales figures, Taylor's industrious postures endeared him to readers as he persevered, aggressively overcoming all obstacles. In the narrative, Taylor is a man of action. His readers could walk alongside him, enjoying his triumphs, sharing his passion for danger and his fearlessness of the unknown. Taylor, self-reliant and strong-willed, offers readers an exciting touring partner—indestructible, inscrutable to the last, the kind of traveler they would want to be. There is no room for leisure-minded, passive tourists.

A friend and fan of Taylor's, Twain knew well the literary and financial benefits of creating an engaging persona, but unlike Taylor, he also recognized the comic value of mocking such postures.[11] In this context, Twain's quasi-adventurer takes on an additional feature: the persona provides a vital point of parody for both tourism and travel writing. In *A Tramp Abroad,* Twain sets up a conscious, carefully crafted pattern that capitalizes on readers' familiarity with the adventurer pose. As was his preference with many travel-writing conventions, he takes well-established forms and makes them his own. His manipulations do, however, depend on reader recognition of the convention. In this case, he builds on the characteristics of the adventurer. Yet, Mark Twain is hardly a stock adventurer.

Twain first indicates the plan for *A Tramp Abroad* in a letter to Frank Bliss, his publisher, dated 20 August 1878: "I have instructed Twichell[12] to keep the title and plan of the book a secret. I will disclose them to you by letter, presently, or through Twichell—but I do not want them to get into print *until the book is nearly ready to issue from the press.*—They are in themselves a joke—and a joke which the public are already prepared for is no joke at all" (Hill, *Twain's Letters* 109). From the beginning, he intended to structure *A Tramp Abroad* around the adventurer pose, and the premise is simple: no matter how often he insists on posing as a strong, energetic, fearless traveler, he ultimately switches and becomes, more accurately, a weak, lethargic, fearful tourist—a new breed of American traveler, a lover of leisure and comfort rather than excitement and danger. The title itself would be a lie according to Twain's plan. He would promise a walking tour, much in the same spirit as Taylor's *Views A-Foot,* but would offer something quite different. A new generation requires a new type of adventurer, one more reflective of the times. Taylor constructed his persona around an image of a strong, determined, rugged narrator who sets out to face a physically demanding ordeal; over thirty years later, Twain would promise in the scope of *A Tramp Abroad* the same adventure, but he would make the pose comically absurd. Quite simply, Twain had neither the desire nor the energy to walk across Europe. He did, however, recognize the potential of implying such an intent.

Originally, Twain planned to inform his readers of the book's true nature and the irony of its title. In an unused preface, he writes:

> When I chose my book's title, I only intended it to describe the nature of my journey, which was a *walk,* through foreign lands,—that is, a tramp; but the more I think of how little I cared whither I went, or how long it took me to go, or whether I saw anything or found out anything when I got there, so long as I had a lazy, delightful, irresponsible high-holiday time on the road, the more I perceived that in using the word Tramp I was unconsciously describing the walker as well as the walk. (qtd. in Hill, *Twain's Letters* 109–10)[13]

Of course, there was nothing unconscious about Twain's use of the double entendre of "tramp" or his plan to undercut himself as an adventurer. In the conception Twain would promise to "tramp" across Europe, but in practice he would almost always avoid such hard work. Whenever possible, he would take any more convenient and inevitably more leisurely alternative that offered itself. Twain used laziness as a pose throughout his career, and it is a prominent character trait that he projected both within and outside his books. Yet by combining his feigned inveterate laziness with a vastly popular travel-book persona, he made his joke all the more shrewd and effective. No adventurer, Twain was a consummate leisured tourist, a man of his gilded age. In a letter to William Dean Howells, Twain shares further clues to his narrative plan: "In my book I allow it to appear,— casually & without stress,—that I am over here to make the tour of Europe *on foot*. I am in pedestrian costume, as a general thing, & *start* on pedestrian tours, but mount the first conveyance that offers, making but slight explanation or excuse, & endeavoring to seem unconscious that this is not legitimate pedestrianizing" (qtd. in Smith and Gibson 249). Twain's use of "costume" provides an interesting parallel to his manipulation of the adventurer pose in that it is itself a mocking costume of sorts throughout the narrative. He is also in leisure costume throughout, and the two poses work together to mock behavior and undermine accepted definitions of "legitimate" tramping in the Tourist Age.

Ultimately, Twain chose not to include his confessional preface, thereby allowing his joke to reveal itself within the narrative proper. He opted, instead, to open with a conventional introduction within the first chapter, in which he immediately assumes the adventurer costume: "One day it occurred to me that it had been many years since the world had been afforded the spectacle of a man adventurous enough to undertake a journey through Europe on foot. After much thought, I decided that I was a person fitted to furnish to mankind this spectacle. So I determined to do it" (17). This beginning paragraph bestows a subtle bow to Taylor's *Views A-Foot,* the original tramp across Europe, a reference that many of his readers would have recognized.[14] It is important to note that Twain's opening accomplishes two tasks: it sets up the adventure context on which the narrative's structure depends and points out that for this tour of Europe, the "spectacle" will not be the Old World but Twain himself. As a modern tourist, Twain is the subject of our gaze.

In just a few lines below the opening assertion, Twain undercuts the narrative persona and provides readers with their first clue to the full nature of his peculiar version of the adventurer: "After a brief rest at Hamburg, we made preparations for a long pedestrian trip southward in the soft spring weather, but at the last moment we changed the program, for private reasons, and took the express train" (17). Such an avoidance of actual walking establishes the joke and sets in motion the running gag that ties *A Tramp Abroad* together. He puts on the costume of the adventurer, but almost immediately he hints to readers that, like other disguises, this one is a travel-book pose, if not a standard one. In reference to tourism, Twain's premise also sets up for parody touristic practices at large, wherein American tourists spread across Europe adorning a variety of costumes seemingly oblivious to the vacuousness of their behavior. For Twain as tourist, walking across Europe requires, first, the ambition to assert the goal, and second, the willingness to dress properly for the occasion; it does not necessarily require walking. Fidelity must be applied to the details of presentation rather than actual exertion. Amusingly, Twain conducts his most extensive "walk" as he looks desperately for a sock in his room in the middle of the night (chapter 13). The pedometer he is wearing at the time indicates he travels a total of forty-seven miles during his search (114–21). After introducing his primary theme using the adventurer, Twain splices the running joke and his satire throughout the narrative using several approaches as touchstones and reminders while also fulfilling other travel-book conventional requirements.

Eventually, Twain and his agent, Harris, propose "to make a pedestrian tour" up the shores of the Neckar River to Heilbronn from Heidelberg. Twain details their extensive preparations and touts the value of the enterprise for a writer, noting that since no one has taken such a route by foot, it remains "virgin soil for the literary pioneer." He meticulously and enthusiastically prepares for the journey, mimicking the excitement usually expressed about such adventurous undertakings: "What a glorious morning it was, and how the flowers did pour out their fragrance, and how the birds did sing! It was just the time for a tramp through the woods and mountains" (102). Then Twain clarifies the picture and reasserts the primary focus of his "pedestrian tour":

We were all dressed alike: broad slouch hats, to keep the sun off; gray knapsacks; blue army shirts; blue overalls; leathern gaiters buttoned tight from knee down to ankle; high-quarter coarse shoes snugly laced. Each man had an opera glass, a canteen, and a guide-book case slung over his shoulder, and carried an alpenstock in one hand and a sun umbrella in the other. Around our hats were wound many folds of soft white muslin, with the ends hanging and flapping down our backs,—an idea brought from the Orient and used by tourists all over Europe. (102)

The attention to detail Twain grants to his pedestrian costume as opposed to, say, the relative dearth of description of the scenery around the river emphasizes his primary focus. He and Harris are the objects of our scrutiny. In reference to Veblen's distinctions, Twain is clarifying his intention to perform a conspicuous act, which demands that he at least dress for the occasion. He does not, it seems, feel obligated to actually perform the task itself. Perfectly outfitted, having made all the correct costume choices, Twain the adventurer is ready to embark, but Twain the tourist makes an astute, practical observation: "When we got down town I found that we could go by rail to within five miles of Heilbronn. The train was just starting, so we jumped aboard and went tearing away in splendid spirits. It was agreed all around that we had done wisely, because it would be just as enjoyable to walk *down* the Neckar as up it, and it could not be needful to walk both ways" (103). Of course, Twain never walks *down* the Neckar either. He places readers on the verge of adventure only to skirt it at the first opportunity, preferring leisure over challenge and easily rationalizing away the implicit failure. Twain's theory of the tourist class is simple, as illustrated by this redefining of "pedestrian tour." The value is in the costume. In order to realize such an adventurous plan—walking up the Neckar, in this specific instance—Twain as tourist dons the proper accoutrements, and once that picture is complete the actual walking is negotiable—up and down, up or down, or neither. Twain rationalizes that *down* is sufficient, but by extension it is not "needful" to walk at all. Twain makes similar choices throughout the narrative, dressing for adventure and enjoying leisure. Twain pushes one step further by introducing several members of a German family on the train who are "greatly interested in our costumes," which, as they see it, are out of place for the terrain (104). They assume, then, that Twain and Harris are heading for "other rugged country." Of course, the family is unaware that the two adventurers are on a virtual pedestrian tour wherein plainer outfits hold little interest. There is really very little need for walking in a pedestrian tour according to Twain's understanding of touristic practices. When the family asks if the two adventurers find walking in such warm weather to be fatiguing, they answer truthfully: "We said no" (104).

In addition to avoiding walking during a pedestrian tour of Europe, Twain intersperses other methods of undermining the adventurer and updating its characteristics to the new age. He does, however, allow for stock excitement, by proxy. He employs surrogate adventurers to do the work for him, gaining the narrative excitement without placing himself under any strain. Harris becomes his primary substitute. For instance, upon noting that his itinerary does not include the Furka Pass, the Rhone Glacier, the Finsteraarhorn, and the Wetterhorn, and also upon discovering from his guidebook that they are important, he calls upon Harris to make an excursion to include each sight so Twain can insert the experience into his book. Moreover, he also wants Harris to take along a courier because, as Twain writes, "I must insist that as much style be thrown into my journeys as possible" (311–12). Twain is reasserting that, in a touristic context, actually doing something is not required to claim the experience as one's own. In his theory of the leisure class, all he needs to do is claim the experience—"my journeys." He also continues his play with the self-indulgence of such behavior, wherein the tourist becomes the focus of attention, the sight. His own *style* is a defining feature of the experience, not the act itself.[15] Later, as they travel through the Gemmi Pass in Switzerland (chapter 35), Twain refers to the "Ladders" built into the face of a precipice "two or three hundred feet high." Local peasants, according to Twain, climb these ladders in their daily routines, but he sees the potential danger of such a climb for someone unfamiliar with them. Twain the adventurer senses that danger is afoot, and he is eager for the challenge of such an exploit. Alas, Twain the tourist recognizes the same potential but prefers a more passive role:

> I ordered Harris to make the ascent, so I could put the thrill and horror of it in my book, and he accomplished the feat successfully, through a sub-agent for three francs, which I paid. It makes me shudder yet when I think of what I felt when I was clinging there between heaven and earth in the person of that

proxy. At times the world swam around me, and I could hardly keep from letting go, so dizzying was the appaling [*sic*] danger. Many a person would have given up and descended, but I stuck to my task, and would not yield until I had accomplished it. I felt a just pride in my exploit, but I would not have repeated it for the wealth of the world. I shall break my neck yet with some such fool-hardy performance, for warnings never seem to have any lasting effect upon me. (397–98)

Twain directly mocks the adventurer pose—and readers' expectations, for that matter—by claiming the thrills and dangers of the experience for himself just as his readers would, vicariously. Simultaneously, he undermines both his own pretense as adventurer and his role as a travel writer. Although everybody remains safe—reader in an armchair, writer at his desk, tourist on the ground—all participants, no less, claim the adventure as their own. They do, after all, pay for it. More important to his overall structure is the continuance of his satirical assertion that proxy experience equals actual experience. For the travel writer and the tourist, there is nothing "fool-hardy" about his vicarious trip up the ladders, but there is value in the "performance" dressed in full tourist costume.

Twain also appropriates the adventures of other travel writers, and the strategy is the same as with Harris. As he travels more deeply into the Alps, the opportunities for danger inevitably increase, and Twain taps into the potential risks to continue his mock-adventure and to maintain the vitality of his structural joke. Noting that approaching the Alps offered a "chance for blood-curdling Alpine adventure," Twain claims that the Great Altels, specifically, are "daring us to an ascent" (371). Again outfitted with stock language and determination, Twain proposes to climb the mountain, placing his readers on the threshold of yet another adventure. Consistent with his pattern, however, he hesitates, claiming that he needs to study the experiences of others in order to prepare himself for his own climb. At this point, Twain introduces his next surrogate adventurer, Thomas Hinchliff, whose *Summer Months among the Alps* (1857) provides the excitement and danger typical of Alpine mountaineering.[16] Twain cites Hinchliff's descriptions of his ascent of Monte Rosa and, using extensive quotations and paraphrases, quite simply transfers Hinchliff's adventures directly into *A Tramp Abroad*. Twain uses Hinchliff in much the same way that he uses Harris (and his "sub-agent"); they both help him capture the adventurous spirit he has promised readers all along. Of course, Harris as proxy helps Twain satirize the convention and create a comic touristic approach to adventuring; Hinchliff, on the other hand, represents the convention in its pure form and thus serves as the standard pose against which Twain can counter his passive, leisure-loving tourist. As he summarizes Hinchliff's narrative, Twain carefully emphasizes its perils and thrills, and he compliments the fortitude of the climbers. It is worth noting that Twain refrains from ridiculing Hinchliff; moreover, he highlights especially daring and shocking passages by placing them in italics. This lengthy usurpation of adventure contains no hint of irony or satire. His method, however, accomplishes two crucial tasks: he gives readers the adventures they enjoy, and he sets up the convention for subsequent parody as he turns the focus back on himself as the tourist. Assuming the role of reader (of Hinchliff), Twain learns about the dangers of *actual* adventuring, and just as he finishes the narrative, Harris interrupts, announcing that preparations for their own climb are complete. Twain balks and responds as the tourist: "I said I believed I wouldn't ascend the Altels this time. I said Alp-climbing was a different thing from what I had supposed it was, and so I judged we had better study its points a little more before we went definitely to it" (379).

Twain opens the following chapter (35) with a conventional description of his newfound passion for mountain climbing:

A great and priceless thing is a new interest! How it takes possession of a man! how it clings to him, how it rides him! I strode onward from the Schwarenbach hostelry a changed man, a reorganized personality. I walked in a new world, I saw with new eyes. I had been looking aloft at the giant snow-peaks only as things to be worshiped for their grandeur and magnitude, and their unspeakable grace of form; I looked up at them now, as also things to be conquered and climbed. (381)

The adventurer reemerges, complete with courage, enthusiasm, and exclamation points, a man ready to face any peril, to earn any experience. It is important to note, however, that the passage focuses not on the Alps but on Twain's "reorganized personality." He is reformed, this time fully in the garb of Hinchliff, a true adventurer. As tourist, moreover, Twain keeps the attention where it resides normally —on the self. Twain sees "with new eyes" that satirically serve more to mirror his touristic identity than to understand the Alps. By defining their "grandeur and magnitude" as "things to be conquered and climbed," Twain firmly infuses the peaks with his self-image, a dramatic overlay that heightens his comic shallowness. The new picture of the Alps has the tourist in the foreground: "I followed the steep lines up, inch by inch, with my eye, and noted the possibility or impossibility of following them with my feet. When I saw a shining helmet of ice projecting above the clouds, I tried to imagine I saw files of black specks toiling up it roped together with a gossamer thread" (381).

His passion reestablished, Twain confronts another opportunity for adventure and again opts for a surrogate. This time he cites Edward Whymper and his *Scrambles amongst the Alps* (1871).[17] As he does with Hinchliff, Twain claims he must learn more about climbing, so he quotes and paraphrases Whymper at length. Assuming the role of reader, Twain incorporates Whymper's perilous adventures into his own narrative. His reaction to his reading is important not only for its self-parody but also because it belies the pretense of a changing self-image. A man now ready for his own adventure comments: "I was no longer myself; I was tranced, uplifted, intoxicated, by the almost incredible perils and adventures I had been following my authors through, and the triumphs I had been sharing with them" (418). A standard trope of Alpine travels, the real-life perils of mountain climbing find their way into Twain's narrative and accomplish two tasks: first, the excerpts from Hinchliff and Whymper offer readers what Twain could rightfully assume would be interesting material and thus valuable as informative and sensational content; second, together they provide an immediate springboard for the leisure tourist. Also, by overstating his "intoxication" with Whymper's (and Hinchliff's) escapades and reasserting his own adventurer pose, Twain is ready for an extended parody of the conventional demands of the adventurer and typical desires of the tourist. He begins by making a supposedly startling proposal. Riding the crest of excitement provided by his surrogates, Twain announces, "I WILL ASCEND THE RIFFEL-BERG" (418). Twain the adventurer has decided to embark on what he proclaims to be a highly dangerous journey, and although Harris begs him to desist, he remains constant to his intentions ("I was already wrestling with the perils of the mountains"). Thus begins Twain's mock-epic adventure—the ascent of the Riffelberg.

Putting together an expedition worthy of true adventure (and true parody), Twain gathers "198 persons, including the mules; or 205, including the cows," and among his troop are four surgeons, fifteen barkeepers, and four pastry cooks (419). In addition to the comically absurd proportions of the expedition, the massive scale of the adventure helps create a sensation, the true goal of the leisure tourist, who wants to be the spectacle. As the long procession ("3,122 feet long") gets ready to leave, Twain emphasizes the explicit value of the ascent: his performance. Isn't it an Alpine picture? With many tourists and townspeople along the roadside, Twain begins his show with the simultaneous raising of 154 umbrellas. "It was a beautiful sight, and a total surprise to the spectators. Nothing like that had ever been seen in the Alps before. The applause it brought forth was deeply gratifying to me, and I rode by with my plug hat in my hand to testify my appreciation of it" (422). This burlesque expedition (mounted on donkeys, Twain and Harris, appropriately, are the only ones not walking) quickly becomes a comedy of errors, riddled with failures and absurdities. But when the climbing party finally reaches its goal seven days later, Twain—seeming ever oblivious to the illegitimacy of his endeavors—using stock language, declares the mission a success and, for those readers unfamiliar with the Riffelberg, completes his extended joke: "At noon we conquered the last impediment—we stood at last upon the summit, and without the loss of a single man except the mule that ate the glycerine. Our great achievement was achieved —the possibility of the impossible was demonstrated, and Harris and I walked proudly into the great dining room of the Riffelberg Hotel and stood our alpenstocks up in the corner" (445). Although his cadence matches that of Whymper and Hinchliff (as well as Taylor), the conspicuous lack of substance illustrates his true intent. The meaningless double-talk—"achievement was achieved" and the "possibility of the impossible"—serves to record, again, the primary characteristic of his pedestrian tour of Europe: leisure. Moreover, he playfully reasserts that he (along with Harris) is the focus of attention as he walks "proudly into the great dining room." The mock-pride derives from the touristic assumption that the style of the performance is all and, no matter the comic failures of the climb, the success of the endeavor is marked by the quality of his entrance into the hotel. The alpenstocks placed in the corner, their badges of courage, substantiate their "achievement." Twain regrets climbing in evening dress, however, because of the wear and tear the ordeal placed on the clothing; as a result, "the general effect was unpleasant and even disreputable" (445). This mistake is the only blemish on an otherwise successful performance. He continues: "There were about seventy-five tourists at the hotel,—mainly ladies and little children,—and they gave us an admiring welcome which paid us for all our privations and sufferings. The ascent had been made, and the names and dates now stand recorded on a stone monument there to prove it to all future tourists" (446). Of course, the ascent, as Twain emphasizes, represents no true "achievement" at all. The punch line for his parody depends on simple facts: "the Riffelberg" is a hotel, not a dangerous mountain, and, moreover, it is populated by "ladies and little children" who have obviously themselves made the "climb" before Twain. Still, his tattered gentleman's clothing aside, Twain affects a grand entrance and gains from the pseudo-ordeal what he has sought all along, "an admiring welcome" and a "monument" to himself as the quintessential tourist. Maintaining the mock-solemnity of the occasion, Twain undermines his own "achievement" as he informs his readers that he can only claim to be a tourist, a man of leisure seeking out Veblen's "immaterial evidences" to justify his unremitting idleness. Twain adds factual information on the Riffelberg Hotel walk taken from the guidebook. According to *Baedeker's* guide book, the walk from Zermatt to the hotel takes three hours (Twain takes seven days), the road is unmistakable (Twain gets lost), and guides are unnecessary (Twain has seventeen). Indignant, Twain concludes that the guidebook is wrong, claiming that "the road *can* be mistaken. If I am the first that did it, I want the credit of it, too" (450).

The conspicuous self-indulgence of the Riffelberg ascent illustrates in the specific what Twain parodies in general throughout *A Tramp Abroad:* his own theory of the tourist class. Touristic behavior, as Twain shows, depends on the overriding desire to place oneself in the pictures that define the world, in this case Europe. Placing himself in many of those pictures requires of Twain a willingness for self-delusion and a belief that actual experience is irrelevant to and, moreover, undistinguishable from touristic experience. In this sense, he follows with an ascent of Mount Blanc, the highest peak in Europe, that parallels his ascent of the Riffelberg in that its primary characteristic is Twain's ability, as the tourist, to insert himself into the frame of experience. In this satire of touristic behavior, Twain uses an ideal symbol, the telescope, which becomes another proxy for him to incorporate an adventurous spirit. The telescope can perform two significant illusions: it can bring the viewer's eyes to the top of Mount Blanc without demanding any exertion (other than pulling three francs from one's pocket), and it can provide a ready-made frame into which Twain can place himself. Twain writes: "I wanted to stand with a party on the summit of Mount Blanc, merely to be able to say I had done it" (515). As he looks through the telescope and watches a climbing party reach the top of the mountain, Twain mentally places himself with them and thereby gains the experience, in a purely touristic sense: "Presently we all stood together on the summit! What a view was spread out below!" (519). He then takes the delusion one step further by describing the view not through the telescope but from the perspective of the climbers, his proxies: "The eye roved over a troubled sea of sun-kissed Alps" (520). Interestingly, Twain uses the singular "eye," but to which eye is he referring—the unified eye of the actual climbers or the eye of Twain squinting through the telescope? It is neither, of course, because Twain's understanding of the eye of the tourist renders the question moot. No matter the origin of "the eye," it sees a wonderful Alpine picture, one the tourist can "remember" always. Nearing the end of this section of his pedestrian tour of Europe, Twain asserts yet again his own vision of touristic experience and provides a tongue-in-cheek tourist's philosophy: "Nothing is gained in the Alps by over-exertion; nothing is gained by crowding two day's [sic] work into one for the poor sake of being able to boast of the exploit afterward. It will be found much better, in the long run, to do the thing in two days, and then subtract one of them from the narrative. This saves fatigue, and does not injure the narrative. All the more thoughtful among the Alpine tourists do this" (531). The goal of the tourist, according to Twain's astute satirical eyes, is to obtain a "narrative." Aside from its self-referential nature to Twain as the travel writer ever vigilant for content to include in his own work, this observation reasserts the self-referential obsession of tourists on the whole, for all tourists perform this deception. Reality in the Tourist Age is always negotiable.

In *A Tramp Abroad,* Twain, like most tourists, is no adventurer, but, again like most tourists, he can pretend to be one and enjoy wearing its costumes. As a thrill-seeker of a vicarious and thoroughly passive sort, Twain endeavors throughout the narrative to gather his "immaterial evidences" to justify his claims to adventure and solidify his status as a man of leisure, as a modern tourist. True to his satire and his structural plan for *A Tramp Abroad,* Twain closes out his pedestrian tour of Europe as he opens it—saving "shoe leather"—thereby concluding both his ambitious "tramp" and his extended joke upon the leisured dreams of the American tourist.

Traveling to the Old World, the mid-nineteenth-century American tourist moves back in time. Twain's versions of such time travel in his two narratives to Europe apply this nostalgia to the Tourist Age. Tourism—a process of commodifying cultures, peoples, and places—is also a process of reformatting the past into the recognizable present, a consumable present. The strengths of *The Innocents Abroad* and *A Tramp Abroad* derive from Twain's intuitive ability to illustrate this reordering of the world into a touristic context. Far more complex than youthful nationalistic exuberance or middle-age complacency, the perspectives within these two narrative tours hold the promise as well as the failure of the Tourist Age, the new way of seeing the world based primarily on deception and self-delusion. Twain makes a provocative observation in the middle of his tour, one of the few remarks on tourism at large and its effects on European culture:

> What a change has come over Switzerland, and in fact all Europe, during this century. Seventy or eighty years ago Napoleon was the only man in Europe who could really be called a traveler; he was the only man who had devoted his attention to it and taken a powerful interest in it; he was the only man who had traveled extensively; but now everybody goes everywhere; and Switzerland, and many other regions which were unvisited and unknown remotenesses a hundred years ago, are in our days a buzzing hive of restless strangers every summer. But I digress. (345)

Twain does not digress here. More accurately, the passage illustrates his understanding of the true power of the "restless strangers" definitive of the Tourist Age. As *The Innocents Abroad* and *A Tramp Abroad* demonstrate, the great popular movement of tourists, placed astutely in context with the conquering army of Napoleon, sweeps across Europe, remaking everything in the process. Twain plays with the ridiculous notion that Napoleon traveled alone, but, of course, he traveled with armies behind him. His transformative power derived from sheer numbers as much as desire as he moved through Europe in order to call it his own. This new army of "restless strangers" ultimately carries more power, and its influences, as Twain recognizes, will long outlive those of Napoleon. There is no Waterloo for the Tourist Age.

4
Touring the New World

The Search for Home in *Roughing It* and *Life on the Mississippi*

Like his travel books to the Old World, Twain's two books westward into the New World explore touristic experience. Added to that context, however, is a pressing search for home. *Roughing It* and *Life on the Mississippi* stand out for their peculiarly autobiographical focus. Of course, all travel books are autobiographical by definition, but these two narratives stretch the connections between the two genres significantly. In *Roughing It,* Twain consciously attempts to follow up *The Innocents Abroad* with a logical companion, "The Innocents at Home."[1] Yet the narrative does not derive from a specific, self-contained trip like the *Quaker City* pleasure excursion; rather, it covers a series of "vagabondizing" adventures that occurred several years before the idea of the narrative itself. It thus resembles memoir, influenced by a nostalgia for the material on which it is based. Yet its final form reveals Twain's recognition of its narrative and thus economic potential to the author as a travel book proper. Twain specifically constructed and manipulated this autobiographical clay and molded it to fit the conventions of the genre—behold the memoir transformed into the travel book. The generative essence remains that of memoir, however. Whereas in *The Innocents Abroad* Twain derives touristic experience from a specific itinerary, in *Roughing It* he applies a specific itinerary to a non-touristic experience. While built around the same travel-book formulas that worked so well in *The Innocents Abroad,* it is a work of more distant memory, a text separated from the actual travels not by weeks or months, but by years. So in shaping the history, Twain, eager to relive the success of *The Innocents Abroad* more so than his life in Nevada and California, essentially revises the material and presents it as a "pleasure excursion," at least in the expectation he sets out with in the opening chapter. As such, the narrative content of *Roughing It,* even though its autobiographical action, so to speak, occurs before that of *The Innocents Abroad,* could only follow Twain's (and readers') first tour. Twain simply grandfathers the western experience into the Tourist Age that began with *The Innocents Abroad.* The proposed "three-month" tour ultimately lasts "six or seven uncommonly long years," but it is important to note that it retains the guise of a tour throughout, and *Roughing It,* therefore, evokes the character of a seven-year pleasure excursion, nonetheless.

Life on the Mississippi is by no means an expansion of the purely autobiographical "Old Times on the Mississippi," a series of autobiographical essays Twain published in 1875 in the *Atlantic Monthly.* To view it as such diminishes Twain's vision for his travel book, which was wholly different from that of "Old Times." There is no doubt that the earlier text helped to encourage Twain to explore further his Mississippi River life and even to go back; however, the return trip itself and the travel-book structure it provides are the crucial, formative characteristics of *Life on the Mississippi,* for which "Old Times on the Mississippi" lends support and breadth, not underpinning. Unlike *Roughing It,* this tour through the author's life derives from a specific trip and, moreover, an anthropological context for mapping the Mississippi River basin culture. For this travel book, then, the recounting of Twain's childhood and adolescence is essential but not generative.

In both narratives, however distinct their differences, Twain is deeply connected personally to "place" (time and geography) and to "self" (his own identity) represented by each place—the West and the Mississippi River, his youth in each. The tourist struggles to find balance between the unavoidable feelings of displacement definitive of tourism and the nostalgic longing so typical of remembrances of things past. Unlike the Old World travels of *The Innocents Abroad* and *A Tramp Abroad,* wherein there is a clear separation of self and place, Twain's narrative tours of the West and the Mississippi River are connected with a sense of self inevitably and inextricably tied to places that helped to form the writer. Twain faces the difficulty of having to visit his personal past in the process of creating a travel narrative. It is a daunting task, forcing him to see not only with the eyes of the tourist but also with the eyes of the native, both of which conspire to be myopic at best, delusional at worst. The two narratives in their individual scopes and in their total personal context offer special challenges to Twain as tourist and travel writer, and they beg two synchronous questions: Can a tourist go home? Can a travel writer write about it?

As a result of this basic conflict within both *Roughing It* and *Life on the Mississippi,* these two narratives also prove problematic for readers, who must sense the ambivalence that often haunts our guide, conflicted by his own struggle to define place and thus himself. Moreover, the historical and instructive content of both works carries with it a much keener sense of urgency—of capturing a lifestyle and a culture quickly ebbing away or perhaps already lost. But because of Twain's connection, the urgency also has a desperation—most poignant in *Life on the Mississippi*—because the self, a past self, goes with the place. The tourist sees himself fading away. Unlike the information prevalent in the two Old World travel books (and subsequently in *Following the Equator*), in *Roughing It* and *Life on the Mississippi* it is personal. What happens when a travel writer goes home? For one thing, his need to respect the place helps to make the instructive content more vital and intrinsic to the narrative movement. Yes, there is parody and satire, but in the balance both narratives represent a comprehensiveness that far exceeds that of Twain's other travel books. He is writing about his history, his self, and the resulting narratives tour (and detour) into a recording of failure.

ROUGHING IT AND EXPERIMENTS IN TOURISTIC IDENTITY

Unique in its subject matter if not structure within Twain's travel-writing canon, *Roughing It* presents youthful meanderings remembered from the eyes of the older, more settled man. Twain works, for the most part, with the same travel-book formulas that worked so well in *The Innocents Abroad,* yet this narrative demands the reorganizing of material from remembrances of years long gone. Although it depends often on Twain's (and his brother Orion's) partial reconstructions of distant travels, *Roughing It* is presented, nonetheless, as a conventional travel book.[2] Twain applies these often disparate experiences to his current touristic perspective, newly learned and newly available for satire. Once the narrative tour begins, the autobiographical context is largely irrelevant. In constructing *Roughing It,* Twain is not so much nostalgic as shrewd in remaking his past into travel narrative, into a tour of the mythic West, and updating it, as it were, for the Tourist Age. As such, the narrator reenters and redefines the experience (bringing his readers along) from one dominant perspective—that of the tourist.

Sensing the mutability of place and the nature of change within himself, Twain, as the tourist, seeks to reform himself, stop touring, and put down roots, thereby placing his mark on the West. This dream, the ultimate dream of authenticity in the Tourist Age, can only fail. The tourist of *Roughing It,* like all tourists, is an outsider who searches for a home based on a misguided notion that both his romantic, imaginary West and his professed commitment to it are real. The pretense of a personal connection to place provides no lasting protection against the failure of experience so prevalent in *The Innocents Abroad.* The connection remains an illusion, and any notion of self depends on self-delusion. *Roughing It,* then, reveals the desperate attempts of a tourist to stay put, to belong while inevitably moving with the westward tide across a promising but ultimately unforgiving landscape. The only destiny made manifest by the Tourist Age is not settlement but indeterminacy—"vagabondizing."

Twain, however, transfers great expectations of place to great expectations of self. The place will alter the self and thereby accept the mark of the tourist narrator on the landscape and culture. As the tourist miner, Twain must dig to make his mark, his claim to the land and his presence; as the travel writer, he must revise his life during those seven years and establish himself as the tourist to acknowledge that his claims were temporary and smacked of conceit and failure. As a result, *Roughing It* offers a satirical look at how delusions of self and illusions of place work together to create touristic failure. Romantic expectations arise not from historical associations but primarily, as Twain illustrates, from dreams of the future. The Old World offers the Euro-American tourist a chance to witness the past; the West offers the chance to make the future. Twain thus participates in the mythic West while demonstrating its limitations and deceptions. It is revisionist history at its touristic best. And the resulting narrative tour westward pretends to be an emigration wherein Twain pretends to transform himself into a local citizen and to reenact the winning of the West. In this sense, the narrative records how the West was lost.

A vital key to reading *Roughing It,* then, is to consider the tourist's passivity in this loss. As he had in *The Innocents Abroad* and would later in *A Tramp Abroad,* Twain explores, comically, the characteristics of the tourist as a passive leisure seeker. Although the West stands in the popular imagination as antithetical to such indulgence in the traveler, *Roughing It* shows that the tourist indeed can move through the epic, mythical West without achieving any substantive "transforming experience," as Henry Nash Smith calls it.[3] Most readers, following Smith's astute lead, have noted that *Roughing It* can be viewed as an initiation wherein the narrator experiences some authentic change, a significant move from the naive tenderfoot to the wiser old-timer.[4] Within the tenderfoot/old-timer theme, the failures that permeate the text become learning experiences. As a result of viewing the narrative from this critical perspective and seeing it as an "embryonic novel,"[5] the balance of the text, a weighty balance at that, becomes problematic and even bothersome to readers. The instructive material so crucial to a travel book and so pertinent to the touristic experience (whether internalized or not) intrudes upon and distracts from a smooth narrative tracing the development of a tenderfoot. The newspaper extracts and anecdotal asides, as well as excerpts from historical accounts and the Sandwich Islands section, seem cumbersome and tangential. It may be helpful to consider, however, that a travel book, by definition, must offer much more varied and even seemingly incoherent content than the tenderfoot/old-timer theme can allow. Readers can only be dismayed by the lack of unity, as if the text were an imperfectly designed novel. Another approach may be to read *Roughing It* as a travel book, as was Twain's intention, and place it more firmly in the Tourist Age, for which *The Innocents Abroad* had been a clarion call.

Roughing It possesses a clear and definitive point of view, that of the tourist, who learns nothing in seven years, who consistently seeks fresh experiences, or at least the image of them. This narrator makes no demands of his travels other than the prototypical dream of the Tourist Age, a search for authenticity without facing too much discomfort. The title implies a "rough" life, but the goal throughout is to avoid such roughness whenever possible. As he had shown in *The Innocents Abroad* and would later expand on in *A Tramp Abroad,* leisure is the tourist's primary goal (if not the stated one), and that standard inescapable wish thus moderates the craving for raw experience. As a consequence, the imagination—not actual physical experience—must become preeminent in order to salvage the tour. Although Twain, the tourist-narrator, tries ostensibly to find a *home* in the West, he cannot escape his basic nature—to watch, to pretend deep involvement while remaining inactive and distant. The failures in the text, then, may not necessarily be those of a naive tenderfoot but of the self-delusioned tourist.

The opening chapter introduces immediately the notion of romanticized travel and Twain's eagerness for his impending participation. The tourist is eager to see "the curious new world" (19), an interesting choice of words, echoing the dramatic romantic ideal of touring westward—the "new world." So Twain defines typically high, if vague, expectations similar to those of *The Innocents Abroad,* but he also grants himself the role—self-deceptive, of course—of the discoverer, the new world open to be explored (and, by implication, conquered). Then he adds to the epic proportions the seemingly antithetical definition of the journey as a "pleasure excursion," reminiscent of the *Quaker City* tour, to juxtapose the true overriding nature of the ensuing narrative. Twain embarks upon a new voyage of discovery, not of the true West, but of the West as one big tourist sight. The tourist travels to fulfill expectations not necessarily connected to any real place, however, so Twain marks this tour by the outlandish, dreamlike quality of his expectations. Filled with hyperbole, *Roughing It* begins with innocent dreams (bolstered also by the illustration called "The Miner's Dream" which precedes the title page). But Twain lets readers know that expectations are thwarted in this tour: "I little thought that I would not see the end of that three-month pleasure excursion for six or seven uncommonly long years" (20). So in the opening, the tour is similar to that of *The Innocents Abroad,* though shorter (three months as opposed to five). It is intended to be, nonetheless, a "pleasure excursion," the new mode of exploration in the Tourist Age. Yet the West, unlike the Old World, offers a different type of pleasure. Twain hopes to encounter "buffaloes and Indians, and prairie dogs, and antelopes, and have all kinds of adventures, and may be get hanged or scalped" (19).[6] With this manic recital of common western stereotypes, Twain begins the tour. The immersion into the myth takes very little time to begin to undermine the tourist's dream. Immediately, Twain must begin altering himself to meet the demands of this new place, discarding the costume that identifies him as the easterner because its weight is not permitted on the stagecoach. He must leave much of his eastern accoutrements behind. The restrictions on the stagecoach not only separate the tourist from the comfort of his possessions but also symbolically force him to renew himself in a different guise and submit wholly to the exigencies of the new place; there is no turning back.

Twain and his brother keep their dictionary, which proves to be a painful decision. Although attempting to bring language (civilization) into this wild West, Twain does little more than put himself at risk, as the book proves to be quite dangerous as it is tossed around the stage and onto the passengers. The words between the book's covers, and all that they may describe, take a beating on the tour to the West, and the tourist, moreover, is punished for his confidence in those words. The words are not only those that may potentially be used to describe the touristic experience; they are also those of previous tourists, the earlier mythmakers who have put their lies into the tourist's dreams. Not only is the holding on to the unabridged dictionary a hopeless and ineffectual choice; it is also a silly, ignorant one, since another could have been purchased in San Francisco (22). The weight of the dictionary is wasted, the words useless and unnecessary; the tourist has made his first mistake.

It is important to note as well that Twain's complaints of stagecoach travel take on an especially conscious touristic context as he compares it later with railroad travel in one of his supposed confusions between the tenderfoot's perspective and the old-timer's. Although Twain shifts from the two points of view, he does so while emphasizing his topic from the perspective of the tourist and notes particularly how the railroads have both shortened the time necessary to cross the continent and lessened the discomfort. These changes emphasize improvements in touristic apparatus, Tourist Age amenities. This touristic perspective supports his choice to include the *New York Times* article "Across the Continent" (46–47). Throughout the overland journey, Twain highlights the distance traveled, noting with enthusiasm how the time required to make such a trip has lessened consistently with the march of civilization. In this sense, Twain methodically keeps before the reader the inevitable shortening of travel time that symbolically shortens distance. The occurrences of such time and space references are numerous: "*fifty-six hours out from St. Joe*" (46); "four hundred and seventy miles from St. Joseph" (59); "our stage had come in *eight days and three hours*—seven hundred and ninety-eight miles!" (97); among others.[7] This inevitable minimizing of time and space provides the underlying message of *Roughing It:* the death of the mythic West, for which the tourist is the true harbinger.

Constant movement is the key. The tourist's fascination with the Pony Express riders offers a further development of the metaphor. It illustrates the basic premise of the mythology of the West as a land of unbridled opportunity for the enterprising, energetic, and industrious, characteristics that form a clear counterbalance to Twain's touristic persona: dull, passive, and lazy. "[The rider] must be always ready to leap into the saddle and be off like the wind!" (70), and Twain continues, "There was no idling-time for a pony-rider on duty." There is the rub. Twain must balance his romantic fascination for such energy with his touristic impulse for leisure, which, in order to move "like the wind," requires the help of a stagecoach driver, not his own drive. Twain is in the West on tour to see the sights, and at this point in the narrative he is eager to do just that. His earliest "sights" are people, characters who fill his touristic canvas. The most formidable character is none other than the epitome of western myth, the desperado Slade.

Slade serves as an ideal romantic figure of the West in all its potential touristic glory, so Twain focuses on him carefully and at length, fully exploiting his interest value and describing him in terms that both expand on his mythic proportions and emphasize the narrator's expectations. The thematic centrality of placing Slade in such a touristic context, a spectacle to be seen, a tourist sight, is evident in Twain's descriptions. They take two basic forms: the reactions of the tourist and the "factual" information taken both in paraphrase and quotation from Thomas J. Dimsdale's *The Vigilantes of Montana.*[8] For our consideration here, the tourist's reactions to the spectacle called "Slade" are especially pertinent: "Here was romance, and I sitting face to face with it!—looking upon it—touching it—hobnobbing with it, as it were! Here, right by my side, was the actual ogre who, in fights and brawls and various ways, *had taken the lives of twenty-six human beings,* or all men lied about him!" (87). Twain presents this encounter as the ideal, authentic tourist experience, and by using the pronoun "it" he clearly places the impetus for the feeling where it belongs—not on the man, Slade, but the image, "Slade," *it.* Moreover, once Twain introduces the experience to readers ("Here was romance"), rhetorically he keeps the focus on himself, the tourist gaining experience by being close to "Slade" ("I sitting face to face with it!—looking upon it—touching it—hobnobbing with it"). Twain closes this moment with a telling phrase: "or all men lied about him!" This is no throw-away line, nor is it an effort to question the veracity of the "facts" of Slade's killing record; rather, it slyly reaffirms the irrelevance of the truth to the touristic experience. This seems to be the case especially when considering his use of the exclamation point, a strange punc-tuation mark to employ if he wants to undermine the accuracy of the Slade myth. Whether or not Twain is "sitting face to face" with a lie is ultimately unimportant. The enthusiasm that begins the paragraph carries through to the end without slowing down to consider the le-gitimacy of the experience of meeting the West, "touching it."

The desperado character is by no means the only sight crucial to a successful western experience for the tourist.[9] The natural wonders seemingly omnipresent in the landscape had been well established as central to the western mythology the tourist is so eager to see, and Twain is ready to grant that part of the experience to readers, as he does throughout his travel-writing career. Nearing Salt Lake City, he writes: "At four in the afternoon we arrived on the summit of Big Mountain, fifteen miles from Salt Lake City, when all the world was glorified with the setting sun, and the most stupendous panorama of mountain peaks yet encountered burst on our sight. We looked out upon this sublime spectacle from under the arch of a brilliant rain-bow! Even the overland stage-driver stopped his horses and gazed!" (106). This description reinforces the touristic way of seeing, a "pano-rama," which could just as easily be indicative of the broad landscape paintings so popular in the nineteenth century as of a generalized wide-open space, a template of sorts for a geography of seemingly infinite possibilities. This is Twain's effective literary application of the idea behind the popular Claude Glass, a gilded frame that sight-seers could hold and through which they could view natural beauty as if it were a painting, a "sublime spectacle" framed by "the arch of a brilliant rainbow." Twain further legitimizes the experience by not-ing that the stagecoach driver, a local, is equally mesmerized by the sight.

The romance of nature has its limitations, and the reality of "roughing it" soon begins to wear down such enthusiasm. The pri-mary concern for such travel to an undeveloped tourist location de-rives from the almost absolute absence of comforts normally required by the tourist. Twain's first significant disappointment occurs in an unnamed alkali desert: "It was easy enough to cross a desert in the night while we were asleep; and it was pleasant to reflect, in the morning, that we in actual person *had* encountered an absolute desert and could always speak knowingly of deserts in presence of the ignorant thenceforward. And it was pleasant also to reflect that this was not an obscure, back country desert, but a very celebrated one, the metropolis itself, as you may say" (142–43). The mind of the tourist is a simple one when it comes to gaining experience, as we have seen. Well aware of the characteristic need of the tourist to chalk up experience as authentic in the most flexible terms, Twain plays on his own touristic "encounter" with an alkali desert fully in relation to touristic expectations. The ideal experience in this context, then, would be to travel across a desert at night, therefore claiming the experience as real (authentic) without suffering any privations whatsoever (and without seeing anything). Twain points out the true value of touring: status, establishing oneself as having been there. Also, he puts that value to work by "speak[ing] knowingly of deserts" to the "ignorant," a word that could apply to ignorance of the desert itself or of exactly how the tourist had gained the so-called experience, in this case while sleeping; either way, it does not matter to the tourist—no pain, much gain. Moreover, they have traveled over a notable desert, one that people had surely heard of. This offers substantial status for the tourist. Crossing it, the tourist claims by extension its celebrity for himself. Similarly to his encounters in the Holy Land, wherein the cover of darkness helped Twain hold on to his romantic images, the nighttime in the alkali desert allows him to maintain the romance of "touching" one (as he had with the desperado via Slade).

The daytime brings a different response, as the tourist must face the desert under the sun's full glare and heat. Twain carefully sets up the inevitable disappointment and reasserts the romantic expectations: "All this was very well and very comfortable and satisfactory—but now we were to cross a desert in *daylight*. This was fine—novel—romantic—dramatically adventurous—*this*, indeed, was worth living for, worth traveling for! We would write home all about it" (143). His mock-eagerness for the danger, even unpleasantness, pretending to want to be "face to face" with a desert as he had with "Slade," awake to the realities, soon withers: "This enthusiasm, this stern thirst for adventure, wilted under the sultry August sun and did not last above one hour. One poor little hour—and then we were ashamed that we had 'gushed' so. The poetry was all in the anticipation—there is none in the reality" (143). The "poetry" perhaps, more accurately, derives from the touristic imagination, fueled by the myth of the West. Here Twain takes a moment not just to mock himself as the tourist but also to debunk the myth—or at least this portion of it—and set the record straight. Following this admission of shame, Twain, in one of his most lyrical and effective descriptive passages, honest and free from satire, follows with four paragraphs of detailed reality of desert conditions wherein the tourist in effect wishes desperately for nighttime, for sleep, for romantic dreams. The passage deserves quoting at length:

Imagine a vast, waveless ocean stricken dead and turned to ashes; imagine this solemn waste tufted with ash-dusted sage-bushes; imagine the lifeless silence and solitude that belong to such a place; imagine a coach, creeping like a bug through the midst of this shoreless level, and sending up tumbled volumes of dust as if it were a bug that went by steam; imagine this aching monotony of toiling and plowing kept up hour after hour, and the shore still as far away as ever, apparently; imagine team, driver, coach and passengers so deeply coated with ashes that they are all one colorless color; imagine ash-drifts roosting above moustaches and eyebrows like snow accumulations on boughs and bushes. This is the reality of it.

The sun beats down with dead, blistering, relentless malignity; the perspiration is welling from every pore in man and beast, but scarcely a sign of it finds its way to the surface—it is absorbed before it gets there; there is not the faintest breath of air stirring; there is not a merciful shred of cloud in all the brilliant firmament; there is not a living creature visible in any direction whither one searches the blank level that stretches its monotonous miles on every hand; there is not a sound—not a sigh—not a whisper—not a buzz, or a whir of wings, or distant pipe of bird—not even a sob from the lost souls that doubtless people that dead air. And so the occasional sneezing of the resting mules, and the champing of the bits, grate harshly on the grim stillness, not dissipating the spell but accenting it and making one feel more lonesome and forsaken than before. (143–44)

Rhetorically, Twain carefully tries to bring readers into the reality of the desert, directly encouraging them by repeating the word "imagine." But this word also reaffirms the crucial role the imagination plays for the tourist and how it has created the West. During the earlier part of the desert crossing—during the night—Twain's touristic imagination has filled his picture of the desert, allowing him to reaffirm his own mythic, romantic expectations of a desert's characteristics, a vital part of the West according to the tourist's understanding. In the phase of the crossing represented by the passage above—during the day—however, Twain subverts the touristic imagination by pushing readers to "imagine" the reality of the alkali desert. Methodically appealing to readers' senses, he demonstrates how harsh and brutal the crossing is; this is not a spectacle, not a fun time to "write home all about." This is no fun at all. And the dominant image is one not of charming, picturesque romance but of death ("dead," "ashes," "waste," "lifeless"). It is the myth that Twain seeks to destroy. He closes out the extended object lesson in reality by returning to the readers' senses and showing how the desert overwhelms them physically and thus symbolically obfuscates from view the desert of the imagination: "The alkali dust cut through our lips, it persecuted our eyes, it ate through the delicate membranes and made our noses bleed and *kept* them bleeding—and truly and seriously the romance all faded far away and disappeared, and left the desert trip nothing but a harsh reality—a thirsty, sweltering, longing, hateful reality!" (144). Face to face with the alkali desert, there is no way for the tourist to speak ("cut through our lips"), no way to see ("persecuted our eyes"), no way to breathe ("made our noses bleed"). It makes very little literal sense to call the experience of the desert crossing "reality" unless Twain is consciously dismantling the mythic imagination. Stripped of the touristic expectations, for which he had "gushed," the experience, not the desert itself, has been altered. The tourist has met the desert "face to face," and he does not like it. He can only hate the "desert trip" and its "reality," not so much for its essence as for its intrusiveness, its forced entry into his pleasure excursion. Unable to deny the harsh effects the desert causes to his too solid flesh, the tourist prefers the nighttime crossing in that it preserves the more alluring illusion of the desert. As the tourist becomes blocked physically from seeing (smelling, tasting, as well as touching) the actual desert, he also loses the touristic way of seeing (smelling, tasting, and touching) the imagined desert, a more painful loss.

The desert as tourist sight proves a formidable disappointment, and its position as the practical end of the overland journey provides an ideal context for Twain, the freshly disillusioned tourist, to begin to alter his self, to adjust the touristic self to the new place. Exhausted by the traveling, newly arrived in Nevada Territory, Twain begins his makeover to become a local, ostensibly transforming himself from a tourist identity to that of a permanent resident. As in all touristic endeavors, this metamorphosis is merely playacting. It is important to note that in pretending to become a local, the tourist simply refocuses his touristic imagination and places himself within the frame, or on the stage. The play's the thing. Twain changes costumes in effect and becomes the homesteader. A theoretical basis may be helpful here to best establish Twain's efforts to go native. In the balance of *Roughing It,* after the overland journey, the narrator adopts a mode of touristic behavior that mirrors what Erik Cohen has termed "experimental." In differentiating between five general modes of touristic behavior, Cohen notes:

> The traveller in the "experimental" mode engages in [local] authentic life, but refuses fully to commit himself to it; rather, he samples and compares the different alternatives, hoping eventually to discover one which will suit his particular needs and desires. In a sense, the "experimental" tourist is in "search of himself," insofar as in a trial and error process, he seeks to discover that form of life which elicits a resonance in himself; he is often not really aware of what he seeks, of his "real" needs and desires. His is an essentially religious quest, but diffuse and without a clearly set goal. (189)

Cohen's experimental tourist provides an accurate and helpful template for examining Twain's pretense of finding a new home and a new identity in the West. Twain immediately begins to assume local costume and plays a local citizen in a typical touristic dramatic production by engaging in what he perceives to be an authentic moment of living. As the narrative illustrates again and again, he is consistently unable to "commit himself," using Cohen's phrase, and as a result he moves from identity to identity—what Twain calls "vagabondizing" in the preface—all the while "hoping eventually to discover one which will suit his . . . needs and desires." Since the tourist needs leisure and desires novelty, his hope truly derives from his unstated but definitive goal of seeking novelty and amusement; he can only meet with failure in the American West.

The opening of chapter 22, coming after he completes the rigorous overland journey, clarifies Twain's impending experimental tourism: "It was the end of August, and the skies were cloudless and the weather superb. In two or three weeks I had grown wonderfully fascinated with the curious new country, and concluded to put off my return to 'the states' awhile. I had grown well accustomed to wearing a damaged slouch hat, blue woolen shirt, and pants crammed into boot-tops, and gloried in the absence of coat, vest and braces" (168). Ceremonially casting off his eastern (outsider) clothing during the initial stages of the journey, the tourist decides to remain in the garb of a local (insider), thus beginning the experiment. True to a touristic sense of authenticity, he assumes that donning the costume equates with becoming a local citizen. Twain believes he belongs to this place, this new home. Well aware of the faults inherent in his experiment, he follows with: "It seemed to me that nothing could be so fine and so romantic" (168). The essential problem with experimental tourism, as Twain intuits it, is that it is based on a flawed premise that authenticity is possible for the tourist, and this weakness becomes patently absurd when the tourist remains enamored of the romantic, mythic West and defines the costume and thus himself as "fine" and "romantic."

Twain's undercutting of this experimental vision in the balance of the narrative clarifies the basic structure that informs *Roughing It*. Honing his perspective for the narrative, Twain establishes a satirical persona that derives from what he learned in his first grand tourist experience chronicled in *The Innocents Abroad*. Although the actual travels that make up *Roughing It* occurred before the *Quaker City* pleasure excursion, the narrative depends heavily on Twain's trip to the Old World and his manipulation of touristic imagination in the earlier text. He is applying the same ways of seeing the Old World to the new. The tourist is now eager to experiment with his self-identity as a way to "touch" the mythic West and become a part of it. It is a fool's errand, as Twain well knows. But it is important to note, as well, that his desire to become a local evolves from the tourist's romantic understanding of the West, not any clear sense of place as true immigrants would perhaps understand it. Like tourists in general, Twain travels to see an ideal of place, a cultural production learned from earlier travel writers and dime novelists, and it is into this mythic idea that he wants to immerse himself, a true believer of his own flawed experiment. The confession that follows the passage above helps solidify this false sense of *self* in *place*. Twain notes that he does nothing in his official capacity as an "officer of the government": "I had nothing to do and no salary." Although the title affords a certain "sublimity" for his identity, its primary value is that it allows him to claim a local identity, a title, while also freeing him to spend the bulk of his time pursuing "amusement" (168). Thus begins Twain's lengthy experimental tour of the mythic West playing the role of homesteader, a touristic reenactment of local identity.

Paramount to the western myth of possibilities is the desire, or even the expectation, to strike it rich. For this portion of the dream, the tourist spends much of his experimental fervor, ostensibly associating himself with his peers, all of whom, it would seem, have the same goal—definitive of the place—to grab a fortune out of the ground itself. One problem: the romantic vision as set out in the opening chapters is, of course, a lie. Before the trip, Twain establishes his faulty assumptions that his brother would "see the gold mines and the silver mines, and maybe go about of [*sic*] an afternoon when his work was done, and pick up two or three pailfuls of shining slugs, and nuggets of gold and silver on the hillside" (19). Interestingly, his brother would find these riches *after* work, thus implying that the gathering of gold and silver is a leisure-minded activity, that it is not work to fill those pails, and that it can be done casually with little effort. Also, the passage importantly illustrates that the tourist believes the gold and silver to be simply scattered "on the hillside," no digging required, no depth necessary. Having arrived in the West and survived the overland journey, Twain intends to put those expectations to the test (seemingly wholly unaware that they may fail such a test). Right away, he faces work and toil trying to homestead on the shores of Lake Tahoe, where he hopes (expects) to pick up his first pailful of riches in the form of a "wood ranch."

Twain's early reactions to Lake Tahoe are crucial ones to consider from his touristic perspective and as central to his experiment. His first description is standard touristic fare: "As it lay there with the shadows of the mountains brilliantly photographed upon its still surface I thought it must surely be the fairest picture the whole earth affords" (169). True to touristic seeing, Lake Tahoe is a "picture," with mountains "photographed" on its surface. Carefully framed, the lake is ready for consumption, a commodity not only of visual imagery but also of potential personal wealth, a veritable paradise of riches there for the taking.

The lake's beauty, however, would prove to be at risk almost immediately upon the tourist's intrusion; this experiment has consequences to place as well as self. The land faces destruction as the tourist's first attempt to homestead fails miserably, not because of any inherent inadequacy of place or opportunity but because of a weakness of self. Despite all desires to become a local man tied to place, the tourist fails at the first experiment due to his basic visitor mentality, governed by his romantic assumptions nurtured from afar. This perspective inevitably stands in contrast to the local reality. The overwhelming struggle Twain faces in even reaching the lake hints at the potentially catastrophic disparity between the romantic ideal of place and its actuality, but what ensures the tragedy is the tourist's behavior —characterized by a comedy of errors definitive of the tourist who assumes after all that the place exists for his consumption. The "fairest picture" in which the tourist frames Lake Tahoe represents only the beginning of the destruction of place. Once compartmentalized, the lake is ready for "mining," ready to offer its riches to the experiment. Twain immediately incorporates one of his favorite character traits, laziness. But considering its touristic context helps to illustrate how this humorous trait (to which he refers throughout his career) complements the experimental tourist and his inevitable failure. Assuming the full role of leisure tourist (by definition passive), Twain puts his companion ("Johnny K") into the role as server, usually the role taken by locals as part of any touristic apparatus. For example, Twain humorously claims his entitlement to leisure even in a small rowboat: "I got Johnny to row—not because I mind exertion myself, but because it makes me sick to ride backwards when I am at work" (169). This joke serves an additional purpose beyond its obvious humorous value; it also solidifies Twain's role here as the tourist. In the absence of locals, someone (in this case, Johnny) must serve the tourist and guarantee his expectations of leisure, his entitlement. Ironically, being served by a "local" helps move the experiment forward by helping Twain play local without exerting himself. Johnny goes on to gather wood for the fire and cook while Twain "supervises." The absence of locals proper helps maintain the illusion that the two are local themselves and that Johnny's servitude does not allow Twain to be the leisure tourist while playing homesteader. As long as Johnny is amenable to doing the work, there is no problem; the performance is safe.

In order to claim the land for their proposed "wood ranch," law requires that they post "notices" announcing the claim and build a fence surrounding it. Here is the first unexpected catch in Twain's experiment. Becoming part of place, it seems, demands not simply an imaginative, self-indulgent desire to be rich but a significant outlay of physical effort. Twain responds as the tourist and thus seals the failure of the experiment. At first they claim three hundred acres, a nice round and big number in the abstract, in the mind of a tourist. "It was necessary to fence our property or we could not hold it. That is to say, it was necessary to cut down trees here and there and make them fall in such a way as to form a sort of enclosure (with pretty wide gaps in it)" (171). There are "pretty wide gaps" in this scheme as well. Even in its inception, Twain balks at making an actual fence; the work it would demand makes it simply out of the question. So he chooses, rather, to cut down trees to *resemble* a fence—one with plenty of "gaps in it," an effort determined to be good enough to satisfy the law and their simplified aesthetic sense, and no more. With such a piecemeal, haphazard effort, the tourist could both support a legal claim to the land and secure his claim to locality by reenacting the homesteading experience. But this effort is short-lived, as anyone who has ever chopped down a tree would expect: "We cut down three trees apiece, and found it such heart-breaking work that we decided to 'rest our case' on those; if they held the property, well and good; if they didn't, let the property spill out through the gaps and go; it was no use to work ourselves to death merely to save a few acres of land" (171–72). Twain does not want a fence, necessarily, but something very like a fence, the image of a fence to "hold" the property, or more accurately, to hold the broader mythic image of western riches. It seems, however, that the fortitude of the tourist has a few gaps as well. "Heart-breaking" is a revealing term in that it illustrates the emotional frustration born not solely from the act of chopping, but also, with each swing of the ax, from slowly realizing how many more swings will be required. With each exhausting chop, the romantic dream "spill[s] out through the gaps" of his vision. It breaks the tourist's heart as well as his back. This is the first lesson for the tourist, the first data to inform the experiment in progress: to establish a home, to be local, requires hard, sustained work. This, however, is not a lesson the tourist is ready to accept or even acknowledge, so he decides, rather, to "rest" his case on what work he has done, no longer interested in saving "a few acres of land," especially if saving the land would mean losing the dream.

The failure is due to the faultiness of the dream as well as to Twain's inability to reconcile an implicit conflict within the experiment: making a claim on the land does not retain it without performing substantive work far beyond the pale of typical touristic behavior. In this persona, Twain cannot fully invest himself in the place—place must always be a "picture." In such a scenario, then, a few acres lost through the gaps do not represent a fatal blow to the overall image. The same paradigm occurs as Twain attempts to build a house, the second legal requirement to homesteading the Lake Tahoe "wood ranch." Of course, the same failure is inevitable, and the proposed "substantial log-house" inevitably degenerates into a "'brush' house" —a poor one at that—a "half-way sort of affair" that all in all bears a "strong family resemblance to the surrounding vegetation" (172). Twain is simply unwilling or unable to conduct the work necessary to construct a legitimate log home. Although he is confident, as with the "fence," that the "'brush' house" of saplings may satisfy the law, it in no way satisfies the aesthetic dream of a log home. In true delusory touristic fashion, Twain declares himself a landowner "within the protection of the law," if not in reality. With the legal claim established, however shabbily, Twain moves forward in reenacting homesteading.

The opening of the next chapter (23) represents a view of Lake Tahoe from a purely touristic perspective. The opening paragraph is a rapturous, romantic reverie on the natural splendors of the new "home," calling it a "noble picture." He closes the paragraph: "The view was always fascinating, bewitching, entrancing. The eye was never tired of gazing, night or day, in calm or storm; it suffered but one grief, and that was that it could not look always, but must close sometimes in sleep" (173). Twain emphasizes here the true object of touristic interest, his eye that "never tire[s] of gazing." Caught in his touristic gaze of Lake Tahoe, Twain dreams that it all belongs to him, that its enchantment is part of his new self. But the illusion would soon go up in flames as the homesteading experiment wholly collapses.

Twain starts a campfire that, due to his ignorance and carelessness, immediately gets out of control and spreads violently. It quickly consumes the camp and billows into the forest. Significantly, the fire itself becomes yet another spectacle for the tourist to watch: "We stood helpless and watched the devastation" (176). Moreover, despite the horror of the conflagration—which on its surface destroys the dream of homesteading by burning the "fence," the "house," and the "ranch" land itself—Twain iterates its visual appeal, thus its touristic appeal: "It was wonderful to see with what fierce speed the tall sheet of flame traveled!" (176). Twain incorporates the exclamation points that come in exceptionally handy in capturing any spectacle, and he watches "spellbound" as the fire of his creation consumes the land. In one of the most evocative descriptive passages in the narrative, Twain details the scene before him and provides a striking contrast to the heavenly "noble picture" with which he opened the Lake Tahoe experiment (discussed above), now become a "reflected hell": "Every feature of the spectacle was repeated in the glowing mirror of the lake! Both pictures were sublime, both were beautiful; but that in the lake had a bewildering richness about it that enchanted the eye and held it with the stronger fascination" (176). Ever the tourist, Twain reveals himself less distraught over losing his home than thrilled by the chance to see such destruction, albeit at his own bumbling hands. This passage is especially telling in that the tourist consistently prefers, even while standing before a massive forest fire, to watch its image here reflected in the water. The picture of the fire, not the fire itself, captures his imagination more effectively. And for the tourist, the difference between the actual fire and the image of it is simply irrelevant. By extension, the tourist can prefer to watch the reflection of the fire rather than the fire itself in the same way that he can distance himself from the damage to the "ranch" and his experiment physically; therefore, he can distance himself from the consequences of his carelessness—a destruction that would be disastrous to a true homesteader. Fortunately for Twain, he is simply playing local; what he loses in the fire, he gains in spades in the spectacle as he sees—always—with the eyes of the tourist. This provides quite a show and, we should note, good copy for the travel writer, especially one who enjoys the wonderfully hopeless and hapless world of the tourist. There will be other experiments.

For the tourist, as is the case in *The Innocents Abroad* and *A Tramp Abroad,* the imagination provides the definitive assessment of touristic experience. No experimental homesteading can alter that basic tenet of tourism. After the fire moves beyond the tourist's gaze, Twain and his companion revert to being "homeless wanderers again." The self-image again takes on the basic essence of movement. Of course, Twain never relinquishes his tourist persona; the delusion continues. With the tool of touristic memory, moreover, he can remake the very recent past, and with all its imaginative redefining power he can lament the loss as he chooses to define it: "Our fence was gone, our house burned down; no insurance. Our pine forest was well scorched, the dead trees all burned up, and our broad acres of manzanita swept away" (177). There was no actual fence, and there was no actual house. He does, however, have the "insurance" of his touristic vision and can replace any actual loss in his mind. He easily pads his list of lost possessions, claiming, with the repetition of "our," not only a fence and a house but also the pines and manzanita. The tourist, it seems, owns all he surveys with his ever-roaming eye. Nonetheless, Twain defines the loss of the legal claim on the land as an actual, substantive loss of a homestead. The experimental tourist must move on.

His next locality involves prospecting for silver. The dream of riches inherent in the mythic West quickly changes in its specific details but not its essence. Twain as the experimental tourist has found another way to play local. After explaining the effects of "silver fever," Twain writes, "I succumbed and grew as frenzied as the craziest" (194). His self-identity has altered to match the demands of a new place, the mine regions of Nevada, and in the process Twain reenacts the experiences of the prospector caught up in the local mining boom. He reiterates his simple, romantic expectations, similar to those offered in the opening of the narrative: "I confess, without shame, that I expected to find masses of silver lying all about the ground. I expected to see it glittering in the sun on the mountain summits" (204). Celebrating his "delirious revel" (205), Twain becomes "full of dreams." Of course, readers know this tourist has come to the West full of illusions. In his first mining effort, he believes that he finds gold but instead learns rather embarrassingly that he has only mica not "worth ten cents an acre!" (208). The tourist reacts simply: "So vanished my dream." But the dream disappears only momentarily, pausing merely to remake itself.

Twain stretches this central theme through several variations, all of which reaffirm the tourist's basic and inescapable inability to achieve a local identity. Each version of the experiment fails. And each time the failure derives from the lack of willingness to put forward substantive effort, but more intrinsically, the failure is predicated by the overall perspective of the experimental tourist. Authenticity is unavailable, yet the tourist keeps looking. The mythic West promises opportunity to re-create oneself, but tourism promises no such thing. The tourist must always be the outsider, and Twain as the tourist—fully immersed in its own mythology—can never be at home. Opening chapter 29, Twain notes: "True knowledge of the nature of silver mining came fast enough" (209). Alas, after a week of digging and obtaining not riches but sore muscles and frustration, Twain quits; the tourist moves on: "One week of this satisfied me. I resigned" (213). Then the prospector tries tunneling: "I resigned again." Twain cleverly elaborates on the role of speculation in mining, and it perfectly mirrors the role of imagination in tourism. It lacks substance and depends on expectations and self-assertion for sustenance, not silver, not any substantive understanding of locality. He writes: "We were stark mad with excitement—drunk with happiness—smothered under mountains of prospective wealth—arrogantly compassionate toward the plodding millions who knew not our marvellous canyon—but our credit was not good at the grocer's" (213). The sense of wealth as well as of self derives from the manipulation of appearances. It seems the whole culture is a tourist culture; he is by no means alone. However, Twain methodically balances the romantic speculation with the hard reality of daily life. No matter how rich they plan to be, they do not enjoy a basic entitlement for a local citizen, credit to buy food. Later, Twain fully realizes the potential power of such speculation and embraces it: "We never touched our tunnel or our shaft again. Why? Because we judged that we had learned the *real* secret of success in silver mining —which was, *not* to mine the silver ourselves by the sweat of our brows and the labor of our hands, but to *sell* the ledges to the dull slaves of toil and let them do the mining!" (217). Again, the need for work alters the experiment, so Twain and his fellow tourists embrace the image of mining rather than reality. Thus mining becomes another form of tourism, a way to tap into the mythic West without losing the dream or, for that matter, doing any work. As with leisure tourism, the *"real* secret of success" resides in the manipulation of experience, of gaining a self-proclaimed authenticity by celebrating the image of it, what Twain calls *"real."* Therein is also the secret of success for the experimental tourist: the most effective way to gain the experience of mining is *not* to mine, according to Twain. This conclusion builds on the same premise he offers in the overland journey, that a desert is most enjoyable when seen at night while sleeping.

All in all, *Roughing It* is a satirical record of the tourist believing he is authentically local, a man assuming that superficial knowledge and romantic expectations are sufficient not only to become part of a place but to succeed there. It is the myth of the Tourist Age, the false promise that, by traveling to a place, one "experiences" it, understands it, and can thus check it off as if it were on a knowledge ledger. Again and again, Twain illustrates failures due to ignorance combined with hubris, and this litany of failures throughout the narrative is in essence a mocking of touristic expectations, both that the self can be so easily modified (as easy as changing a costume) and that place can be so easily modified to allow such a romantic possibility. A significant difference between a leisure tourist and a naive tenderfoot, then, is that the former creates and perpetuates his illusion and celebrates his mental gymnastics by claiming authenticity. As a result, there is no need (as the tourist would define it) to change behavior or to learn from experience. The tourist willingly and eagerly changes costumes to match place without caring to recognize that such a change is superficial and, in fact, inauthentic, a failed experiment in its conception. "When in Rome, do as the Romans" may be a popular mantra for tourists, but it should not imply that by doing so one *becomes* Roman. So desperate is his search for home, for riches, and for the West that the experimental tourist-narrator of *Roughing It* refuses to make this distinction (or at least to admit that the difference is relevant). As such, Twain, in this tourist persona, comically attacks such myth-building by tourists (and travel writers). Self-delusion, again and again, builds from place-illusion; the result of each experiment can only be a failure of the experiment. Whether it is wood ranching, mining, milling, or any other form of the get-rich-quick fever that informs Twain's efforts to play local, each version of the experiment adds together to build not a new self in the new world, but simply the same old touristic pretense in new costumes, what Twain calls his "slothful, valueless, heedless career" (277). This "career," though, is more accurately leisure-minded playacting, an extended pleasure excursion, for which sloth, lack of values, and heedlessness should be expected.

This series of experiments culminates in the "blind lead" debacle. Twain abandons mining and milling, and the formerly wealthy prospector takes a manual labor job "at ten dollars a week and board." The apparent opportunity offered by the "blind lead," however, reinfects Twain with the fever and reignites the dream. The experiment is back on. The expectations of the experimental tourist rise and ostensibly alter the place, and "the floorless, tumble-down cabin" becomes "a palace" (281). Rescued by the hope of the blind lead, the tourist regains his mythic wonder for the possibilities of the West, but there is a catch. He needs to "do a fair and reasonable amount of work" (284). It is the wood ranch all over again, the experiment still flawed, the tourist still passive. Local law would again require what the tourist is ill-equipped to provide: work, a true commitment to the land. Mining—digging into the land itself, its substance—is an apt symbol for both the desire of the tourist and the failure of the experiment. Digging requires actual engagement with the land (digging into the land, immersing one's self into the ground), and the action of digging is in itself a metaphor for the experiment. The tourist, however, travels always on the surface; he has no other option. The result can only be disappointment. As a metaphor for the West itself, the blind lead *leads* nowhere because the tourist is blind to the true depth and complexity of the region and of making a home there. Twain writes: "We would have been millionaires if we had only worked with pick and spade one little day on our property and so secured our ownership!" (291). It bears noting that according to our narrator, they fail not because they did not mine the rock but because they did not produce (perform) the image of working even for "one little day." Even in hindsight, the tourist only partially recognizes the actual failure and focuses on the image, the pretense of working and thus *owning* the land, as the sad oversight, as if it would have truly been that simple to prevent their loss. In the mind of the tourist, the loss derives from a truncated performance—"work" for one day-long show. Of course, he forgets that working with pick and ax earlier was far from simple and easy. Although he recognizes that the lack of work destroys the dream of the blind lead, the tourist holds on to his claim to the identity fostered by that claim, or the image of it: "I can always have it to say that I was absolutely and unquestionably worth a million dollars, once, for ten days" (291). Like a true tourist, the significance—beyond the sting of losing potential for money and stature—remains in gaining the ability to claim experience and identity, and moreover, that such a claim is substantiated by the "official records of Esmeralda District." Twain the tourist "can always have it to say," in much the same vein (pardon me) that he can say he crossed the alkali desert (even though at night). All disappointment aside, the play's the thing, and the tourist knows his lines.

The delusion continues as Twain runs through a variety of local identities—grocery clerk, law student, blacksmith, bookseller's clerk, drug store clerk, printer. All of them fall short because he does not want to work, especially "after being so wealthy" (292). (The narrator makes a direct reference to Benjamin Franklin but seems, tongue-in-cheek, unaware that Franklin's success depended on industry and self-discipline.) After failing at one more attempt to be a miner, Twain becomes a newspaperman and thus changes his costume again, shifting his experiment from digging into the land for local identity to digging into language and thereby defining the place with words rather than action. In an effort to find a better way to gain a sense of home, Twain sets aside the pickax and takes up the pen.

Significantly, his local identity as city editor for the *Virginia City Territorial Enterprise* affords Twain a special opportunity to become directly and fully involved in the city, but in the end it simply perpetuates his speculation. He adorns himself in a new garb but learns that authenticity within his writing is no more relevant—for the tourist —than it is with mining and the other versions of his experiment. In short, like the tourist, the city editor can create any world he wishes. He can make "affluent" use of any subject of his gaze, the gaze of the tourist (296). Playing journalist in this context, like the homesteader, miner, and so forth, Twain relies on image, on appearances: "I could add particulars that would make the article much more interesting" (297–98). The place is his for the making, and without losing any sweat from his brow.

An important portion of *Roughing It* follows the beginning of Twain's experiment as the local-color journalist, whereby he offers an exhaustive, informative, and highly comic overview of life in Nevada Territory—all thoroughly consistent with travel-book convention. Much of the material comes from anecdotal asides and his actual *Enterprise* articles.[10] This previously published material takes on a metaphorical role within *Roughing It* as well, in that it provides a supposed depth of understanding of a place for the tourist. In the costume of the "journalist," Twain is also collecting data for his experiment. Once he follows formula to provide a substantive narrative tour (sometimes factual, sometimes burlesque) of Virginia City and its environs, he returns to his restlessness as a tourist, tired again of playing local (but also, it bears emphasizing, only after fulfilling travel-book convention). Having grown bored with this locality and this identity, the tourist is eager to move on to find new novelties, new selves: "I began to get tired of staying in one place so long" (398). Herein Twain captures the basic conflict, and structuring principle of the narrative as a whole, for the experimental tourist who wants to become a local citizen: the tourist craves the continuous novelty promised by movement; the local—by definition—stays put. The only option, then, is for the tourist to continually change his definition of what "local" means, thereby maintaining the illusion of the play. Bemoaning the lack of "satisfying novelty," Twain heads for San Francisco. Tellingly, he notes, "I wanted—I did not know *what* I wanted" (398). The important point here is not his confusion but his unrelenting desire for novelty. The tourist always *wants*. Moreover, he is not sure *who* he wants to be, but he does want change, and he must once again adjust the parameters of his experiment.

In San Francisco, Twain the tourist enjoys "an entirely new phase of existence—a butterfly idleness; nothing to do, nobody to be responsible to, and untroubled with financial uneasiness" (419). This is the ideal touristic dream, enjoying the pretense of a new local identity. His image is an apt one—"butterfly idleness"—in that it emphasizes the change, the tourist emerging from a cocoon of sorts, an enclosure defined in this case by a job in Nevada and increasing local sensibilities. And "idleness" is always attractive. The butterfly's life is a short one, however. The speculations of the mine sale back east fall through (again as a result of his inattention to detail), and his stocks plummet. "It was the 'blind lead' over again" (427). The tourist must get a job.

Twain loses his newspaper post due to laziness (he does no work), then goes back to mining (pocket mining, which is supposedly easier), and after seven months he returns to San Francisco. "Too mean and lazy . . . to work on a morning paper," he takes a position as the Pacific Coast correspondent for the *Virginia City Territorial Enterprise.* He gets out of debt, but after five months his "interest in [the] work was gone"; the tourist itches for more novelty. "The vagabond instinct was strong upon me," he confesses (444). "Vagabond" for *Roughing It* is synonymous with "tourist," and it is a learned behavior rather than an instinctual one. Twain sets up the next stage of his experimental tour of the mythic West, moving the myth further westward and into the paradise of the South Seas, the Sandwich Islands (Hawaii). For the first time since the opening chapters of the overland journey, traveling itself takes the foreground. The Hawaiian Islands become a logical extension of the romantic West and offer novelty and possibly another chance to go native. San Francisco, a "paradise" for the butterfly tourist, is replaced by a new paradise, but the troubles inherent in this new experiment quickly undermine the tourist's search for place and self. Once on the islands, Twain notes, "it was such ecstacy to dream, and dream—till you got a bite. A scorpion bite" (457).

If there is any inconsistency between the bulk of the narrative and the Sandwich Islands section, it derives from Twain's shift from being the experimental tourist to being the more typical recreational tourist.[11] He no longer seeks to pretend to be a local, perhaps inhibited by his racial separation from the native population as well as his defined role as roving correspondent on temporary assignment. Since he is employed in San Francisco, he does not have the same perspective that informs *Roughing It* up to this point, and this shift hinders the Sandwich Islands chapters and alters the consistency of the narrative as a whole. This change is not inherent in the place; it is Twain's self that does not attempt to alter to become local or adapt to a new costume consistent with regional custom. Still, the material presents solid travel writing, offering a wealth of romantic descriptions of natural beauty and plenty of historical and cultural information, culled mainly from James Jackson Jarves's *History of the Sandwich Islands.*[12] This portion of the narrative, however, provides a crucial transition and informs the experimental tourist's motivation and mounting frustration on the whole. One passage in particular illustrates the tourist's dilemma. On the top of Haleakala Volcano, Twain provides an interesting reaction and creates a powerful and telling image: "I felt like the Last Man, neglected of the judgement, and left pinnacled in mid-heaven, a forgotten relic of a vanished world" (550). Homeless and seemingly without substantive self-identity, the tourist acknowledges his failed experiment and, in turn, the condition of the tourist, bereft of locality, lost and separate from the world he endeavors so eagerly to see and belong to. The tourist has gone to the ends of the mythic West and has yet to find home, is yet to find himself even in the garden paradise of the Sandwich Islands.

"After half a year's luxurious vagrancy," Twain returns to San Francisco, a city he now calls "home," though he has lived in San Francisco for a shorter time than in the Sandwich Islands. It is delusion. The local claim upon San Francisco further clarifies why the Sandwich Island section appears disjointed from the whole. It is not that the South Seas are too far from the American West, nor that the section derived directly from the letters published long before *Roughing It* was written; it is Twain's perspective that is inconsistent in relation to the tourist's experiment that defines the balance of the narrative and is conspicuously absent from the Sandwich Islands, which seem too foreign for the tourist to consider, even imaginatively, home.

Back "home" in San Francisco, Twain dons a new identity, lecturer, that proves successful. It is important to note that his lecture subject, the Sandwich Islands, helps to solidify his touristic pretense of being local by emphasizing the exotic value of the South Seas. In lecturing as the tourist about a foreign land, Twain is automatically part of the audience—one of "us"—as he describes "them." But the benefits of his growing local identity and popularity are not, alas, vigorous enough to keep the tourist in his adopted home, for all in all he remains the tourist, reenacting locality and growing restless for novelty all the while. He proposes a "pleasure journey to Japan and thence westward around the world," in effect continuing the travel westward he had started years ago in St. Louis. This plan falls through and he heads back to the East, "to see home again" (569). What is *home* to this tourist? San Francisco has never been anything but a resting place for the tourist to play local, as is the West as a whole—the land and the idea. And the perpetual tourist tells readers his stay at home was a brief one—Twain had no home—as he set out on the *Quaker City* pleasure excursion which he would make famous in *The Innocents Abroad*.

Twain closes with a moral that effectively wraps up his western travels for readers and closes his failed search for home, the primary unifying theme of *Roughing It*. It is the experimental tourist's moral, based on a delusion of self that goes beyond the self-deprecation of the joke: "If you are of any account, stay at home and make your way by faithful diligence; but if you are 'no account,' go away from home, and then you will *have* to work, whether you want to or not" (570). As the tourist playing local, Twain, of course, has taken on neither task; he has performed little work, nor has he stayed at home. In the end, it would seem, the moral simply does not apply to the tourist who will nevertheless and always seek to "go away from home" and often in hopes of finding one. In this sense—especially considering Twain's initial plans to travel around the world—the tourist bears an uncanny resemblance to Melville's Ishmael in *Moby-Dick,* the wanderer, the outcast never at home but endlessly seeking to trace the round (circle the globe) again. The experimental tourist, like Ishmael, remains forever homeless and forever restless, and the travel writer survives to tell the tale in any manner he or she sees fit.

THE NOSTALGIC TOURIST IN *LIFE ON THE MISSISSIPPI*

Modern readers of *Life on the Mississippi* benefit from an especially astute and insightful monograph, Horst Kruse's *Mark Twain and* Life on the Mississippi, which methodically examines its composition and structure. Although Kruse does not concern himself with travel writing as a genre, his analysis nonetheless recognizes intuitively the nature of travel writing and examines the text with an illuminating perspective that respects its conventions. Most importantly, Kruse reminds readers of Twain's original intent to produce a "standard" work on the subject of North America's largest river basin and shows clearly how the "padding" throughout the text—often dismissed by readers with novelistic sensibilities—reflects Twain's vision, not his desperation for material.[13] Kruse notes that Twain considered himself the "only privileged and authoritative historian" of the river (6). In discussing Twain's plans to return to the river for research purposes, however, Kruse does not address a crucial context for such a trip. Certainly, Twain would gather information as a travel writer, but he would also do so as a tourist.

Always the conscientious professional, of course, Twain eagerly sought out information, but he returned to the Mississippi River foremost as the tourist who hoped to gain experiences that would be of value to him personally and professionally as a travel writer. It was a working tour since he was actively putting together text for a narrative, but that is simply what travel writers do. It should be recalled that all of Twain's travel books, with the exception of *Roughing It* (which capitalized on a previous trip), derived from specific tours with explicit intentions of producing travel narratives. Twain as a travel writer and tourist always endeavored to "read up" on a place and share this information with his readers (see Kruse 7–9). A more potentially illuminating way to read *Life on the Mississippi,* then, may be to *read* the narrative as Twain had to *reread* the river itself in 1882, with the eyes of the tourist. As a result, we may see in the narrative tour up and down the Mississippi that he approaches his former haunts with nostalgia rather than his more typical cynicism. And this nostalgic tourist, homesick for the river culture of his youth, becomes increasingly wistful as he realizes that, indeed, the tourist cannot go home again.[14]

Instead of opening with a conventional travel-book preface explaining in general the logic and purpose of the journey and the subsequent narrative, Twain in *Life on the Mississippi* opts to begin with an excerpt from the "Editor's Table," *Harper's Magazine* (February 1863). This is our first indication that Twain, in this his fourth travel book, may be altering his entrance to the genre. His choice is a compelling if idiosyncratic one. In "The 'Body of the Nation'" he offers, if not a standard prefatory remark, a thoroughly suitable one for the text. The title itself, *Life on the Mississippi,* indicates the perspective within the narrative proper that will make this travel book unique in Twain's canon, and perhaps in nineteenth-century belles lettres. Unlike his other travel-book titles, *Life on the Mississippi* does not foreground the tourist's perspective as the center and true subject of the text. This narrative does not derive from the eyes of an "innocent" or a "tramp"; it does not record Twain "roughing it" or "following the equator." Rather, this title focuses on the place itself and the "life" that defines it. If this title does not really fully suggest the text with absolute fidelity, it nonetheless represents a significant thematic change of course for Twain, an alteration testifying to the powerful pull this particular place has for him. The "life on the Mississippi" River, its status as the geographic, symbolic, and, for Twain, emotional "body of the nation," names this narrative and serves as its unifying thematic thread. The river itself not only sets the parameters of the tour, which must logically follow the river's course, but also offers its own justification for such a tour; life on the Mississippi, according to Twain, is the center of the life of the nation at large, and is, indeed, "well worth reading about."

Still, as a travel book by Mark Twain, *Life on the Mississippi* does have an authorial perspective, a multifaceted one that at times seems wholly part of the river culture and at other times seems baffled by it. The narrative differs from his others in this confusion as Twain moves toward that "body" as a nostalgic tourist who inevitably has two competing perspectives: the tourist/autobiographer and the travel writer/historian. These two points of view, in all travel narratives, are symbiotic; the tourist is to the travel writer as the autobiographer is to the historian. In each split role, the subjective eye is paired with the ostensibly objective: the tourist with the travel writer, the autobiographer with the historian. These roles traditionally intertwine in travel writing, yet the difficulties inherent in such a balancing act force themselves to the forefront in a work like *Life on the Mississippi* because Twain's relation to his topic is so close, so personal. The two mantras of the travel writer—*self* and *place*—are here taken beyond their normative constraints and contexts. As a result, the self—as tourist, as travel writer, as autobiographer, as historian—is confused from the beginning because it is unclear which voice should dominate or at least take the lead. The fusion of past and present blurs the narrator's eyes throughout as Twain comes upon conflicting images of the present Mississippi set against those of his own past, his childhood and adolescence. This place, the river, is not a tourist sight in Twain's mind; it is *home*. But he is a tourist, nonetheless. What, then, exactly happens when a tourist comes home?

"The 'Body of the Nation'" closes with the following: "*As a dwelling-place for civilized man it is by far the first upon our globe,*" the italics provided by Twain. "As a dwelling-place," as a home, the Mississippi River basin is unparalleled, according to the editors of *Harper's,* but more importantly, it is likewise so pronounced and emphasized by Twain. His acknowledgment, however, is much more personal; this tourist/autobiographer, this travel writer/historian describes his childhood home. Within his narrative, this direct emotional connection must coexist with the goal of Twain as the historian who wants to put together a "standard" work. In a letter to his wife, Olivia (27 November 1871), long before commencing on the narrative, he indicated his early plans for such a book: "When I come to write the Mississippi book, *then* look out! I will spend 2 months on the river & take notes, & I bet you I will make a standard work" (Fischer and Frank 499).[15] Such a task requires a new brand of narrative, one that captures the life on the Mississippi as well as Twain's own life on the Mississippi.

Despite the multiple motives with which Twain explores the Mississippi River basin, he still faces many of the same limitations and frustrations that he engages in other travel books. He is always the tourist, even though he may be dominated by the sense of nostalgia typical of a native. Throughout the tour he must remain, unalterably, an outsider, separated by time and space. He seeks the authentic, but as we have seen, that authenticity is unavailable directly. *Life on the Mississippi* is a sincere nostalgic search for self and history, a hauntingly intimate journey into the psyche of the tourist. For the first time in his narrative travels, Twain faces his own fractious identity head-on, a confrontation hardly encouraged by the Tourist Age with its adherence to superficiality and touristic faith. The inevitable tension bears itself out within the narrative tour. As a result, *Life on the Mississippi* is intermittently both the most intensely personal of his travel books and the most passionless and distant, almost clinical as the autobiographical impulses fail to merge smoothly with the duties of a historian. While readers are made well aware of Twain's emotional connection to this place, he rarely lets readers within his various psyches, even comically, for very long, preferring to retreat frequently into the objective cover of the historian. While aiding his goal of producing a standard work, the historian's eye that informs the narrative also shields both Twain and his readers from the potential discomforts of a close encounter with the body of the nation so recently torn apart in the Civil War and so intrinsically connected with the recollections of a man who escaped that conflict.

So Twain is not only forced to take readers along on his journey down and up the river but also along his journey into his own past and into the full meaning implied by the Mississippi River history and culture. A standard work must naturally be comprehensive, and therein lies both the beauty and failure of *Life on the Mississippi*: Twain's heartfelt love for the river is not altogether sustainable within the theoretically objective purpose of history. All in all, Twain, perhaps aware of the dangers of simultaneously traveling to the river and writing a "standard" history as well as a standard travel book, blends the two often competing impulses quite well and produces an ostensibly dispassionate record spliced with highly personalized touches as well as a narrative that offers what a travel book in the nineteenth century should, that is, a little bit of everything.

Still, there is trouble ahead for the tourist and autobiographer counterparts to the travel writer and the historian. To know the river, to offer it to readers with a comprehensive and scientific detachment, risks losing the wonder and majesty of it for the tourist by too often short-circuiting his desire for invoking his imagination to sketch his experience and the river itself. Not coincidentally, Twain's struggle to learn the river as a cub-pilot serves as a model for his struggle as tourist/travel writer. He hopes that we will read the book as we ought to read the river, understanding all the while the risk he runs as he tries to balance the objective with the subjective, the autobiographical with the historical. The passage wherein he ponders this implicit difficulty warrants quoting at length:

> The face of the water, in time, became a wonderful book—a book that was a dead language to the uneducated passenger, but which told its mind to me without reserve, delivering its most cherished secrets as clearly as if it uttered them with a voice. And it was not a book to be read once and thrown aside, for it had a new story to tell every day. Throughout the long twelve hundred miles there was never a page that was void of interest, never one that you could leave unread without loss, never one that you would want to skip, thinking you could find higher enjoyment in some other thing. There never was so wonderful a book written by man; never one whose interest was so absorbing, so unflagging, so sparklingly renewed with every re-perusal. The passenger who could not read it was charmed with a peculiar sort of faint dimple on its surface (on the rare occasions when he did not overlook it altogether); but to the pilot that was an *italicized* passage; indeed, it was more than that, it was a legend of the largest capitals, with a string of shouting exclamation points at the end of it; for it meant that a wreck or a rock was buried there that could tear the life out of the strongest vessel

that ever floated. It is the faintest and simplest expression the water ever makes, and the most hideous to a pilot's eye. In truth, the passenger who could not read this book saw nothing but all manner of pretty pictures in it, painted by the sun and shaded by the clouds, whereas to the trained eye these were not pictures at all, but the grimmest and most dead-earnest of reading-matter. (118–19)

In celebrating the complexity of the river, Twain also develops an apt metaphor for the travel writer who hopes to read the river *and* write it successfully and with some depth of understanding. In this passage there are two rivers, one seen from the informed, conscientious eye and the other seen from the tourist's (passenger's) eyes. Twain wants to share his reverence for the river's history and significance, but he must attempt that narrative task ultimately from the perspective of a tourist, who is like the cub-pilot again trying to "learn" the river that has changed dramatically since his childhood. And for his readers who can only see "faint dimples on its surface," Twain desperately wants to "italicize" that text (river), and so his entire text (*Life on the Mississippi*). It is certainly understandable for Twain, the native son, to wish to *italicize* the entire book for readers, but his prickly task is to do so without draining its wonder and magnificence. He knew well the risk: "Now when I had mastered the language of this water and had come to know every trifling feature that bordered the great river as familiarly as I knew the letters of the alphabet, I had made a valuable acquisition. But I had lost something, too. I had lost something which could never be restored to me while I lived. All the grace, the beauty, the poetry had gone out of the majestic river!" (119). Twain follows this lament with a lengthy romantic description of a sunset he once saw as an innocent. But the point is clear; as an experienced pilot, with a duty to be objective and matter-of-fact, he could elicit no splendor in such a sunset. Knowledge siphons all the colors from the picture. *Life on the Mississippi,* then, represents an effort to balance both ways of seeing, of knowing. In a sense, the author tries to pilot the narrative safely down (and then up) the river without running aground. This river, though, has plenty of snags. Likewise, the time travel to his old stomping ground places Twain, as it would anyone, in a difficult position as he tries to mesh the imaginative pictures of memory he holds so dear with the present tour and its unadorned pictures. He thus faces the same dilemma that he had in the Holy Land of *The Innocents Abroad.* Some memories may be best untouched. The travel writer can never escape his role as the tourist, as we have seen, but making his additional roles of autobiographer and historian prominent rather than complementary throws the balancing act of travel writing off kilter.

In this context, it is important for readers to recognize that *Life on the Mississippi,* as a travel book of the Mississippi River basin, parallels the cub-pilot's experience. Twain intends, he announces, to capture both the factual history and his personal history, to combine the fine brushstrokes of his own life with the broad strokes of the river's culture. As the author of a travel book, a "standard book," Twain adopts the same intention as his mentor Horace Bixby, who says to young Sam Clemens: "When I say I'll learn a man the river, I mean it. And you can depend on it, I'll learn him or kill him" (111). Unlike his other travel books, then, this tour is no pleasure excursion; Twain sets out determined to "learn" us the river.

The vastness of the Mississippi River and the significance of the varied life that feeds off it can overwhelm any potential historian. Likewise, the inherent poignancy of delving into one's past could stifle any autobiographer. As both, Twain faces a daunting task, especially considering his recognition (already demonstrated in his other travel books) that a tourist can never fully understand anything, neither life at large on the river nor his own life on the river. The organization of the narrative tells of the struggle. Twain does not provide a personal preface (as in *The Innocents Abroad* and *Roughing It*), nor does he include an authorial introduction and justification in the opening paragraphs of the first chapter (as in *A Tramp Abroad* and *Following the Equator*); *Life on the Mississippi* stands alone in his travel-book canon for this omission of travel-book convention. Moreover, there is no mention of pleasure or leisure, and the strong implication early on is that history will be preeminent and autobiography will be complementary. Significantly, the first "I" appears in the tenth paragraph of chapter 1, and it exists only to promise more historical information (25). The next "I" occurs in chapter 3 as Twain introduces the subject of keelboats and inserts text from the in-progress *Adventures of Huckleberry Finn.*[16] To clarify the strictly historical information on keelboats and steamboats (that "I have been trying to describe"), Twain begins, "I remember the annual processions of mighty rafts that used to glide by Hannibal when I was a boy" (42). This remembrance leads him to the *Huckleberry Finn* raft passage, which he includes, legitimately, for its informative value. The excerpt serves a purpose similar to that of the numerous anecdotes and myths that appear in the rest of the narrative and his other works. In addition, such material taken from his own fiction further establishes his credibility on the subject of the narrative. It reminds the reader, again, that this writer *knows* the river, and readers will benefit from such depth of knowledge far beyond typical travel books. He writes: "By way of illustrating keelboat talk and manners, and that now-departed and hardly-remembered raft-life, I will throw in, in this place, a chapter from a book which I have been working at, by fits and starts, during the past five or six years, and may possibly finish in the course of five or six more" (42). His personal eye (and "I") reveals itself only to establish authoritative context for the information illustrated by the following scene. Otherwise, the first three chapters are wholly written from the ostensibly objective and distant eye of the historian.

Chapters 4–20 are pure autobiography lifted almost directly from "Old Times on the Mississippi" (1875) to explain the "science" of piloting to readers. Twain inserts into the "Old Times" chapters numerous references to the "science of piloting" both to justify its inclusion within the larger narrative and to remind readers of his historical authority and technical expertise.[17] In opening chapter 10 he illustrates his intentions: "Whosoever has done me the courtesy to read my chapters which have preceded this may possibly wonder that I deal so minutely with piloting as a science. It was the prime purpose of those chapters; and I am not quite done yet. I wish to show, in the most patient and painstaking way, what a wonderful science it is" (122). Intending to "learn" us the river, Twain apparently believes that any autobiographical material or any fictional material from a novel in progress which helps to achieve that primary goal belongs in *Life on the Mississippi* and will cohere. As he admits, "I have felt at liberty to take up a considerable degree of room with it" (123). Under the auspices of this narrative goal, the keelboat section from *Adventures of Huckleberry Finn* and "Old Times on the Mississippi" work well to add to the mosaic Twain is trying to construct. Interesting and fun reading on their own, these insertions succeed also by advancing the historical task of *Life on the Mississippi*.

Chapter 21 serves as a brief transition to bring readers up to the current steamboat tour, and chapter 22 (247 pages into the book) begins the tour proper as Twain returns to his "muttons." Notably, the current "I" steps forward incognito, in effect attempting to deny the authority established by the preceding text and to sublimate the personal connection to the place. This "I" can only see with the eyes of the tourist. The opening twenty-one chapters have laid a significant context for the actual tour, but they have not removed Twain's inevitable role as a tourist, as he finally moves physically along the river basin. As an especially knowledgeable tourist, Twain is able to remind readers again and again of his own relationship to the place, and he does so, ironically and in contrast to normal travel-writing circumstances, by overtly playing the tourist, as opposed to reentering as the favorite son, the prodigal come home. For the only time in his travel-book career, he dons a fully self-conscious tourist identity, imposed to protect his *true* identity as a native. Twain clearly feels local, but he fails to realize, it seems, that the river is no longer his home, in space or in time, that his tourist identity is not a mask but his current essential self. As a result of this narrative tension between selves, Twain tours two Mississippi River cultures, the one of his memory and the one of the present. They are destined to be in conflict.

In chapter 22, Twain provides, finally, a typical travel-book opening: "After twenty-one years' absence, I felt a very strong desire to see the river again, and the steamboats, and such of the boys as might be left; so I resolved to go out there. I enlisted a poet for company, and a stenographer to 'take him down,' and started westward about the middle of April" (247). He follows with his justification for concealing his identity. In a sense, in addition to denying Samuel Clemens, a famous native son, he is also trying to lose his identity as Mark Twain, a famous travel writer/tourist.[18] In a travel narrative, however, such a denial is impossible, so not only does the pretense of the incognito fail almost immediately (he cannot keep track of *who* he is: Smith, Jones, or Johnson), but his essential role as a tourist intrudes itself in unintentional ways. Unlike his other travel books, wherein Twain enjoys manipulating the foibles of tourist behavior and experience, here he is caught between being a tourist and acknowledging it. Since he does not feel like a tourist, at no time in *Life on the Mississippi* does Twain feel any need to costume himself in local garb, as he does so often in other narratives; rather, his efforts to keep his identity secret betray his assumption that he *is* local, that he must endeavor to hide that reality (as he sees it) in order to gather the best possible experiences. Built on a false assumption, this pretense cannot last. After his incognito efforts fail, his first contact with the pilothouse explodes his game as well. Having played tourist to an old friend and encouraging that friend to lie, Twain admits that he cannot fool anyone, and this episode gives him the chance to reenact his life as a steamboat pilot, thereby participating actively in his nostalgic tour. It is a staged production wherein Twain creates the opportunity to be a pilot and thus re-creates his past, but in order to take the wheel he first must be the tourist, a visitor motivated by nostalgia.

His knowledge of the river and steamboats helps him to recognize when he is being lied to, unlike typical tourists, but it does not protect him from the fact that the river he once knew no longer exists. Of the several instances wherein Twain is taken to be wholly ignorant of steamboats and the river, one is especially illustrative of his dual existence. A young man from Wisconsin lies to Twain about the boat, mocking him as he would an ordinary recreational tourist, "an innocent stranger from a far country" (329). This fellow, after amusing himself at Twain's expense, later sees Twain piloting the boat, thus learning that he himself has been made a fool. Twain has methodically reasserted his special status as a local, not a typical tourist at all. However, he follows this with a lengthy description of a "summer sunrise on the Mississippi," viewed with the eyes of the tourist, framing the scene at length and creating for himself and readers "one of the fairest and softest pictures imaginable" (332). He closes out the description with "you have seen something that is worth remembering." Twain does not seem to be referring to a specific sunrise here, since the description merely begins with the comment that "one cannot see too many summer sunrises on the Mississippi," and continues, "they are enchanting" (331). Is Twain describing from memory one of the sunrises of his youth or a specific spectacle from this trip? Or is he giving to his touring partners at home a universal picture of a sunrise, beautiful and neatly framed? It is difficult to determine his perspective in this passage, and it seemingly contradicts earlier reservations of the cub-pilot who had lost any sense of enchantment in such a scene because of his tiresome immersion in pilot science. Who are readers learning from here? The teacher seems to be the nostalgic tourist, picturing for himself and readers one sunrise, every sunrise. He continues: "All this stretch of river is a mirror, and you have the shadowy reflections of the leafage and the curving shores and the receding capes pictured in it" (332). Twain sees in shadows and in reflections the romantic imagination of a tourist traveling through time and memory. He is enchanted by it all. Throughout *Life on the Mississippi,* Twain struggles between his multiple perspectives and never achieves a comfortable balance. This tension derives from the intrinsic problem for the travel writer who is too close to his subject and the tourist who expects to be at home.

Twain's persona, caught in playing local while also playing tourist, truly disintegrates when he returns to Hannibal. Past and present collide and form a narrative dissonance that represents *Life on the Mississippi* at its best and worst. Whereas Kruse astutely argues that the Hannibal chapters do not follow the pattern of the narrative as a whole and undermine its status as a standard work, I believe that these chapters and their explicit disconnectedness serve as a culmination of the book's implicit structure.[19] The problem intuited by Kruse rests not with any inconsistency inherent in the context of the Hannibal chapters but with the perspectives inherent in the act of a travel writer who goes home. The Hannibal chapters do not signify a loss in structural integrity; rather, they clarify Twain's split selves integral to his efforts to write a standard work. It is that structure which inevitably leads to Hannibal. Twain's multiple perspectives—tourist, travel writer, autobiographer, historian—enjoy a peaceful but uneasy coexistence in the balance of the narrative, but that existence cannot hold when Twain returns to his direct link to the river. Twain's multifarious points of view float lost in time. Readers of an avowed comprehensive work, as a result, must face disappointment as the Hannibal of 1882 remains conspicuously absent and its character elusive. There is no way for Twain to maintain his illusion of belonging to a home that no longer exists. And there is no way for the writer to explore anything else but his past.

Upon reaching Hannibal ("where my boyhood was spent"), Twain comments that "the only notion of the town that remained in my mind was the memory of it as I had known it when I first quitted it twenty-nine years ago," noting, "that picture of it was still as clear and vivid to me as a photograph" (524). He makes a crucial distinction here upon first seeing his boyhood home, a "picture" in his mind, a "photograph" of a town from the past—his past—not of the present. The nostalgic tourist finds what he is always searching for, poignancy and pathos. Is the struggle of Twain as the tourist in Hannibal the same as in any other place? Is he trying to balance his imaginative expectations borne of the past with reality borne of the present? If so, he prefers, as in *The Innocents Abroad,* the imagination as a way to see what the tourist wants to see, to preserve memory. Twain immediately frames a Hannibal picture in the same manner as he frames "oriental pictures" in *The Innocents Abroad,* for example; even in his boyhood home, then, he sees with the eyes of the tourist. There is a difference here, however. Twain does have a physical, specific history here (unlike the virtual historical expectations of Europe and the Holy Land), so his memory derives from personal, firsthand knowledge. But as we have seen, this distinction, though important to the historian, matters little, in the end, to the tourist's imagination.

Twain registers his feeling of being lost in time as he enters the town: "I stepped ashore with the feeling of one who returns out of a dead-and-gone generation" (524). Curiously, he chooses the perspective that he is moving *out* of a "dead-and-gone" Hannibal (of his childhood years) and entering the present Hannibal of 1882. Of course, he does no such thing. As the tourist driven by nostalgia, he tours his past, and the present can only get in his way. Rhetorically, for the travel writer, the admixture of past and present is an evocative and compelling theme in that it can allow him to capture a Hannibal that is timeless and provide a valuable foundation for his historical mission by highlighting specific cultural changes over time. The historian, obviously, must be familiar with the outlines of time past. Yet Twain, the tourist, makes a poignant choice in how he sees Hannibal: "I saw the new houses—saw them plainly enough—but they did not affect the older picture in my mind, for through their solid bricks and mortar I saw the vanished houses, which had formerly stood there, with perfect distinctness" (524). Ingeniously, Twain avails himself of the ploy of confessing the trouble with seeing a place as a tourist, wherein the "too tangible walls of stone" that similarly intruded into his experience in the Holy Land are again imagined away and replaced with the picture of a "dead-and-gone" time. Here he recognizes the present but dismisses it by looking *through* it to the past, perfect and distinct. The tourist sees what he intends to see, ultimately, with only slight acknowledgment of conflicting reality. This strategy attains one of the most compelling moments in *Life on the Mississippi,* and it vividly displays the underlying crisis of self that makes autobiography and history so difficult to mesh for the travel writer touring home. Twain, no matter his intentions for history, no matter his personal knowledge of place, can only view Hannibal as the tourist, tied to the pictures in his mind, no less limited by memory and expectations than the tourist in Paris or the Holy Land, the Alps or the West. Yet, because the tourist site this time is Hannibal, the narrative carries with it a heightened, bittersweet emotional quality. His hometown now exists only as a series of pictures in the mind of the tourist, an outsider.

Not quite history, not quite autobiography, chapter 53 in any case is impressive travel writing. Although the following Hannibal chapters, dominated by anecdotal memories of death and guilt, do little to move the narrative forward, they should not divert our attention from these chapters' centrality to Twain's touristic experience on the Mississippi. Like many other travel writers, Twain decides to gain a panoramic view of Hannibal. "I passed through the vacant streets," he writes, "still seeing the town as it was, and not as it is, and recognizing and metaphorically shaking hands with a hundred familiar objects which no longer exist; and finally climbed Holiday's Hill to get a comprehensive view" (524). But the tourist can never gain a "comprehensive view," even if that tourist grew up in the town he wishes to understand; can the historian? the autobiographer? the travel writer? Twain moves as the tourist, though he himself does not feel like one. Yet he has the sense of being lost and confused. His understanding of the narrative moment seems clear as he offers up a monologue while physically looking over the town and also consciously, energetically *overlooking* the town at present—seeing, rather, into his past. For this nostalgic tour, the present at best serves simply as a catalyst for emotional time travel. If Twain here seeks to comprehend Hannibal, it is only the town of his youth that engages his interest. As he walks the streets, he "metaphorically" touches his past; he does the same on Holiday's Hill, touching it in one touristic embrace. He continues: "The whole town lay spread out below me then, and I could mark and fix every locality, every detail. Naturally, I was a good deal moved" (524). By marking and fixing "every detail" he reconstitutes not the current Hannibal but the town of his youth, the town he wants to see. Only that town could truly affect him emotionally.

Twain can maintain the illusion as long as he focuses on the town from a distance amid the natural landscape, "one of the most beautiful on the Mississippi" (525). The satisfying quality of the surrounding topography is enhanced by its immutability; it looks the same as it did in his childhood. People, however, cause annoyances (as locals do for tourists worldwide); they intrude upon the lovely pictures. They themselves change, and they cause other changes; they inevitably shatter the illusion of timelessness, making it impossible for Twain to remain "convinced . . . that [he is] a boy again." It would seem that Hannibal—like Naples, Damascus, Constantinople, and Jerusalem, among other locales in *The Innocents Abroad*—is best seen from a distance. In Italy, Twain mocked the saying "See Naples and die"; now touring the Mississippi, an apt phrase could be "See Hannibal and die," for Twain metaphorically appears to wither during his tour of his boyhood home.

Almost everybody else in the town of Twain's youth is dead and gone. Twain meets "an old gentleman" who illustrates the problem with the people of Hannibal. Despite several examples of relative success or happiness, the majority of those former residents about whom Twain inquires turn out to have met with misfortune, some manner of failure or heartache, or death—"killed in the war." Significantly, the main problem of the people of Hannibal, on the whole, is that, "marked with their griefs and defeats," they can offer "no upliftings of spirit" (525). But who really needs uplifting here—the travel writer/historian? No, it is the tourist/autobiographer who is facing a crisis of self and needs revivifying. The disappointment initiated by coming *down* from Holiday's Hill and leaving the protective shield of distance sends Twain into morbid memories of childhood. These stories add little to any "comprehensive" overview, though they do serve a logical purpose for the tourist; they offer a chance to escape wholly into the past. The stories may focus on death, but not Twain's; he is back in his youth and the time and place are alive again, not "dead-and-gone." He does, before closing out his Hannibal experience, acknowledge how it affects him: "During my three days' stay in the town, I woke up every morning with the impression that I was a boy—for in my dreams the faces were all young again, and looked as they had looked in the old time—but I went to bed a hundred years old, every night—for meantime I had been seeing those faces as they are now" (540). The experience of seeing present-day Hannibal via his old friends overwhelms Twain and moves him to exclaim hyperbolically that he feels "a hundred years old." There is solace only in a dream, the dream of a tourist. Although he claims subsequently to have adjusted to the change, he never really does, and stays mostly off the topic, or, when writing autobiographically, employs a particularly morbid slant. He closes this chapter (55) with a reference to "an interesting cave a mile or two below Hannibal" that had been turned into a mausoleum of sorts for the body of the fourteen-year-old daughter of the cave's owner. The girl's body is suspended in a copper cylinder filled with alcohol. Short of time (pun intended), Twain chooses not to take his readers there, but he points out that the "baser order of tourists" like to "drag the face into view and examine it and comment upon it" (547). In the balance of the Hannibal chapters, he has been doing much the same thing by remembering primarily the horrors of childhood, accentuated by death—by drowning, by fire. The child's face that he stoically drags into view, however, is his own. Here, Twain does not simply dabble in morbid fascination; he acts under a spell of nostalgia. The experience, though, seems no less disturbing for the tourist who does not want to think of himself as one.

Twain quickly concludes his tour following the Hannibal chapters, providing standard if brief vignettes of the upper Mississippi, sprinkled liberally with anecdotal information and Indian legends. He returns wholly to the objective travel writer/historian angle of vision; the energy of the autobiographer/tourist, after touring his childhood home where his "boyhood was spent," seems itself spent. Twain's final paragraph is a telling one, especially his comments concerning Chicago, and they parallel both his implicit reactions to his Mississippi River life and to *Life on the Mississippi*. "It is hopeless," he writes, "for the occasional visitor to try to keep up with . . . the Chicago you saw when you passed through the last time" (593). Although he is not directly applying this sentiment to the Mississippi, it fits his experiences as tourist/travel writer and autobiographer/historian. Twain's problem throughout the narrative has been the overwhelming change he has been forced to encounter, if not reconcile. In exasperation, he can only explain that it is impossible "to keep up." The nostalgic tourist, like all tourists, seeks a world that does not exist, an experience that is unavailable because, alas, he is always the "occasional visitor" to places undergoing change. The Mississippi River, like Chicago, is never the river that one passed before, whether the tour occurred twenty-one years earlier or only twenty-one hours. The river flows on; it buries, it builds, it destroys. But it always flows on.

Life on the Mississippi is Twain's most personal travel book, but for that reason perhaps it is also the most difficult for readers to join. Their traveling narrator, with his conflicted perspectives mired in the past and flustered by the present, seems overwhelmed by the vastness of Mississippi culture and history and underwhelmed by how his own life fits within (and without) it. Chapter 4, "The Boys' Ambitions," is emblematic of Twain's ambivalence. In recounting how the townspeople of Hannibal in his childhood reacted to the arrival of a steamboat, Twain also provides an analogous appraisal of his tourist-self in *Life on the Mississippi:* "Before events, the day was glorious with expectancy; after them, the day was a dead and empty thing" (63). The long-awaited "expectancy" of writing a standard work, of touring the Mississippi, of seeing his home again, is initially thrilling. Disappointment, however, soon sets in and deflates his buoyancy; the autobiographer seems unable to face the changes caused by the ebb and flow of the mighty river, and the historian becomes distracted. Twain's only recourse is to his incomparable imagination, reassuring himself that "after all these years I can picture that old time to myself now, just as it was then" (63), and as it always *is,* in the mind of the tourist.

5
Touring the Round

Imperialism and the Failure of Travel Writing in *Following the Equator*

"Whenever it's a damp drizzly November in my soul, I quietly take
to sea."—Ishmael

Herman Melville, *Moby-Dick*

"You feel mighty free and easy and comfortable on a raft."—Huck

Mark Twain, *Adventures of Huckleberry Finn*

Mark Twain ended his travel-writing career much as he began it, producing a successful narrative based on a highly publicized tour with a specific itinerary, a farewell tour for America's most popular tourist. *Following the Equator* comes the closest of his travel books in its form and structural execution to matching *The Innocents Abroad* as representative of this vastly popular genre. This heralded tour provides a fitting closing bookend to his canon. Unified and coherent, it re-creates a specific journey for readers, and it is the most typical of Twain's travel books since *The Innocents Abroad* became the prototype narrative for the Tourist Age. Almost thirty years after his initial astounding success, Twain with *Following the Equator* offers readers yet another companion to *The Innocents Abroad* and illustrates wholly how he recognized the vagaries and idiosyncracies of the genre throughout his career and how he mastered its demands. Still, *Following the Equator* is often the least readable of his travel books, and it never matches the humor and energy of its predecessors. It has comic moments, but its humor is more likely to garner a smirk or bemused acknowledgment than the boisterous laughter evoked by *The Innocents Abroad* (and the others). As such, the narrative may be less like a formal closing to a century of "innocent" travel and more like a sad, if cynical, acknowledgment of what is to come, a watershed narrative marking the close of the first phase of the Tourist Age and an end to willful ignorance of its dark, imperialistic context.

If the markedly different reading experience does not derive from the structure or application of travel-writing conventions, or even from effective and powerful writing, it must come from the mind of the tourist and his changing ways of seeing the world. This final narrative, then, is Twain's most ethically conflicted travel book. He is forced to grant his readers a tour of the world through the eyes of the tourist, as he has for thirty years, while also for the first time becoming acutely conscious that the tourist is by no means a harmless if indulgent visitor who enters, roams, and departs from a landscape and culture without leaving a lasting trace. At the close of the century he is not only trapped again by the vacuousness of touristic experience (the primary source of Twain's playfulness throughout his career) but also openly aware of his complicity in the imperial culture he has come to abhor so vehemently. If *The Innocents Abroad* heralded the beginning of the Tourist Age, complete with obnoxious but relatively harmless Americans, *Following the Equator* announces the end of its first phase. The vandals have evolved into oppressors.

As a result, despite its formalistic coherence, *Following the Equator* is rather schizophrenic in that on the one hand it reaffirms the imaginative core of touristic experience explored in each of his other travel books, while on the other hand it rejects the imperialistic component of the great popular movement that sets the stage for such touristic play. The tide of tourism has circled and, indeed, engulfed the world, and its affectations have remade it according to its simplistic and self-indulgent vision. Though similar in its structure to *The Innocents Abroad, Following the Equator* is of a wholly different time and has a far darker tone throughout, a point of view that allies Twain more with the modernists of the twentieth century than with his fellow Victorians, or with his earlier tourist self. The figure in this carpet is Twain's struggle to reframe his relationship to native populations as the tourist. As the travel writer, he confronts a similar crisis in this his last narrative. Twain, for the first time, applies the implications of touristic experience directly and at length to the nature of narrative itself. The many years and experiences that intervene between the two texts not only offer evidence of his mastery of travel-writing formula but also his ultimate disenchantment with the limits of language. As the tourist, Twain can no longer play the innocent; he can no longer ignore his inevitable connection to the misdeeds of an aggressively imperialistic culture and his complicity as its most pernicious representative—the tourist in full. As the travel writer, he can no longer salvage the experiences in words—the writer on empty. If there is no social or political escape from the imperialistic context for mass tourism, then there is, likewise, no refuge for the writer in his craft.

IMPERIALISM AND THE DREAM OF COLOR

We should begin reading *Following the Equator* as a typical Twain travel book and recognize it as yet another formidable example of his mastery of the genre. On the whole, he is in complete control of his material and of our experiences as readers, and the narrative holds within it a carefully structured tour of Australia, New Zealand, India, and South Africa that balances information, entertainment, and comfort conventional to the genre and endemic to Twain's understanding of reader needs. The various stops are all tied together by the peace of an ocean voyage that traces the round in search of a cure for Twain's artistic and personal malaise. The adherence to a well-proven formula deserves some consideration, especially since *Following the Equator* contains much to illuminate Twain's continuing desire to build on his travel-writing skill and his interest in the characteristics of touristic experience even in his farewell narrative. *Following the Equator* follows his established patterns, but that is not to say that it is a cookie-cutter narrative wherein he simply plugs in local jokes and images along a grooved narrative plank, as he had once recommended for his speeches.[1] While it does follow a successful formula, it also builds upon his understanding of both travel writing and touristic experience.

Early in the narrative, after having missed a stopover in the Hawaiian Islands due to a cholera outbreak onshore, Twain comments on the equator as the ship nears it, his first reference to the namesake of the narrative: "Those of us who have never seen the equator are a good deal excited. I think I would rather see it than any other thing in the world" (65). The joke is, of course, that there is nothing to see. The equator serves as a watery geographical reference point and offers hardly anything to see that differs from the surrounding region. Yet Twain comically illustrates what he has been manipulating during his entire travel-writing career: that the lack of actual sights bears little on the potential for developing tourist sights. Once informed by the ship's crew of the equator's exact location, the tourists can provide the desired experience on their own—water, water everywhere but not a drop to demand reverence until it is defined in a touristic context, with a renowned location. Suddenly, and somewhat arbitrarily (given the tourists' ignorance of the place), *this* water in *this* place is worth seeing and commenting on; it means something for the tourist. Twain's mocking joke represents perhaps the touristic center of *Following the Equator*, that the equator, the tour, and the experience are all constructs of reality based on imaginary lines, imaginary experiences, and the touristic desire to accumulate them. One of Twain's working titles for the narrative, "Imitating the Equator," then, is an astute one beyond his assertion that his tour mimics the line by roughly (very roughly) following it; the tourist also imitates the experience of seeing what is not there, of seeing an idea, a metaphor of the imagination.[2] His wish, likewise, to see the Southern Cross restates the basic touristic approach to experience and the search for novelty at its core. He writes:

> Yesterday evening we saw the Big Dipper and the north star sink below the horizon and disappear from our world. No, not "we," but they. They saw it—somebody saw it—and told me about it. But it is no matter, I was not caring for those things, I am tired of them, any way. I think they are well enough, but one doesn't want them always hanging around. My interest was all in the Southern Cross. I had never seen that. I had heard about it all my life, and it was but natural that I should be burning to see it. (78–79)

Predictably, Twain sets up the standard tourist trope, eager for novelty, urged on by overblown, hyperbolic expectations ("I supposed it would need a sky all to itself") and followed by the inevitable disappointment ("not large, and not strikingly bright") (79). Hardly an easily ascertained cross in the sky, the so-called Southern Cross is barely worth the effort to seek it out. This is familiar and comfortable ground for Twain's readers. But as we have seen, Twain does not overwhelm his fellow tourists—his readers—with disappointment; there is also a wealth of pleasure available in pictures, controlled and contrived images of reality.

Twain is consistently adept at providing compelling touristic pictures for his readers, images with which they are already familiar on some level. *Following the Equator* is no exception, populated with many paradigms of travel writing especially powerful in Twain's able hands. The Fiji Islands offer one such opportunity for Twain as the ship passes by for a Kodak moment:

> Yesterday we passed close to an island or so, and recognized the published Fiji characteristics: a broad belt of clean white coral sand around the island; back of it a graceful fringe of leaning palms, with native huts nestling cosily among the shrubbery at their bases; back of these a stretch of level land clothed in tropic vegetation; back of that, rugged and picturesque mountains. A detail of the immediate foreground: a mouldering ship perched high up on a reef-bench. This completes the composition, and makes the picture artistically perfect. (91–92)

Twain takes a literary snapshot and gives it to readers, explaining in the process how he (and readers) can compose the image for consumption. He indicates that the picture is standard and has already been "published." One may wonder to which "picture" he refers, one from his memory, stored from earlier reading, or the one at the touristic moment as the ship sails near the islands. In the end, it does not matter. What he sees (we must assume as readers) is what he shows, yet he describes the scene as a postcard, a carefully constructed image based on his and his readers' already well established image of Fiji, one everyone can "recognize." Twain thereby makes not only the narrative picture "artistically perfect" but also the experience of seeing it, reading it, imagining it, or even remembering it as "artistically perfect." This is effective travel writing, not because it endeavors to be fresh but because it builds on common if abstract expectations, thereby making the foreign familiar and within limits of understanding.

The travel writer never really paints a picture out of whole cloth, but depends on images already in the tourist's mind and imagination. Twain often laments that he is haunted by those preconceptions and rejects how they alter his experiences by, in most cases, creating in his imagination an unrealistic, overblown expectation well beyond the limitations of reality. This is a prominent motif in all of his travel books, but he never really acknowledges that he depends on those same images in the minds of his readers. However, perhaps the most difficult challenge for the travel writer is to capitalize on those expectations and to mock them on occasion without alienating readers. Twain most often succeeds on both counts.

Implicit in the narrative act of turning landscapes and human-made structures into touristic pictures is the tourist gaze, an objectifying look toward locals that readily incorporates them into such pictures.[3] The native populations under such a gaze become subservient, actors in a play constructed by the touristic imagination, important only in how they add to or subtract from the aesthetics within the frame. In addition to working with typical touristic pictures, Twain also represents the ever-present tourist's gaze, establishing locals as sights, people valuable for their novelty only, and he does so in much greater depth of understanding than in earlier narratives. India offers the best illustration of this common touristic way of seeing. For example, in Bombay ("*Bombay!* A bewitching place, a bewildering place, an enchanting place") Twain describes the crowds of people in a park across from his hotel: "It does not seem as if one could ever get tired of watching this moving show, this shining and shifting spectacle" (345). Then he focuses specifically and at length on the views at Scandal Point, a seaside vista that has "handy rocks to sit on and a noble view of the sea on the one hand, and on the other the passing and repassing whirl and tumult of gay carriages, are great groups of comfortably-off Parsee women—perfect flower-beds of brilliant color, a fascinating spectacle" (346). After describing typical male clothing and stature, he focuses on the Parsee woman: "She is so straight, so erect, and she steps with such style, and such easy grace and dignity; and her curved arm and her brazen jar are such a help to the picture—indeed, our working-women cannot begin with her as a road-decoration" (347). This description is supported by a photograph of a Parsee woman in the pose Twain details; the picture is identified as "Road Decoration" (347). This passage along with the illustration reflects a decidedly male gaze that objectifies women (is Twain playing with the notion of her as a "working" woman to conjure up thoughts of prostitution?). In any event, however, it is the touristic gaze that dominates the narrative moment. The crucial term is "road-decoration." Twain's primary point of view derives from his perspective as a tourist, not a man; the title defines her and Twain, both of the "road," Twain as tourist, the woman as sight. She exists in the narrative to decorate the landscape for the consumption of the tourist reader, and she offers something pleasant to look at while on the road. Her gender and comeliness ultimately add to her touristic value as a spectacle for, in this case, a male tourist.[4]

These examples represent the typical though no less thoughtful Twainian touristic experience so evident in earlier narratives, as we have seen. However, such images rarely exist alone in their innocence; other scenes intrude upon the tourist and force him to face the more painful connections to the imperialistic (racist and classist) components of the Tourist Age, wherein the delight of watching "spectacles" often becomes intertwined with indignities and horrors at the fringe of the frame, just beyond the standard touristic gaze.

The most powerful instance of such peripheral awareness occurs in the same chapter as the scene above (chapter 38) when Twain witnesses a German supervisor strike an Indian servant (351). Twain's reaction to the violence is an interesting one for its relevance not only to his autobiography and his growing understanding of the brutality of racism he witnessed as a child, but also for how the tourist experiences the world. Twain observes and marvels at his own thinking process and how his mind (via the memory and imagination needed to make the connection) constructs experiences beyond physical restrictions. As he watches the German hit the Indian servant, Twain travels emotionally and mentally back to the antebellum Missouri of his youth. He describes honestly and with clear self-awareness the violence and degradation of slavery that he saw but could not comprehend as a child. But for the touristic content, his marveling at how his own mind works illustrates the best of how the tourist may react to such a stimulus as well:

> It is curious—the space-annihilating power of thought. For just one second, all that goes to make the *me* in me was in a Missourian village, on the other side of the globe, vividly seeing again these forgotten pictures of fifty years ago, and wholly unconscious of all things but just those; and in the next second I was back in Bombay, and that kneeling native's smitten cheek

was not done tingling yet! Back to boyhood—fifty years; back to age again, another fifty; and a flight equal to the circumference of the globe—all in two seconds by the watch. (352)

Twain writes of "all that goes to make the *me* in me" and moves free from physical realities and restrictions; emotional and mental gymnastics characterize his personal and touristic reaction to the violence. This passage, then, both undercuts touristic experience and rejuvenates it in a deeper, more engaged context. The shift comes from Twain's direct connection to the violence, since the German was in effect punishing the Indian on the tourist's behalf; both the supervisor and the servant were, after all, serving Twain. The affirmative part of the experience comes from Twain's thoughtful and empathetic response; he understands. This is a compelling moment for readers, as they gain a touching insight into their narrator's past and their past as well, one that is candid and unpleasant. The time travel has only a tangential relationship to India, which had sparked a personal memory. Yet this is gripping travel writing, not simply because it offers a shameful memory of antebellum Missouri but because it brings the past forward into Twain's current life. The two pictures—one Indian, the other American—are variations on the same theme of racism. In both, Twain, the little boy or the older man, is a spectator who is nonetheless connected to the violence, whether he comprehends it or not. The travel writer recognizes the synchronicity and tries to give both pictures—as one image—to readers. "It is curious—the space-annihilating power of thought," he says—and of pain and injustice, all within a narrative frame of a servant's stinging cheek. So, on the one hand, this touristic moment reaffirms typical behavior by illustrating how the tourist interprets experience on his own terms and within his own imagination, while on the other hand it also demonstrates the remarkable potential for the tourist who may, after all, learn something by making such connections. There is something to be proud of in *Following the Equator* for the old tourist/travel writer; he has matured in recognizing the inequality and blatant mindlessness of racism and is now able to use the power of thought to recognize and convey a sense of injustice done not only to the servant but also to the slaves of his youth.[5] Such thought, of course, cannot effect a change of condition for the slave or the servant, but it can ameliorate the mind of the tourist capable of entering the picture with empathy.

This growth also causes the tourist difficulty. How much emotional space should the tourist allow for this expansion of consciousness? Can the tourist recognize fully the consequences of imperialism and still remain an enthusiastic tourist? Does the tourist need to stay home? *Following the Equator* probes this dilemma, which manifests itself most specifically in the manner in which Twain evades certain connections to imperialism; the tourist can travel at peace only by escaping into a dream of color.[6]

We need to go back to the beginning of the narrative, which opens typically enough. After a "snail-paced march across the continent," Twain and his entourage take to sea, beginning in earnest his around-the-world tour. Despite the tortured land journey (the specifics of which he opted to leave out of the narrative), once at sea Twain feels comfortable: "We closed the field-glasses and sat down on our steamer chairs contented and at peace" (26). The comfort is short-lived: "But they went to wreck and ruin under us and brought us to shame before all the passengers" (26). This is customary Twainian self-deprecation, but it also sets up two pertinent themes. The most evident one presents Twain as a spectacle, the famous man touring the world while everyone watches, listens, and participates. No longer the innocent or the tramp, Twain is the world-famous man of letters, a celebrity of the first order. Another theme (and more directly applicable to this inquiry) illustrates the sharp contrasts between leisured comfort and embarrassment while also exploring their inevitable interconnectedness. For the first time, Twain faces not merely the laughable (and often annoying) contexts of tourism but the darker and powerful effects of imperialism, for which tourism serves a crucial codependent role. In this apt beginning, Twain establishes himself comfortably only to be humiliated by falling to the deck; the chair on which he rests is weak, and his complacency is undermined. Symbolically, the grand old tourist in tracing the round cannot avoid facing how his touring is complicit in the imperialism that he is coming to loathe by the end of the century. His intellectual and moral recognition of his relationship to imperialism via his whiteness does not, however, prevent him from playing the typical role of the tourist, that of an escapist. In fact, it impels the wish for escape forward with greater urgency.

According to Erik Cohen, traveling beyond one's own home landscape and culture (one's "life-space") "assumes that there is some experience available 'out there,' which cannot be found within the life-space, and which makes travel worthwhile" (182). A tourist endeavors to move—temporarily—out of the domestic arena and into another space for some perhaps vague or specific purpose that holds forth the promise of pleasurable and/or instructive experiences. Cohen identifies five types of tourists: recreational, diversionary, experiential, experimental, and existential. Whereas recreational and diversionary tourists seek no involvement in cultures they visit beyond their ability to provide rest or diversion, the other three types make an effort to engage on some level of active participation, however brief or shallow. The experiential and experimental tourists hope to gain different experiences foreign to their own, with the latter being more of a seeker longing to find a new self (as we have explored in *Roughing It*). Neither is committed to the long term. The existential tourist, however, is devoutly looking for a complete change of self, a complete altering of existence. The tourist of *Following the Equator* most resembles this mode.

The problem, as Twain realizes, is that the act of touring is implicitly an act of escape from one's home, but it is also an inescapably political act. Mary Louise Pratt, in a seminal work on travel writing and imperialism, *Imperial Eyes* (1982), coins the term "contact zone" to refer to "social spaces where disparate cultures meet, clash, and often grapple with each other, often in highly asymmetrical relations of domination and subordination" (4). Here is the rub: in traveling out of one's "life-space," the tourist must move into the spaces of others; these newly crowded spaces constitute "contact zones." On the political level, the imperial culture spreads its influence throughout the world; on the personal level for the tourist and travel writer, the act of sightseeing—defining and commodifying place—is also an act of domination, no matter the intention or comprehension of the tourist, since the sights are subordinated to the primary goal of gaining touristic experience. In an imperialistic context—the primary and unavoidable situation for the Tourist Age—such movement, in any mode, can have unforeseen and dire consequences. The touristic assumption that expanding one's horizons is intrinsically and invariably salutary can bring about malignant effects, no matter how benign the personal wish may be. *Following the Equator*, Twain's last travel narrative, represents his first attempt to reconcile this basic touristic dilemma in a substantive fashion.[7] He methodically assesses the results of the "contact zones" on indigenous peoples in Australasia, India, and South Africa and is rightly appalled. Yet, in recognizing the complications of a Tourist Age that is no longer innocent, the awakening tourist nonetheless remains a captive of the overwhelming tide of this popular movement, and he concludes that there is no way to alter his existence as the tourist, no way to move around the world without leaving an altered physical and cultural landscape in his wake.

Our first indications of the escape wish occur on the ocean, as Twain rhapsodizes about the romantic promise of the South Seas, a symbolic extension of the mythical American West:

> Indeed, the Island Wilderness is the very home of romance and dreams and mystery. The loneliness, the solemnity, the beauty, and the deep repose of this wilderness have a charm which is all their own for the bruised spirit of men who have fought and failed in the struggle for life in the great world; and for men who have been hunted out of the great world for crime; and for other men who love an easy and indolent existence; and for others who love a roving free life, and stir and change and adventure; and for yet others who love an easy and comfortable career of trading and money-getting, mixed with plenty of loose matrimony by purchase, divorce without trial or expense, and limitless spreeing thrown in to make life ideally perfect. (100)

This is quite an amoral reverie, and we may be tempted to wonder which of these men might be Twain's alter ego, or more accurately, whether they are all part of him. The escape wish, with its implicit hope for new beginning, for freedom, pervades this dream. After this fantasy, he writes, "We sailed again, refreshed" (100). "We" seems to be all of the men in the reverie, all part of Twain, and it is the dream that refreshes the old tourist. In other words, Twain begins the tour in the existential mode of tourism, in that he is seeking another life, a full escape from the world as he knows it. If the tour itself for Samuel Clemens began as an effort to escape from debt, the narrative begins with a metaphorical effort to escape all forms of restrictiveness (even marital), to celebrate freedom. Symbolically, like Melville's Ishmael (or even his own Huck Finn), Twain seeks the openness and peace implied by taking to open water. Twain the old tourist wants peace, mainly: "Three days of paradise. Warm and sunny and smooth; the sea a luminous Mediterranean blue. . . . One lolls in a long chair all day under deck-awnings, and reads and smokes, in measureless content" (324). There are two major parts to Twain's version of the existential tourist: on the one hand, he shows his anger concerning the political and cultural effects of imperialism, to which tourism and travel writing are contributing factors; on the other hand, he dreams of escape to the best that travel has to offer—idleness, peace, freedom from restrictions. So he struggles alternately between disparaging imperialism and participating in it—the white man's burden becomes the tourist's burden—or running away from it all. He is trapped because, for the tourist, running away, ironically, perpetuates imperialism.

To deny complicity is unacceptable to Twain; to escape from it all still holds sway—and hope. He offers numerous attacks upon imperialism and its effects, despite his general belief that the British Empire represents much of the best mankind has to offer the world—not a strong recommendation considering his mounting distaste for mankind.[8] Twain is resigned to the inevitability of colonialism, yet he mourns the losses and despises the arrogance of Western civilization even as he acknowledges its unmatched power, for both good and evil. Twain's general attitude of anti-imperialism remains virulent, and these two themes work together to shape his dream of escape. He comments acidly on population figures for aboriginal peoples in Australia and how European "appliances of civilization" have decimated them: "The white man knew ways of keeping down population" (208). He alludes to the murderous inclinations that follow civilization, and closes the chapter with a pithy and summary judgment: "There are many humorous things in the world; among them the white man's notion that he is less savage than the other savages" (213). Twain, it should be noted, does believe that brutality and violence are endemic not just to European culture but to human history: "No tribe, howsoever insignificant, and no nation, howsoever mighty, occupies a foot of land that was not stolen" (623). Be that as it may, Twain is also certain that the late nineteenth century's version of real estate theft far outstrips any previous efforts in its efficiency at overwhelming indigenous cultures on a global scale. If he is resigned to the inevitability of such imperialism and persuaded that the British

Empire offers the most beneficent the world has to offer, he is by no means impressed by that accomplishment as any momentous improvement on how humans treat one another.

The most memorable manifestation of this vitriolic attack on white civilization is presented most passionately, if indirectly, through an elaborate dream of color.[9] Although this vision exhibits itself in various ways, clothes become a central metaphor as Twain once again becomes obsessed with costume. This time, however, rather than focusing on how the tourist can try on local costumes to alter—symbolically or superficially—a sense of identity, Twain in his imperial tour focuses on the striking differences between Western clothing and native costume and uses these differences to explore the distinct and inescapable futility of his dream of escape into color. He appears almost blinded by his whiteness. Twain registers his hatred for the restrictiveness of white civilization's clothing styles, and he rejoices in the vibrant hues of the clothing of nonwhite cultures. In short, clothing becomes his preferred metaphor for the innate values of both cultures at large. Longing to change his costume, he never does so directly, resigned to his lot; Twain is no Gauguin, no Melville. Clothing becomes synonymous with the restrictions of Western civilization, and perhaps this is itself an imperial conceit, the dominant race bemoaning its lack of freedom (forgetting that he has the economic power—even during bankruptcy—to travel around the world) and pining for the freedom of local populations, who may very well be struggling with extreme poverty. His references to clothing permeate the narrative and are indicative of his existential mode of tourism, his dream of escape to color. An early example involves Twain's observation of a Fijian butler in native dress: "This man was clothed in flowing white vestments, and they were just the thing for him; they comported well with his great stature and his kingly port and dignity. European clothes would have degraded him and made him commonplace. I know that, because they do that with everybody that wears them" (96). For Twain, the man's simple dress reflects his dignity. Part of imperialistic culture is the imposing upon the local population the intruder's value systems, in this case clothing. Twain voices his opinion that European clothes, and all that comes with them, can only degrade the native. But he does not stop here. Rather, he turns the criticism back onto European culture at large and, more specifically, upon himself as a wearer of such clothing. The tourist, the representative of that imperial culture, stands "degraded" and "commonplace." This reversal becomes a central technique of assessing the effects on imperialism, and as he enters into Indian culture, especially, the dream of color takes hold of his imagination in full.

Arriving in Ceylon, Twain invokes the dream in his standard touristic way of seeing—in pictures. He writes:

> The walking groups of men, women, boys, girls, babies—each individual was a flame, each group a house afire for color. And such stunning colors, such intensely vivid colors, such rich and exquisite minglings and fusings of rainbows and lightnings! And all harmonious, all in perfect taste; never a discordant note; never a color on any person swearing at another color on him or failing to harmonize faultlessly with the colors of any group the wearer might join. (340)

This is a utopian vision, a dramatic contrast of the spectrum alongside white, colorless, lifeless clothing. The dream of color carries within it an implied escape from his own "degraded" and "commonplace" clothing. Twain revels vicariously in the freedom that the tourist believes the native population enjoys, capturing their own "rainbows" and "lightnings." All is harmony. He continues at length, and his reactions remain upbeat, emphasizing that the color affects him physically in that it "made a body catch his breath, and filled his heart with joy" and "made the heart sing for gladness." The heart of the tourist, it seems, can "sing with gladness" and thereby metaphorically join in the harmony through his imagination. Throughout the narrative, two types of experiences consistently thrill Twain: receiving homage from his fans and seeing wonderfully brilliant colors. The adoration of fans has a clear justification for being exciting, but the dream of color becomes much more for him emotionally in that it is intrinsically tied in his mind to freedom, escape. The two stimuli, then, are not so far apart; both allow him respite from his own troubles. The former reaffirms his fame; the latter reasserts the possibility of a different life altogether. As mentioned above, his reverie on the "Island Wilderness" had captured his dream of escape and elaborated on how color is so intertwined with the dream, "that incomparable dissolving-view of harmonious tints, and lithe half-covered forms, and beautiful brown faces, and gracious and graceful gestures and attitudes and movements, free, unstudied, barren of stiffness and restraint" (343). Twain is again in reverie, equating the color of clothing with freedom; by implication, this existential tourist wishes to change his restrictive, studied, stiff, and restrained costume. His harmonizing in thought and emotion, however, proves discordant with his true touristic (white) self, and the tune can only go flat. "Just then, into this dream of fairyland and paradise," he writes, "a grating dissonance was injected. Out of the missionary school came marching, two and two, sixteen prim and pious little Christian black girls, Europeanly clothed—dressed, to the last detail, as they would have been dressed on a summer Sunday in an English or American village" (343). Note how he uses "march," an image of control—stiffness, restraint. By implication, missionaries and everything they represent— white, Christian, civilized—destroy Twain's dream of harmony. As with the easy chairs in the opening of the narrative, the comfort of the dream falls to ruin beneath him, for it is built unpicturesquely on imperialism. He continues: "Those clothes—oh, they were unspeakably ugly! Ugly, barbarous, destitute of taste, destitute of grace, repulsive as a shroud" (343).[10] "Shroud," a curious but telling word choice, emphasizes the death of color, and the dream, as well as the innocence and freedom of the young girls. All is lost. Then Twain comments: "I looked at my women-folk's clothes—just full-grown duplicates of the outrages disguising those poor little abused creatures—and was ashamed to be seen in the street with them. Then I looked at my own clothes, and was ashamed to be seen in the street with myself" (343). "Shame" provides the key here; the connection between the lack of color in his and his family's garb reminds him of his connection to the missionaries who have taken the freedom (the color) away from the young girls, "poor little abused creatures." Humiliated by his capitulation to European restrictiveness, he must also recognize that he is linked to the missionaries and their oppressive behavior toward nonwhite natives. That is to say, the shame is more than mere embarrassment at wearing colorless clothes; Twain crosses the bridge to cultural imperialism via the metaphor of clothes. His presence in the streets, spoiling the picture, as it were, is in itself part of the problem. This tourist—no matter his thrilling support for and envy of local costume—nevertheless becomes a significant force of cultural domination, an arm of imperialism under the guise of harmless, if hapless, tourism. Although he never fully formulates this realization in the narrative, Twain seems to intuit that the tourist alters the local, no matter what his intentions. As his clothes announce, he is more aligned with the missionaries than with the natives; his lack of color (whiteness) gives him away. Resigning himself to his visible partisanship, he continues:

> However, we must put up with our clothes as they are—they have their reason for existing. They are on us to expose us—to advertise what we wear them to conceal. They are a sign; a sign of insincerity; a sign of suppressed vanity; a pretense that we despise gorgeous colors and the graces of harmony and form; and we put them on to propagate that lie and back it up. But we do not deceive our neighbor; and when we step into Ceylon we realize that we have not even deceived ourselves. (343)

Clothes, then, explicitly prove the delusory arrogance of white civilization, its false and revealing "pretense" of superiority, and Twain cannot help but walk about exposed; this tourist has no clothes. He goes on to list examples showing how whites in reality love color, then writes: "Yes, our clothes are a lie, and have been nothing short of that these hundred years. They are insincere, they are the ugly and appropriate outward exposure of an inward sham and a moral decay" (344). He claims that the native costume (or even the lack of it in reference to a little boy who wears only a string) is supremely honest, while the restraint in European costume is "odious flummery."

With this caustic analysis, Twain the tourist finds himself in a difficult position once again, for he remains a tourist and travel writer. His only option is to retreat back into a simpler role of the tourist as observer, a failed existentialist unable to change his costume, unable to hide his whiteness. He can only return to his dream of color, knowing that it is but a dream, forced to forego his efforts at harmony and embrace his only respite: touristic imagination. The reverie goes on: "It is all color, bewitching color, enchanting color—everywhere —all around—all the way around the curving great opaline bay clear to Government House, where the turbaned big native *chuprassies* stand grouped in state at the door in their robes of fiery red, and do most properly and stunningly finish up the splendid show and make it theatrically complete" (347). Noting how the locals provide a "splendid show" that is "theatrically complete," Twain retakes his place as the tourist sightseer, and the locals are put back into their role as entertainment sights. Twain uses the dash here to convey the snapshot impressions and symbolically turn his readers's eyes "all around," to take in the color that surrounds him "everywhere." He closes this extended reverie with "I wish I were a chuprassy" (347). He wishes to insert himself, the tourist, into a picture of his own creation. He would thus overlay himself and readers across the middle of the picture, surrounded by color. Twain then utters heartfelt praise, complete with exclamation points for exotic India: "This is indeed India! the land of dreams and romance" (347). The dream of color seems the only escape from imperialism. The white man's burden is not any trumped-up obligation to care for supposed less fortunate or less capable people; rather, in this case, it comes from an awareness of the arrogance of such an assumption; this is Mark Twain's burden. He even extends his attack on whiteness, in effect traveling back to a time before imperialism, before the Tourist Age, before the cultural clash:

> It [white complexion] is not an unbearably unpleasant complexion when it keeps to itself, but when it comes into competition with masses of brown and black the fact is betrayed that it is endurable only because we are used to it. Nearly all black and brown skins are beautiful, but a beautiful white skin is rare. How rare, one may learn by walking down a street in Paris, New York, or London on a week-day—particularly an unfashionable street—and keeping count of the satisfactory complexions encountered in the course of a mile. Where dark complexions are massed, they make the whites look bleached-out, unwholesome, and sometimes frankly ghastly. (381)

Despite the touristic dream of color, in spite of the recognition of the tourist's complicity, the bottom line is that Twain, tourists, whites simply should *not* be there: whiteness can only be bearable if "it keeps to itself." There is no other option that can keep the tourist from appearing "bleached-out, unwholesome, and sometimes frankly ghastly." Yet this tourist is in the middle of a world tour, the travel writer in the middle of his narrative. Grim, it is high time for the tourist to take to sea.

After India, a relieved Twain is back on the ship and regains the peace he craves: "We are far abroad upon the smooth waters of the Indian Ocean, now; it is shady and pleasant and peaceful under the vast spread of the awnings, and life is perfect again—ideal" (609). Still the dreamer, he writes:

> I do not know how a day could be more reposeful: no motion; a level blue sea; nothing in sight from horizon to horizon; the speed of the ship furnishes a cooling breeze; there is no mail to read and answer; no newspapers to excite you; no telegrams to fret you or fright you—the world is far, far away; it has ceased to exist for you—seemed a fading dream, along in the first days; has dissolved to an unreality now; it is gone from your mind with all its businesses and ambitions, its prosperities and disasters, its exultations and despairs, its joys and griefs and cares and worries. They are no concern of yours any more; they have gone out of your life; they are a storm which has passed and left a deep calm behind. (616)

Given the financial troubles that launched Clemens upon the trip, Twain's deep wish for the peace of the ocean, for escape from everything, is natural, and his gratitude for such tranquillity is entirely understandable. But this passage also represents the dream of the tourist who after thirty years of travel is finding it especially difficult to remove himself from his own world of tourism. Moreover, he can no longer enter any other worlds without acknowledging the costs of such intrusion on local cultures. There is no longer any "innocence" in the tour. In the beginning, the Tourist Age promised that one could escape his or her part of the world, explore the rest of the world, and enrich him- or herself, but Twain is finding out that he cannot leave behind his own troubles and, more broadly, that he cannot evade the imperialistic implications of such escapist tourism. This existential tourist wants to change his life but is learning that ultimately he has no place to go, no reality wherein he can hide from his civilization. The dream of color distracts Twain momentarily, but alas he cannot change his costume permanently. Nor does the dream of escape at sea offer any lasting solution, for eventually the ship will reach the next port: "If I had my way we should never get in at all. This sort of sea life is charged with an indestructible charm. There is no weariness, no fatigue, no worry, no responsibility, no work, no depression of spirits.

There is nothing like this serenity, this comfort, this peace, this deep contentment, to be found anywhere on land. If I had my way I would sail on for ever and never go to live on the solid ground again" (616–17). The ideal tour, it seems, would be to travel (move, move, *move!*) but never make landfall (Columbus was innocent until he struck ground in the New World). Perhaps this passage encapsulates the ideal tourist experience—doing nothing, pretending nothing, seeing nothing. The secret to tourism is to have no place to go, just to sail on, trace the round, imitate the equator. This is the final, absolute escapist dream. The existential tourist can find peace, not by moving *to* a place, but by moving *in* place, intruding upon no one's values, trespassing upon no one's land. Otherwise, at the conclusion of the first phase of the Tourist Age, at the end of the nineteenth century, and at the close of Twain's travel-writing career, the tourist can only be one of two deplorable types, two disparate selves: an imperialist or a nihilist. There is no middle ground. The namesake for Twain's narrative, the equator, comes back into play here. In the beginning of the narrative, the tourist wants to see the equator, after all, precisely because there is nothing to see. There the tourist could find peace. There is no land, only an imaginary line that reaches around the world, symbolically holding together its two halves. Indeed, that would be something to see. But even then, the tour must run aground. Like the dream of color, the dream of staying on the sea is unattainable. Twain wraps up *Following the Equator* in the only way he can, with one last acknowledgment of failure and humility:

> It seemed a fine and large thing to have accomplished—the circumnavigation of this great globe in that little time, and I was privately proud of it. For a moment. Then came one of those vanity-snubbing astronomical reports from the Observatory-people, whereby it appeared that another great body of light had lately flamed up in the remotenesses of space which was traveling at a gait which would enable it to do all that I had done in *a minute and a half.* Human pride is not worth while; there is always something lying in wait to take the wind out of it. (712)

The metaphor referring to losing wind derives from a sea voyage. Lacking proper wind, a sailing vessel sits dead in the water, powerless to move. Ironically, this is exactly what the tourist wishes for in the end, to be stranded alone in the island wilderness, an outcast of the Tourist Age. Both throughout his career and within his last tour, Twain had traveled the globe, but the tourist—at long last—saw little of enduring value in the constant search for novel sensations, nothing worthy of "human pride." All journeys must end. The tourist must go home.

"LANGUAGE IS A TREACHEROUS THING": THE FAILURE OF TRAVEL WRITING

If the tourist must stop traveling, what remains for the travel writer? The first of two headings for chapter 59 of *Following the Equator,* from Pudd'nhead Wilson's New Calendar, reads: "Don't part with your illusions. When they are gone you may still exist but you have ceased to live" (567). This advisory may apply to all tourists, since Twain has shown throughout his travel-writing career that tourism depends on such willful self-delusion. Overall, this represents Twain's view of the tourist experience, recognizing its failure while also embracing its potential for escape, for an imaginary pleasure excursion that serves as the enduring allure of the Tourist Age. The tourist travels not to shatter illusions but to maintain them, to cherish them. In the specific case of *Following the Equator,* stripped of illusions of innocence and faced with the limits of his unsustainable dream of color, Twain the tourist must go home and end his touring. But this resignation leaves his touring partners, his readers, in a lurch. If the tourist chooses to go home and shed his globe-trotting identity, what then becomes of the travel writer? Are readers destined to the similar failure of their vicarious dreams?

Following the Equator serves as an appropriate bookend to *The Innocents Abroad.* The narrative builds again on Twain's intuitive and thoughtful notions of touristic faith, but it also achieves a theoretical vision that, in the end, represents a conscious loss of faith also for Twain as the travel writer. Not only is tourism a sham, but writing about it is as well. There were, of course, reasons why Samuel Clemens never attempted another travel book, but it is important to consider that Mark Twain, as is revealed by his ad hoc travel-writing theory in *Following the Equator,* abandoned the genre for reasons purely aesthetic. If he lost his interest in touring because of its imperialistic implications, as we have seen, he lost faith in the travel narrative (language) because of its inability to convey any accurate sense of experience at all. The second heading for chapter 59 reads, "Often, the surest way to convey misinformation is to tell the strict truth" (567). In his thirty years as a travel writer, has Twain put together a remarkable collection of misinformation? In the end, Twain, the man who began his career as a travel-book writer promising to see with honest eyes, doubts his power to render their objects in words. He no longer trusts the travel writer's eyes or the reader's.

In no other narrative does Twain examine the nature of travel writing so methodically and directly as he does in *Following the Equator*. Although in *The Innocents Abroad* he makes several extended references to the maddening limitations of travel writers from his perspective as a critically minded reader, his frustration stems directly from the ineptitude or disingenuousness of the writers themselves, not the literary form. His narrative commentary, likewise, has always offered implicit links to a prototypical touristic theory, as we have seen. Yet in this his last travel book, Twain attempts to cull together an explicit theory of travel writing in chapter 59, and in so doing he is forced to face the severe limits of the form and of language itself. As he tries to explore the travel-writing and travel-reading experience, his theoretical musings, in the end, deconstruct the genre altogether.

Niagara Falls in the United States and the Taj Mahal in India serve as springboards for his dissertation. The famous natural wonder and the world-renowned structure, two of the most oft-described places in the world, offer ideal subjects for his critical exercise, since both have accumulated a wealth of attention over the years and have thereby become emblems of the vagaries of both touristic experience and expression. He begins by explaining his personal touristic relationship with Niagara Falls:

> I had to visit Niagara fifteen times before I succeeded in getting my imaginary Falls gauged to the actuality and could begin to sanely and wholesomely wonder at them for what they were, not what I had expected them to be. When I first approached them it was with my face lifted toward the sky, for I thought I was going to see an Atlantic ocean pouring down thence over cloud-vexed Himalayan heights, a sea-green wall of water sixty miles front and six miles high, and so, when the toy reality came sud-

denly into view—that beruffled little wet apron hanging out to dry—the shock was too much for me, and I fell with a dull thud. (574–77)

Twain is disappointed because his expectations, encouraged by countless travel writers before him, overwhelm the commonsensical reality, so at Niagara he falls—or more accurately, his imagination falls—with a "thud." He continues: "Yet slowly, surely, steadily, in the course of my fifteen visits, the proportions adjusted themselves to the facts, and I came at last to realize that a waterfall a hundred and sixty-five feet high and a quarter of a mile wide was an impressive thing. It was not a dipperful to my vanished great vision, but it would answer" (577). Although Twain does assert that return visits to a sight that holds sharp contrasts between reality and imagination may eventually lessen the sad shock caused by the reality, the real never attains the magnitude of the imagined place, nor does it remove from memory the imagined experience; it merely inserts itself into the tourist's consciousness until, bit by bit, it becomes undeniable and of some value to the tourist, at least enough to "answer." This type of intense visitation, however, is simply not applicable to the Tourist Age on the whole. Twain's evolving relationship with Niagara Falls is an anomaly. His methodical melding of the two Niagara Falls simply breaks the rules of the game by invoking an arduous mental process that eventually reconciles the actual natural falls, what he calls a "beruffled little wet apron," with the tourist landmark, "a sea-green wall of water."

Twain takes this context and applies it to the Taj Mahal, opening with his standard complaint: "I know that I ought to do with the Taj as I was obliged to do with Niagara—see it fifteen times, and let my mind gradually get rid of the Taj built in it by its describers by help of my imagination, and substitute for it the Taj of fact. It would be noble and fine, then, and a marvel; not the marvel which it replaced, but still a marvel, and fine enough" (577). Imagination is more marvelous, yet practicality ensures that the tourist prefers the dream image of the Taj Mahal (or Niagara Falls). For Twain the wealth (or burden) of previous touristic experience overwhelms the real, and only by visiting the sight repeatedly can the tourist establish a relationship with it, an experience all his own. In this scenario, though, the travel writer is nothing but an encumbrance, a destroyer of authenticity.

Twain is beginning to make an important step toward understanding travel-writing and travel-reading experience. The tourist "reads" a place much like a text (a typically simplified text). As a reader, the tourist always characterizes the first draft of experience for the subsequent travel narrator, as the reader becomes writer. Beyond the obviousness of this connection hides an important limitation for the would-be travel writer, especially one who would eagerly separate from a touristic context. In describing his own reading habits (being overly self-critical to emphasize his point), Twain astutely equates the tourist with the travel reader:

> I am a careless reader, I suppose—an *impressionist* reader; an impressionist reader of what is *not* an impressionist picture; a reader who overlooks the informing details or masses their sum improperly, and gets only a large splashy, general effect—an effect which is not correct, and which is not warranted by the particulars placed before me—particulars which I did not examine, and whose meanings I did not cautiously and carefully estimate. It is an effect which is some thirty-five or forty times finer than the reality, and is therefore a great deal better and more valuable than the reality; and so, I ought never to hunt up the reality, but stay miles away from it, and thus preserve undamaged my own private mighty Niagara tumbling out of the vault of heaven, and my own ineffable Taj, built of tinted mists upon jeweled arches of rainbows supported by colonnades of moonlight. It is a mistake for a person with an unregulated imagination to go and look at an illustrious world's wonder. (577–78)

Twain still assumes that the writer (the good writer) provides accuracy, even authenticity. It is the reader who loses the *real* by failing to pay attention, by gravitating toward impressionism. Significantly, the resulting misinterpretation creates a more enjoyable product, "finer" and "more valuable." The mind of the reader (Twain, in this case) is simply the mind of the tourist. Twain's touring and his travel writing must inevitably depend on his "unregulated imagination" as well as those of his readers. The travel writer—any writer, by necessity— seeks on some level to "regulate" the responses of readers and to control experience. These readers, however, often have stubbornly "unregulated" imaginations that, it would seem, put them at cross-purposes with the writer. Readers, like tourists, endeavor to hold on to their illusions when faced with a disappointing reality; the realistic writers are caught in the middle in Twain's scenario, trapped between their initial touristic experience and the equally touristic readers. The pure, honest narrative is orphaned. But Twain knows better. Tourism must be impressionistic; travel writing, then, must also be impressionistic, and there is little room for even the most committed realist. The total effect the sightseer seeks dissolves upon too close scrutiny, as images blur in proximity. Travel writers, likewise, may choose words carefully to capture a self-defined truth of the moment (or is it the moment later at the writing desk?) and daub the experience as a painting in a way to create their own impressions of Niagara Falls or the Taj Mahal. Unless tourists visit each sight fifteen times and gain the peace that passes all understanding of imagination and reality, they are better off holding on to illusions as envisioned on the narrative canvas. The closing lines of this passage help to illustrate Twain's point as he overtly chooses to heighten *his* readers' romantic expectations with his own narrative impressions of Niagara Falls, "tumbling out of the vault of heaven," and "my own" Taj Mahal "of tinted mists upon jeweled arches of rainbows." Twain is not ironic here. Rather, the images come from the travel writer simply resisting regulation. And readers should do the same.

Twain is conflicted and angry at the misconceptions perpetuated by travel writing, but he places the problem on readers' imaginations, hating the moments when that imagination must face reality. Twain recognizes the strict limitations of language to define experience without potentially marring reality by inevitably distorting it in the mind of readers. Therefore, since all tourists have images of everything already in their heads—implanted by well-meaning travel writers among others—there is no escape. The travel writer and reader are caught like the tourist, all craving authenticity and pleasant experiences taken from a broad world, but all knowing at some level that such a quest cannot succeed, that the grail is unattainable. It seems the only recourse may be to tour a spot fifteen times; only then can the imaginative experience be at peace with the real one, though it is not clear from Twain how this transformation takes place. The important point, in any case, is that such repetition forms no substantive part of the Tourist Age paradigm; tourists rarely return even once, much less fourteen times. Barring such intense touring of one sight, the travel writer and the tourist are both trapped, the former desperate to capture and share experiences through language, the latter desperate to match the supposed reality of those who have gone before, and both disappointed inevitably by the whole process.

In looking back to the first heading for chapter 59—"Don't part with your illusions"—perhaps this maxim offers the only way out. This is the message implicit in all of Twain's travel books, and it is the one ultimately stated directly in his final narrative. Either stay at home—with your imagination pure, unadulterated, and unregulated —or travel and hold on to the dream pictures dearly; they may face corrective and intrusive regulations, but they may not necessarily have to succumb to them. Hold on. Travel writers have obligations in this context, though for Twain few writers acknowledge such responsibilities. According to Twain, travel writers owe it to readers to be careful in language or at least take lengths to explain themselves. "These describers are writing for the 'general,' and so, in order to make sure of being understood, they ought to use words in their ordinary sense, or else explain" (581). In short, travel writers must consider how readers may respond to their descriptions.

Twain is especially conscious of how the tourist and reader can easily blur details and thereby miss important portions of informative description. In the following passage, he sets up a standard narrative picture: "The approaches to Ballerat were beautiful. The features, great green expanses of rolling pasture-land, bisected by eye-contenting hedges of commingled new-gold and old-gold gorse—and a lovely lake" (230). Yet Twain appends an important self-reflexive comment: "One must put in the pause, there, to fetch the reader up with a slight jolt, and keep him from gliding by without noticing the lake" (230). Not only does Twain carefully construct a travel image carefully composed of "eye-contenting" colors, but he also highlights his writing process, noting his use of a dash to slow readers down and prevent them from missing the lake. This is an explicit reference to how the travel writer not only shapes the scene, as through a Claude Glass, but also directs how the readers should move around the frame. As the tourists take in the landscape, supposedly moving their eyes across it, so does the reader in following the words across the page.

In visiting Agra and Delhi, Twain chooses not to describe their mosques and forts, claiming that because he had read little about them he enjoyed "a natural and rational focus upon them, with the result that they thrilled, blessed, and exalted me. But if I had previously overheated my imagination by drinking too much pestilential literary hot Scotch, I should have suffered disappointment and sorrow" (570). Twain refuses to share much of his experience with his readers and provides little substantive information as texture for these unexpected sights. He may be saving readers from the type of disappointment he faces by not heating up their imaginations. More likely, however, he moves on because his ire is up. He continues his attack upon his travel-writing forebears, supporting his assertion that travel writing imposes itself negatively upon the prospective tourist. He continues:

> I mean to speak of only one of these many world-renowned buildings, the Taj Mahal, the most celebrated construction in the earth. I had read a great deal too much about it. I saw it in the daytime, I saw it in the moonlight, I saw it near at hand, I saw it from a distance; and I knew all the time, that of its kind it was *the* wonder of the world, with no competitor now and no possible future competitor; and yet, it was not *my* Taj. My Taj had been built by excitable literary people; it was solidly lodged in my head, and I could not blast it out. (570)

This passage repeats the same core lament offered in Twain's other travel books, but it is not clear how the reader is to take the complaint. Is travel reading valuable only as long as one never travels? He also contradicts himself, it seems, as he shifts the blame for the discrepancy back upon the writers—"excitable literary people"—forgetting perhaps that it is his "unregulated imagination" that leads to such disappointments, too. Twain is himself "excitable literary people." He emphasizes the difference between the actual Taj Mahal and the one of his imagination, what he calls "*my* Taj." Such ownership ironically portrays the basic conceit of tourism, that a sight—object, place, people, event—can indeed belong to the tourist, that it can be owned by Twain and his readers. But this ownership, in the end, can exist only in the mind of the tourist, in the imagination, so therein exists both the fascination of travel and its disappointment. Moreover, what Twain most objects to is that *his* Taj Mahal derives from misleading travel writers. He turns his anger away from the real and to those who gave him the imagined. It is not simply the travel writer's fault, however; it is the nature of tourism itself. The tourist can never belong, can never own a sight in the actual. In this scenario, though, the tourist loses not only *his* Taj Mahal as a supposed physical reality, but also the confidence in his imagined one. He no longer owns his imagination. Shaping his developing theory, Twain continues:

> I wish to place before the reader some of the usual descriptions of the Taj, and ask him to take note of the impressions left in his mind. These descriptions do really state the truth—as nearly as the limitations of language will allow. But language is a treacherous thing, a most unsure vehicle, and it can seldom arrange descriptive words in such a way that they will not inflate the facts—by help of the reader's imagination, which is always ready to take a hand, and work for nothing, and do the bulk of it at that. (571)

Twain uses the phrase "by help of the reader's imagination" to build on his own "unregulated imagination" and its influence on touristic experience. In both cases, the willingness of the "readers"—the writer and the reader—to imagine the unknown is crucial. He then goes on to give several brief descriptions culled from other travel writers (Satya Chandra Mukerji, William Wilson Hunter, and Bayard Taylor). Then, after citing various passages, some at length and some briefly, he writes: "All of these details are true. But, taken together, they state a falsehood—to *you*. You cannot add them up correctly. Those writers know the values of their words and phrases but to you the words and phrases convey other and uncertain values" (573). Since he has seen the actual Taj Mahal, Twain feels he can thus interpret these earlier travel writers' words in a manner unavailable to most readers.

In a specially formulated Twainian math system, he takes random italicized lines and assigns to them a numeric value (he does not clarify how he determines those values). He tallies the values of his first three examples to get 19, then asks: "Then why, as a whole, do they convey a false impression to the reader? It is because the reader—beguiled by his heated imagination—masses them in the wrong way" (574). Touristic math, it would seem, is the culprit. The writer, he observes, adds the numbers ($5 + 5 + 9 = 19$), but "the reader masses them thus—and then they tell a lie—559." Furthermore, incorporating the numbers from all of his examples, Twain shows that the writer's sum is 63, whereas the reader's sum is "559575255555." He then comments: "You must put in the commas yourself; I have to go on with my work" (574). Despite the idiosyncratic liberties with mathematical properties, Twain's base point remains sound symbolically as it relates to touristic reader response. Travel writers can never guarantee that their readers are getting their messages; in fact, for Twain it seems that the readers cannot even come close to understanding them. One may wonder, then, what's the point of writing or reading? The same failures of authenticity that define touristic experience also characterize reader experience. Twain seems to anticipate narrative questions intrinsic to twentieth-century theoretical debates on the postmodern; the travel text has no objective reality, lost in its own fun house of touristic imagination. The imagination so intrinsic to touristic experience intrudes upon and shapes the reader's experience. The actual Taj Mahal, no matter the solidity of its marble, stands malleable to the tourist's mind. Likewise, the specific words constructed by the travel writer describing the Taj Mahal are fungible, dependent upon the whims and inclinations of readers. So whose fault is all of this misunderstanding? Are the writers and their imprecise language to blame, or is it the readers and their "heated" imaginations? Both, perhaps, share the blame, but there seems to be no substantive recourse to correct the transmittal of misinformation that derives from an inevitably faulty translation from writer to reader. This problem, though, begins with the inevitably faulty translation from sight to tourist. It is no wonder the numbers never balance.

Twain's line "I have to go on with my work" is especially curious. To what extent is the writer responsible for the mistake and to what extent does the writer depend on the deceptions, on readers' completion of the translation? By omitting the commas and demanding that readers supply them on their own, Twain implies that the writer gladly opens the spaces for readers to fill in as they will. Where will they put the commas? His work—without the commas—seems unfinished, but perhaps that is his point, however playful and comic. In the end, the successful travel writer can only *suggest* image and *suggest* experience. The imaginations of both the tourist writer and the tourist reader always put figures together in a "wrong" manner. And the discrepancies hardly matter. Despite his comic protestations and his absurd numerical system that pretends to assign a specific value to any given descriptive moment, Twain in his inexhaustible and ever-engaging fashion pulls the rug out from under his own joke. He pretends to lack the time to finish his point, leaving readers on their own to complete the task, for he has other work that demands his attention. Yet the work he must get on with is to offer other deeply flawed and corruptible and even illusory touristic experiences for his readers, who may add (and punctuate) the moments as they wish. Mark Twain, America's foremost tourist and travel writer, can do no more.

Notes

1. As mentioned in the preface, the identity struggle between Samuel L. Clemens and Mark Twain has been a standard debate in literary criticism, begun by Van Wyck Brooks's *The Ordeal of Mark Twain* (New York: Dutton, 1920), which charged that Clemens's environment arrested his literary development. Bernard DeVoto's *Mark Twain's America* (Boston: Little, Brown, 1932) answered by asserting that Twain was a fully realized literary artist and that his work did not suffer from opposed literary sensibilities. The scholarly examinations that have added to this type of critical consideration are numerous. Several biographical studies especially conscious of the issue are Everett Emerson, *The Authentic Mark Twain* (Philadelphia: U of Pennsylvania P, 1984) and *Mark Twain: A Literary Life* (Philadelphia: U of Pennsylvania P, 2000); Justin Kaplan, *Mr. Clemens and Mark Twain: A Biography* (New York: Simon & Schuster, 1966); Leland Krauth, *Proper Mark Twain* (Athens: U of Georgia P, 1999); Bruce Michelson, *Mark Twain on the Loose: A Comic Writer and the American Self* (Amherst: U of Massachusetts P, 1995); Henry Nash Smith, *Mark Twain: The Development of a Writer* (Cambridge: Belknap/Harvard UP, 1962); and Jeffrey Steinbrink, *Getting to Be Mark Twain* (Berkeley: U of California P, 1991).

2. Hill provides accurate sales figures, pointing out that Twain and Bliss commonly inflated the numbers of actual sales for the publicity value. Also see Louis Budd, *Our Mark Twain* (Philadelphia: U of Pennsylvania P, 1983) 30. Budd notes that even as late as 1905–7, *Innocents* sold 46,000 copies, which was 5,000 more than *Huck Finn* in the same period.

3. Kaplan notes that mismanagement and the prevalence of pirated Canadian editions affected *Tom Sawyer*'s sales figures, yet even considering the negative influence, the numbers reflect a markedly lower reader interest in

this work than in the travel books, each of which also faced its own publication problems.

4. See also 17n, in which Salamo provides references to letters between Twain and Chatto in London regarding sales. For a formidable study of Twain's relationship with his English publishers, see Dennis Welland, *Mark Twain in England* (Atlantic Highlands, NJ: Humanities Press, 1978).

5. For examples of such commentary, see Bret Harte, rev. of *The Innocents Abroad, Overland Monthly* Jan. 1870: 100–101; unsigned rev. of *Adventures of Huckleberry Finn, Saturday Review* 7 Mar. 1885: 301; and Desmond O'Brien, rev. of *A Connecticut Yankee in King Arthur's Court, Truth* 2 Jan. 1890: 25.

6. The first page of the letter is no longer extant, and Paine gives only 1890 for its date.

7. For excellent discussions of the struggles between genteel characteristics and bawdiness, including the Whittier birthday speech, see Justin Kaplan, *Mr. Clemens and Mark Twain: A Biography* (New York: Simon & Schuster, 1966); Leland Krauth, *Proper Mark Twain* (Athens: U of Georgia P, 1999); and Bruce Michelson, *Mark Twain on the Loose: A Comic Writer and the American Self* (Amherst: U of Massachusetts P, 1995).

8. Twain first made this comparison in his notebook in May 1886, almost a year before his letter to Howells: "My books are water; those of the great geniuses is [*sic*] wine. Everybody drinks water." See Robert Pack Browning, Michael B. Frank, and Lin Salamo, eds., *Mark Twain's Notebooks and Journals,* vol. 3 (Berkeley: U of California P, 1979) 238.

9. Although he recognizes Twain's use of touristic experience, Ziff chooses not to delve into the topic beyond the standard stereotype of tourist behavior. For helpful discussions of Twain and tourism, see Richard S. Lowry, "Framing the Authentic: The Modern Tourist and *The Innocents Abroad,*" *New Orleans Review* 18.2 (1991): 18–28; Bruce Michelson, "Mark Twain the Tourist: The Form of *The Innocents Abroad,*" *American Literature* 49 (1977): 385–98; Hilton Obenzinger, "Authority and Authenticity," *American Palestine: Melville, Twain, and the Holy Land Mania* (Princeton: Princeton UP, 1999) 161–76; and Jeffrey Steinbrink, "Why the Innocents Went Abroad: Mark Twain and American Tourism in the Late Nineteenth Century," *American Literary Realism* 16 (1983): 278–86. Michelson is the first to explore the tourist as a central identity in *The Innocents Abroad,* focusing on how the *Quaker City* pleasure excursion allowed Twain to manipulate notions of "play" (*paidia*) and imagination.

10. Much has been written on Twain's travel books over the years. For a few especially helpful works in addition to those cited within the text, see Philip D. Beidler, "Realistic Style and the Problems of Context in *The In-*

nocents Abroad," *American Literature* 52 (1980): 33–49; John R. Brazil, "Structure in Mark Twain's Art and Mind: *Life on the Mississippi,*" *Mississippi Quarterly* 34 (1981): 91–112; Stanley Brodwin, "The Useful and Useless River: *Life on the Mississippi* Revisited," *Studies in American Humor* 2 (1976): 196–208; Guy Cardwell, "*Life on the Mississippi:* Vulgar Facts and Learned Errors," *ESQ* 29 (1973): 283–93; Stephen Fender, "'The Prodigal in a Far Country Chawing of Husks': Mark Twain's Search for a Style in the West," *Modern Language Review* 71 (1976): 737–56; Leslie A. Fiedler, "An American Abroad," *Partisan Review* 33 (1966): 77–91; Dewey Ganzel, *Mark Twain Abroad: The Cruise of the Quaker City* (Chicago: U of Chicago P, 1968); Obenzinger, *American Palestine;* Robert Regan, "Mark Twain, 'the Doctor,' and a Guidebook by Dickens," *American Studies* 22 (1981): 35–55; Franklin R. Rogers, "Burlesque Travel Literature and Mark Twain's *Roughing It,*" *Bulletin of the New York Public Library* 67 (1963): 155–68; Arthur L. Scott, "*The Innocents Abroad* Reevaluated," *Western Humanities Review* 7 (1953): 215–23, "Mark Twain Looks at Europe," *South Atlantic Quarterly* 52 (1953): 399–413, and "Mark Twain's Revisions of *The Innocents Abroad* for the British Edition of 1872," *American Literature* 25 (1953): 43–61; and Franklin D. Walker, *Irreverent Pilgrims: Melville, Browne, and Mark Twain in the Holy Land* (Seattle: U of Washington P, 1974).

11. See Henry Nash Smith, *Mark Twain: The Development of a Writer* (Cambridge: Belknap/Harvard UP, 1962). Smith's work on Twain is seminal and invaluable, and I cite it specifically only to highlight the fact that even the strongest critical works ignore travel-book contexts and conventions, a problem that has been endemic. The result is that Smith and subsequent critics have undervalued Twain's travel books. For example, in reference to *The Innocents Abroad,* Smith implies that the narrative inconsistencies in point of view and tone ultimately prevent it from becoming a complete work, so, at best, it is "an embryonic novel." What Smith misses is the fact that those same features are exactly the narrative stances and variations that make it a strong travel book. By contrast, in a contemporary review of *Following the Equator,* Hiram Stanley of *The Dial* (16 Mar. 1898) comments that Twain provides "a most brilliant and varied jumble of wit, humor, information, instruction, wisdom, poetry, irony, and jest" (186–87). Stanley understands the requirements for the genre and evaluates *Following the Equator* accordingly. He praises the diversity and episodic structure, whereas a modern critic like Smith isolates similar features in *The Innocents Abroad,* regards them as unfortunate inconsistencies, and concludes that "the various kinds of writing shade into one another in a fashion that baffles analysis" (Smith 22). Of course, Smith is not truly stymied; he is, like so many others, viewing (in this example) *The Innocents Abroad* not for what it is—a travel book—but for

what he wants it to become—a novel. In that context, his reaction is understandable but unfortunate.

For an interesting parallel—and something of a rebuttal—see Twain's letter to Dan DeQuille (4 Apr. 1875), in which he comments on the use of "detached sketches." In advising DeQuille, he writes: "I'll show you how to make a man read every one of those sketches, under the stupid impression that they are mere accidental incidents that have dropped in on you unawares in the course of your *narrative* [Twain's emphasis]." See Oscar Lewis, introduction, *The Big Bonanza,* by Dan DeQuille (1876; New York: Thomas Y. Crowell, 1969) xviii–xix.

12. Boorstin's comments are in the chapter "From Traveler to Tourist," which argues that tourism threatens to undermine our ability to distinguish between reality and image; as a result, we increasingly crave shallow experiences. See also Maxine Feifer, *Tourism in History* (New York: Stein & Day, 1986).

13. The text used throughout this discussion is *The Tourist: A New Study of the Leisure Class* (1976; Berkeley: U of California P, 1999). My discussion also benefits from those critics who have expounded on MacCannell, namely Jonathan Culler, mentioned earlier, and Erik Cohen, discussed subsequently. For other especially helpful discussions of tourist experience in addition to MacCannell and the other critics cited within this chapter, see Paul Fussell, "Travel, Tourism, and International Understanding," *Thank God for the Atom Bomb and Other Essays* (New York: Summit, 1988) 151–76; Jost Krippendorf, *The Holiday-Makers* (Oxford: Heinemann, 1987); and Denison Nash, "Tourism as a Form of Imperialism," *Hosts and Guests: The Anthropology of Tourism,* ed. Valene L. Smith (Philadelphia: U of Pennsylvania P, 1977) 33–47.

14. See also Erik Cohen, "A Phenomenology of Tourist Experiences," *Sociology* 13 (1979): 179–201. Cohen builds on MacCannell and argues for a broader definition of tourists, identifying five modes of tourist behavior: recreational, diversionary, experiential, experimental, and existential. The first two modes center around a partial escape from the daily life of the tourist, and the remaining modes represent varying degrees of the tourist's need to alter identity.

15. For the definitive treatment of leisure, see Thorstein Veblen, *The Theory of the Leisure Class* (1899; Boston: Houghton-Mifflin, 1973).

16. See Bruce Michelson, "Mark Twain the Tourist: The Form of *The Innocents Abroad,*" for an interesting reading of Twain's use of "play" in his role as a tourist.

17. MacCannell, *The Tourist,* offers an extended discussion of authenticity, especially p. 105.

18. For helpful discussions of authenticity see MacCannell, *The Tourist*, especially 14–15; Boorstin, *The Image*, especially 252; Erik Cohen, "A Phenomenology of Tourist Experiences" and "Authenticity and Commoditization in Tourism," *Annals of Tourism Research* 15.3 (1988): 371–86; and Chris Ryan, "The Tourist Experience," *Recreational Tourism* (New York: Routledge, 1991) 35–49.

19. See Ryan, "The Tourist Experience."

20. Mary Mason Fairbanks, "The Cruise of the *Quaker City*, with Chance Recollections of Mark Twain," *Chataugua* July 1892: 429–32.

CHAPTER 2

1. Several instructive book-length studies of American travel literature have recently appeared: James Buzard, *The Beaten Track: European Tourism, Literature, and the Ways to Culture, 1800–1918* (New York: Clarendon/Oxford UP, 1993); Terry Caesar, *Forgiving the Boundaries: Home as Abroad in American Travel Writing* (Athens: U of Georgia P, 1995); Lewis Perry, *Boats against the Current: American Culture between Revolution and Modernity, 1820–1860* (New York: Oxford UP, 1993); William W. Stowe, *Going Abroad: European Travel in Nineteenth-Century Culture* (Princeton: Princeton UP, 1994); and Larzer Ziff, *Return Passages: Great American Travel Writing, 1780–1910* (New Haven: Yale UP, 2000). See also Ahmed M. Metwalli, "Americans Abroad: The Popular Art of Travel Writing in the Nineteenth Century," *America: Exploration and Travel*, ed. Steven E. Kagle (Bowling Green, OH: Bowling Green UP, 1979) 68–82; and Alfred Bendixen, "Americans in Europe before 1865: A Study of the Travel Book," diss., U of North Carolina, 1979.

2. See also Sarah Hale, "The Romance of Travelling," *Traits of American Life* (Philadelphia: E. L. Carey & A. Hart, 1835) 187–208.

3. Christof Wegelin, "The Rise of the International Novel," *PMLA* 77 (1962): 305–10. Wegelin derives his figures from cited government publications and extrapolates the totals for the four majors ports: Boston/Charlestown, New York, Philadelphia, and Baltimore. He lists totals for the remainder of the century: 25,202 for 1870; 36,097 for 1880; 81,092 for 1890; 108,068 for 1900; and 144,112 for 1901. See also Foster Rhea Dulles, *Americans Abroad: Two Centuries of European Travel* (Ann Arbor: U of Michigan P, 1964). Dulles counts all transatlantic passengers, noting that passenger numbers increased at midcentury from "perhaps 5,000 a year to anywhere from 25,000 to 30,000" (44).

4. See Buzard, *The Beaten Track*, especially 47.

5. A revised edition expands the number of entries considerably but

maintains the exclusion of American continental travel. See Harold F. Smith, *American Travellers Abroad: A Bibliography of Accounts Published before 1900* (Lanham, MD: Scarecrow Press, 1999).

6. For a valuable discussion of this issue, see William C. Spengemann, *The Adventurous Muse* (New Haven: Yale UP, 1977).

7. For exceptional treatments of this point, see James Buzard, "A Continent of Pictures: Reflections on the 'Europe' of Nineteenth-Century Tourists," *PMLA* 108 (1993): 30–43; and his *The Beaten Track,* especially chapters 1 and 2. See also Ziff, introduction, *Return Passages* 1–16.

8. For helpful discussions of this issue, see Perry, *Boats against the Current;* Stowe, *Going Abroad;* and Ziff, *Return Passages.* See also Bendixen, "Americans in Europe before 1865"; and Thomas Asa Tenney, "Mark Twain's Early Travels and the Travel Tradition in Literature," diss., U of Pennsylvania, 1971.

9. For a meticulous overview of the American publication history of the seven pamphlets that constituted the initial presentation of *The Sketch-Book,* see William Charvat, *Literary Publishing in America, 1790–1850* (Philadelphia: U of Pennsylvania P, 1959), especially 38–50. See also *The Profession of Authorship in America, 1800–1870: The Papers of William Charvat,* ed. Matthew J. Bruccoli ([Columbus]: Ohio State UP, 1968), especially 29–48. Given the publishing realities (and nightmares) of the fledgling American market, Irving's success was remarkable.

10. Washington Irving, *The Sketch-Book of Geoffrey Crayon, Gent.,* author's rev. ed. (New York: Putnam, 1860). All references are to this text.

11. For a compelling and long-overdue argument for the centrality of Bayard Taylor in American travel literature, see Ziff, "Bayard Taylor," *Return Passages* 118–69. See also Sharon Ann Tumulty, "From Persia to Peoria: Bayard Taylor as Travel Writer," diss., U of Delaware, 1971.

12. Participants in this debate were numerous. For a few examples, see David Phineas Adams, "The Loiterer—No. 1," *The Monthly Anthology, or Magazine of Polite Literature* 1.1 (1803): 3–6; William Cullen Bryant, rev. of *Essay on American Poetry,* by Solyman Brown, *North American Review* 7.2 (1818): 198–211; and for the most explosive British attacks on American letters, Sydney Smith, "Travellers in America," *Edinburgh Review* 31.61 (1818): 132–50, and rev. of *Statistical Annals of the United States of America,* by Adam Seybert, *Edinburgh Review* 33.65 (1820): 69–80.

13. See William Charvat, *Literary Publishing in America* and *The Profession of Authorship in America.* Charvat also discusses James Fenimore Cooper, arguing that both men demonstrated the financial potential for American authors and American subject matter.

14. For a good discussion of this point, see Metwalli.

15. For an extended look at this point, see Bendixen.

16. Although the subject is beyond the scope of this study, travel-book conventions often parallel those of earlier European writers. For valuable discussions on the travel book in Europe see Percy Adams, *Travelers and Travel Liars, 1660–1800* (Berkeley: U of California P, 1962); and Charles L. Batten, Jr., *Pleasurable Instruction: Form and Convention in Eighteenth-Century Travel Literature* (Berkeley: U of California P, 1978).

17. Throughout the following discussion, I have chosen to depend primarily, but not exclusively, on writers who produced multiple narratives. Career travel writers, more so than onetime travel writers, depended on the conventions of the genre and therefore provide a more accurate window into travel-writing forms and practices, especially in relation to meeting audience expectations. If writers failed to please their readers, it is unlikely that they would have published multiple books.

18. Since many of the travel books discussed in this chapter may be difficult to obtain, I have chosen to quote often and at length in order to provide as much textual context as possible and, I hope, to capture adequately the mood and flavor of the narratives.

19. Mark Twain, *The Innocents Abroad* (New York: Oxford UP, 1996). All references are to this text, a facsimile of the first American edition.

20. Browne is referring to *The Land of Thor* (New York: Harper and Brothers, 1868), which is a narrative of Nordic travel. Browne was an exceptionally strong travel writer whose works, unfortunately, have been largely overlooked and forgotten. For a primary bibliography and an instructive discussion of his connections to Mark Twain, see Tenney.

21. As a corollary, Browne's use of extended information on whaling parallels some of the content of Melville's *Moby-Dick,* wherein he meticulously illustrates the science and art of whaling. Melville, of course, built his most popular works around travel-book conventions with *Typee* and *Omoo.*

22. As stated earlier, asides are often lengthy and not readily quoted, but they make up a large portion of Twain's informative material, and he often used the convention to alter or even make up legends for humorous effect. For a few of the many examples of asides, see "The Story of Abelard and Heloise" in *The Innocents Abroad* (141–47); "Across the Continent" in *Roughing It* (46–47); "The Cave of the Spectre" in *A Tramp Abroad* (133–38); "The Professor's Yarn" in *Life on the Mississippi* (387–96); and "Cecil Rhodes' Shark and His First Fortune" in *Following the Equator* (141–50).

23. For a couple of similar examples wherein Twain attacks such anec-

dotal stories while also perpetuating them, see "The Legend of the Queen's Chair" in *The Innocents Abroad* (66–68) and the story of Horace Greeley and Hank Monk in *Roughing It* (151–56).

24. Numerous examples of reveries are present in any travel book. For additional examples see Bayard Taylor's *Eldorado,* which contains a rich description of a western sunset: "we seem floating in a hallow sphere of prismatic crystal" (33–34); and Horace Greeley, *An Overland Journey* (1860; New York: Knopf, 1964), which contains an elaborate description of a gorge: "Had the mountain spoke to me in an audible voice, or began to lean over with the purpose of burying me beneath its crushing mass, I should hardly have been surprised" (258).

25. For an especially adept and helpful discussion of Twain's romantic reveries, see Henry Nash Smith, "Two Ways of Viewing the World" and "Pilgrims and Sinners," *Mark Twain: The Development of a Writer* (Cambridge: Belknap/Harvard UP, 1962) 1–21, 22–51.

26. For an interesting discussion of the prominence of sensational subject matter, see Tenney, especially 37–40. In addition, Tenney offers a highly informed examination of the characteristics and conventions of the genre.

27. For a valuable corresponding look into the Paris Morgue and the catacombs from one of Twain's contemporaries, see Lawrence I. Berkove, ed., " 'An Irregular Correspondent': The European Travel Letters of Mark Twain's Editor and Friend Joe Goodman," *Mark Twain Journal* 35.2 (1997): 1–43, especially 14–21.

28. For a helpful examination of nationalism, see Bendixen, especially 320–23.

29. For solid discussions of how travel writers distinguish between cultures to solidify home identity, see Carolyn Porter, "Social Discourse and Non-Fictional Prose," *Columbia Literary History of the United States,* ed. Emory Elliott et al. (New York: Columbia UP, 1988) 345–63; Eric J. Leed, *The Mind of the Traveler* (New York: Basic Books/Harper-Collins, 1991); and John Urry, *The Tourist Gaze: Leisure and Travel in Contemporary Societies* (London: Sage, 1990).

30. For a helpful discussion of anti–Catholicism in nineteenth-century America, see Sydney Ahlstrom, "Anti-Catholicism and the Nativist Movement," *A Religious History of the American People* (New Haven: Yale UP, 1972) 555–68.

31. Priests were often targets of criticism as well, though such attacks are not discussed here. For examples see Taylor's *Views A-Foot,* in which he calls priests "the greatest beggars" whose "bloated, sensual countenances and ca-

pacious frames tell of anything but fasts and privations" (330). Twain, in *The Innocents Abroad*, notes that monks "look like consummate famine-breeders. They are all fat and serene" (164).

32. Browne makes a similar comment in chapter 17 of *Etchings of a Whaling Cruise*. He refers to an incident in which a sick sailor was mistreated by the Christians in Zanzibar, and Browne claims he would prefer to be uncivilized if their conduct represents "civilization."

33. For clarification on Twain's reference to the Gosiutes, see Franklin R. Rogers, "Explanatory Notes," *Roughing It, The Works of Mark Twain* (Berkeley: U of California P, 1972) 566–67.

34. The article, entitled "Return of the Holy Land Excursionists—The Story of the Cruise," first appeared in the *New York Herald* on 20 November 1867.

CHAPTER 3

1. *The Innocents Abroad* has garnered a wealth of critical attention, much of it highly insightful. For a few exceptional examples that address issues of tourism and travel writing, see Leon Dickinson, "Mark Twain's Revisions in Writing *The Innocents Abroad*," *American Literature* 19.2 (1947): 139–57; Richard S. Lowry, "Framing the Authentic: The Modern Tourist and *The Innocents Abroad*," *New Orleans Review* 18.2 (1991): 18–28, and *"Littery Man": Mark Twain and Modern Authorship* (New York: Oxford UP, 1996); Bruce Michelson, "Mark Twain the Tourist: The Form of *The Innocents Abroad*," *American Literature* 49.3 (1977): 385–98, and "Fool's Paradise," *Mark Twain on the Loose* (Amherst: U of Massachusetts P, 1995) 39–93; Hilton Obenzinger, *American Palestine: Melville, Twain, and the Holy Land Mania* (Princeton: Princeton UP, 1999); David E. E. Sloane, afterword, *The Innocents Abroad* by Mark Twain, The Oxford Mark Twain, ed. Shelley Fisher Fishkin (New York: Oxford UP, 1996) 1–18; Henry Nash Smith, "Sinners and Pilgrims," *Mark Twain: The Development of a Writer* (Cambridge: Belknap/Harvard UP, 1962) 22–51; Jeffrey Steinbrink, "Why the Innocents Went Abroad: Mark Twain and American Tourism in the Late Nineteenth Century," *American Literary Realism* 16.2 (1983): 278–86; and Larzer Ziff, "Mark Twain," *Return Passages: Great American Travel Writing, 1780–1910* (New Haven: Yale UP, 2000) 170–221.

A Tramp Abroad, on the other hand, has been virtually ignored or dismissed. For a couple of especially valuable exceptions that address issues of tourism, see Leland Krauth, "Victorian Traveler," *Proper Mark Twain* (Athens:

U of Georgia P, 1999) 51–77, especially 69–71; and James S. Leonard, afterword, *A Tramp Abroad* by Mark Twain, The Oxford Mark Twain, ed. Shelley Fisher Fishkin (New York: Oxford UP, 1996) 1–14.

2. With the exception of *Life on the Mississippi,* all of Twain's travel books were marketed so as to capitalize on the popularity of *The Innocents Abroad.* Name recognition, for example, was a benefit for subsequent narratives published in Great Britain: *The Innocents at Home* instead of *Roughing It,* and *More Tramps Abroad* for *Following the Equator.* Also, Twain used "Abroad" in his second Old World tour for its resonance.

3. Samuel Taylor Coleridge, *Biographia Literaria,* vol. 2, *The Collected Works of Samuel Taylor Coleridge,* vol. 7, pt. 2, ed. James Engell and W. Jackson Bate (Princeton: Princeton UP, 1983).

4. Discussions of applications of the term *other* in literary and cultural studies are numerous, but for an especially helpful study of tourist behavior see John Urry, *The Tourist Gaze: Leisure and Travel in Contemporary Societies* (London: Sage, 1990).

5. See "The Author's Account of Himself," *The Sketch-Book,* author's rev. ed. (New York: Putnam, 1860) 14–15.

6. He uses the same idea in his description of Naples, mocking the saying popularized by Neapolitans, "See Naples and Die," which carries the assumption that Naples represents the epitome of beauty and charm. As he does with Damascus, Twain notes that the city is beautiful from a distance, but up close the tourist encounters "disagreeable sights and smells" (316).

7. In Egypt, Twain is again frustrated by the unpleasantness of the actual in reference to his imagined pictures, and again he emphasizes that meaning for the tourist must be defined separately from the actual picture: "Why try to call up the traditions of vanished Egyptian grandeur; why try to fancy Egypt following dead Rameses to his tomb in the Pyramid, or the long multitude of Israel departing over the desert yonder? Why try to think at all? The thing was impossible. One must bring his meditations cut and dried, or else cut and dry them afterward" (623).

8. The sociological connections between leisure and tourism form the core of MacCannell's seminal work on touristic behavior, *The Tourist: A New Theory of the Leisure Class* (1976; Berkeley: U of California P, 1999), which incorporates Veblen's title.

9. Taylor's travel books include *Views A-Foot* (1846); *Eldorado* (1850); *A Journey to Central Africa* (1854); *The Lands of the Saracen* (1855); *A Visit to India, China, and Japan in the Year 1853* (1855); *Northern Travel* (1857); *Travels in Greece and Russia* (1859); *At Home and Abroad, First Series* (1859); *At Home and Abroad, Second Series* (1862); *Colorado, A Summer Trip* (1867); and *By-Ways of Europe*

(1869). His sales were consistent and formidable. See S. Austin Allibone, *A Critical Dictionary of English and British and American Authors,* vol. 3 (1871; Philadelphia: Lippincott, 1908) 2340–41. *Views A-Foot* went through twenty editions in ten years; *Eldorado,* eighteen editions in twelve years; *A Journey to Central Africa,* eleven editions in eight years; *The Lands of the Saracen,* twenty editions in eight years. In addition, Putnam's issued the Caxton and Household uniform editions of his works in 1862.

10. *New York Times* 20 Dec. 1878: 1–2.

11. See Alan Gribben, *Mark Twain's Library: A Reconstruction,* vol. 2 (Boston: G. K. Hall, 1980) 687–88. Gribben provides helpful documentary evidence illuminating Twain's admiration for Taylor.

12. The Reverend Joseph Twichell was Twain's companion for much of the trip, but Twain refers to him as his agent, Harris, within the text.

13. Twain never published the preface, dated July 1879. There is no direct evidence available to explain why he chose not to include it (the narrative has no preface), but considering his letter to Bliss forbidding the release of the title and plan for the book, it seems likely that he simply did not want to give his joke away and ruin its potential effect as a structural thread for the narrative as a whole.

14. Significantly, Bayard Taylor traveled to Europe aboard the *Holsatia* during the same voyage that carried Twain and his entourage. Taylor was going to Germany to take his newly appointed post as United States minister to Germany. Also, Twain refers to Taylor directly in chapter 18: "Bayard Taylor, who could interpret the dim reasonings of animals, and understood their moral natures better than most men, would have found some way to make this poor old chap forget his troubles for a while, but we had not his kindly arts, and so had to leave the raven to his griefs" (161–62).

15. See also chapter 33, in which Twain employs Harris to set logs adrift in a swiftly running brook because Twain "needed exercise" (363).

16. Twain refers directly to Hinchliff, giving his title and date of publication in the text.

17. Twain refers to "Mr. Whymper" but does not provide his book's title or imprint information.

CHAPTER 4

1. See Harriet Elinor Smith, introduction, *Roughing It,* The Works of Mark Twain, ed. Harriet Elinor Smith and Edgar Marquess Branch (Berkeley: U of California P, 1993) 797–911. An early title for the narrative was "Flush Times in the Silver Mines, and Other Matters," but Elisha Bliss,

Twain's publisher, copyrighted "The Innocents at Home" on 3 Aug. 1871 (862 n. 190). Bliss later copyrighted "Roughing It" on 6 Dec. 1871 (871 n. 220). British publication by Routledge came out in two volumes, the first as *Roughing It,* the second as *The Innocents at Home* (876–77).

2. For the composition and publication history, see Harriet Elinor Smith, introduction, *Roughing It,* 797–911.

3. Henry Nash Smith, "Transformation of a Tenderfoot," *Mark Twain: The Development of a Writer* (Cambridge: Belknap/Harvard UP, 1962) 52–70.

4. The critical response to *Roughing It* is varied and substantive. For especially insightful analyses in addition to Smith's, see Drewey Wayne Gunn, "The Monomythic Structure of *Roughing It, American Literature* 61.4 (1989): 563–85; Harold J. Kolb, Jr., "Mark Twain and the Myth of the West," *The Mythologizing of Mark Twain,* ed. Sara de Saussure Davis and Philip D. Beidler (Tuscaloosa: U of Alabama P, 1984) 119–35; Richard S. Lowry, *"Littery Man": Mark Twain and Modern Authorship* (New York: Oxford UP, 1996); Kenneth S. Lynn, *Mark Twain and Southwestern Humor* (Boston: Little & Brown, 1959); Bruce Michelson, "Ever Such a Good Time: The Structure of Mark Twain's *Roughing It,*" *Dutch Quarterly Review of Anglo-American Letters* 17.3 (1987): 182–99, and "Fool's Paradise," *Mark Twain on the Loose: A Comic Writer and the American Self* (Amherst: U of Massachusetts P, 1995) 39–93; Forrest Robinson, "'Seeing the Elephant': Some Perspectives on Mark Twain's *Roughing It,*" *American Studies* 21.2 (1980): 43–64; Jeffrey Steinbrink, *Getting to Be Mark Twain* (Berkeley: U of California P, 1991); Henry B. Wonham, afterword, *Roughing It,* The Oxford Mark Twain, ed. Shelley Fisher Fishkin (New York: Oxford UP, 1996) 1–17, and *Mark Twain and the Art of the Tall Tale* (New York: Oxford UP, 1993).

5. Henry Nash Smith, *Mark Twain* 22.

6. This type of opening was not uncommon. For a strikingly similar introduction, see John Ross Browne, *Adventures in Apache Country* (New York: Harpers, 1868).

7. For other examples of references to distance and time, see 146 and 150.

8. In a footnote, Twain identifies his source for the quoted passages as "'The Vigilantes of Montana,' by Prof. Thos. J. Dimsdale" (84).

9. It bears noting that the chapters on the Mormons assume a purpose and perspective similar to those on Slade. Regardless of Twain's opinions of Mormon faith, the Mormons, like Slade, offer part of an exotic western culture for eastern sensibilities, and Twain's descriptions of them serve to furnish another image within the mythic West.

10. For an extended valuable discussion of Twain's use of humorous anecdotes and tall tales, see Wonham, *Mark Twain and the Art of the Tall Tale.*

11. See Cohen, "A Phenomenology of Tourist Experiences." Cohen defines five modes of touristic behavior: recreational, diversionary, experiential, experimental, and existential.

12. James Jackson Jarves, *History of the Hawaiian or Sandwich Islands: Embracing Their Antiquities, Mythology, Legends, Discovery by Europeans in the Sixteenth Century, ReDiscovery by Cook, with Their Civil, Religious and Political History, from the Earliest Traditionary Period to the Present Time* (Boston: Tappan & Dennet, 1843).

13. See Horst H. Kruse, *Mark Twain and* Life on the Mississippi (Amherst: U of Massachusetts P, 1982), especially the introduction (1–4) and "Planning a Standard Work" (5–19). For additional valuable studies of *Life on the Mississippi,* see John R. Bird, "Structure in Mark Twain's Art and Mind: *Life on the Mississippi,*" *Mississippi Quarterly* 34 (1981): 91–112; Stanley Brodwin, "The Useful and Useless River: *Life on the Mississippi* Revisited," *Studies in American Humor* 2 (1976): 196–208; Guy Cardwell, "*Life on the Mississippi:* Vulgar Facts and Learned Errors," *ESQ* 29 (1973): 283–93; Dewey Ganzel, "Twain, Travel Books, and *Life on the Mississippi,*" *American Literature* 34 (1962): 40–55; Lawrence Howe, afterword, *Life on the Mississippi,* The Oxford Mark Twain, ed. Shelley Fisher Fishkin (New York: Oxford UP, 1996): 1–18; Marion Montgomery, "The Old Romantic vs. the New: Mark Twain's Dilemma in *Life on the Mississippi,*" *Mississippi Quarterly* 11 (1958): 79–82; Coleman O. Parsons, "Down the Mighty River with Mark Twain," *Mississippi Quarterly* 22 (1969): 1–18; Henry Nash Smith, "Mark Twain's Images of Hannibal," *Texas Studies in English* 37 (1958): 3–23; and Robert F. Stowell, "River Guide Books and Mark Twain's *Life on the Mississippi,*" *Mark Twain Journal* 16.4 (1973): 21.

14. In defining the five modes of touristic behavior, Cohen does not consider a tourist going home. Here I am defining such a tourist as "nostalgic" since his behavior derives directly from a personal, emotional connection to the place.

15. Kruse makes a solid argument that Twain's substantive plans are realized in the narrative and, moreover, that a return trip—a tour—was essential to his vision all along.

16. Kruse defends convincingly the inclusion of the keelboat section from *Huckleberry Finn* in *Life on the Mississippi*. See 45–48.

17. In addition to the example cited, see also 152 and 166.

18. See Frederick Anderson, Lin Salamo, and Bernard Stein, eds., *Mark Twain's Notebooks and Journals,* vol. 2 (Berkeley: U of California P, 1975). Twain notes being recognized (536); he records that a passenger made note of his river knowledge (526–27); and he mentions using the pilothouse as a scene for abandoning the incognito (467). See also Kruse 26–37.

19. Kruse argues the Hannibal chapters "violate the structure of the book" (109). See 107–9.

CHAPTER 5

1. See Dixon Wecter, ed., *The Love Letters of Mark Twain* (New York: Harpers, 1949) 165–66.

2. See Fred Kaplan, afterword, Following the Equator *and Anti-Imperialist Essays,* The Oxford Mark Twain, ed. Shelley Fisher Fishkin (New York: Oxford UP, 1996) 12–13. Kaplan quotes Twain's letter to Frank Bliss, his publisher (26 Mar. 1897), wherein Twain suggests the title "Imitating the Equator" (along with "Another Innocent Abroad"). Twain preferred the former because the equator, like Twain, "goes around the world."

3. See John Urry, *The Tourist Gaze: Leisure and Travel in Contemporary Societies* (London: Sage, 1990).

4. There are many examples of locals being defined as sights. Such passages are a staple of travel writing. For one other example, see the opening of chapter 50, part of which reads, "You have the monster crowd of bejeweled natives, the stir, the bustle, the confusion, the shifting splendors of the costumes—dear me, the delight of it, the charm of it are beyond speech" (475).

5. Of course, Twain explores such themes in other works, namely *Adventures of Huckleberry Finn* and *The Tragedy of Pudd'nhead Wilson*. But this study concerns itself only with Mark Twain as he exists within the travel narratives.

6. See Larzer Ziff, "Mark Twain," *Return Passages: Great American Travel Writing, 1780–1910* (New Haven: Yale UP, 2000) 170–221. Ziff mentions Twain's enthusiastic response to color as evidence of his growing awareness of the destructive context of imperialism. See especially 213–21.

7. Throughout his travel-writing career, Twain mocked and even admonished bad tourist behavior that intruded upon local custom or betrayed decency, yet the application of such a perspective in *Following the Equator* takes on a far more serious context. His anger and disgust are directed well beyond the mischievousness of individual tourists (or himself) and toward implicating his culture at large.

8. For a valuable study of Twain's understanding of British imperialism, see Howard G. Baetzhold, "The World Tour and After (1895–1897)," *Mark Twain and John Bull: The British Connection* (Bloomington: Indiana UP, 1970) 179–95. Though primarily focusing on Twain's experiences in Hawaii, Amy Kaplan's "Imperial Triangles: Mark Twain's Foreign Affairs," *Modern Fiction*

Studies 43 (1997): 236–48, offers an insightful look at Twain's emerging consciousness of nationalism and imperialism.

9. See Fred Kaplan, afterword 4–5, for brief but insightful comments regarding Twain's excitement in India and South Africa. See also Ziff 213–21 for a compelling discussion of Twain's enthrallment with color.

10. For another helpful example of Twain's disgust toward European clothing, see his remarks in Capetown, South Africa, wherein he sees a group of women wearing "fiendish clothes" (692–93).

Works Cited

Anderson, Frederick, Lin Salamo, and Bernard Stein, eds. *Mark Twain's Note-books and Journals.* Vol. 2. Berkeley: U of California P, 1975.

Beatty, Richmond Croom. *Bayard Taylor: Laureate of the Gilded Age.* Norman: U of Oklahoma P, 1936.

Boorstin, Daniel. *The Image: A Guide to Pseudo-Events in America.* New York: Atheneum, 1985.

Bridgman, Richard. *Traveling in Mark Twain.* Berkeley: U of California P, 1987.

Browne, John Ross. *Adventures in Apache Country.* 1868. New York: Promontory Press, 1974.

———. *An American Family in Germany.* New York: Harpers, 1866.

———. *Etchings of a Whaling Cruise.* New York: Harper & Brothers, 1846.

"Carter's *Letters from Europe.*" *American Quarterly Review* 2 (1827): 539–84.

Channing, William Ellery. "Address on Self-Culture." *The Works of William Ellery Channing, D.D.* 4th ed. Vol. 2. Boston: James Munroe, 1845. 347–411.

Cohen, E[rik]. "A Phenomenology of Tourist Experiences." *Sociology* 13 (1979): 179–201.

Culler, Jonathan. "The Semiotics of Tourism." *Framing the Sign: Criticism and Its Institutions.* Norman: U of Oklahoma P, 1989. 153–67.

Dana, Richard Henry, Jr. *Two Years before the Mast.* 1840. 2 vols. Ed. John Haskell Kemble. Los Angeles: Ward Ritchie Press, 1964.

Fairbanks, Mary Mason. "The Cruise of the *Quaker City,* with Chance Recollections of Mark Twain." *Chatauqua* July 1892: 429–32.

Fischer, Victor, and Michael B. Frank, eds. *Mark Twain's Letters, 1870–1871.* Vol. 4. Berkeley: U of California P, 1995.

Fisk, Wilbur. *Travels in Europe.* 1838. New York: Harpers, 1841.

"Going Abroad." *Putnam's Magazine* 1 (1868): 530–38.

Greeley, Horace. *An Overland Journey.* 1860. New York: Knopf, 1964.

Hall, Mrs. Herman J. [Adelaide]. *Two Travellers in Europe*. Springfield, MA: Hampden, 1898.

Hawthorne, Nathaniel. Preface. *The House of the Seven Gables. The Centenary Edition of the Works of Nathaniel Hawthorne*, Vol. 2. [Columbus]: Ohio State UP, 1971. 1–3.

Hill, Hamlin. *Mark Twain and Elisha Bliss*. Columbia: U of Missouri P, 1964.

——, ed. *Mark Twain's Letters to His Publishers*. Berkeley: U of California P, 1967.

Howells, William Dean. "Mark Twain's New Book." *Atlantic* May 1880: 686–88.

Irving, Washington. *The Sketch-Book of Geoffrey Crayon, Gent*. Author's rev. ed. New York: Putnam, 1860.

James, Henry. "Americans Abroad." *Nation* 3 Oct. 1878: 208–9.

Jarves, James Jackson. *Parisian Sights and French Principles Seen through American Spectacles*. New York: Harper & Brothers, 1852.

——. *Scenes and Scenery in the Sandwich Islands and a Trip through Central America*. Boston: James Munroe, 1843.

Kaplan, Justin. *Mr. Clemens and Mark Twain*. New York: Simon & Schuster, 1966.

Kirkland, Caroline M. *Holidays Abroad; or Europe from the West*. 2 vols. New York: Baker & Scribner, 1849.

Kruse, Horst H. *Mark Twain and* Life on the Mississippi. Amherst: U of Massachusetts P, 1982.

Lewis, Oscar. Introduction. *The Big Bonanza*. By Dan DeQuille. New York: Thomas Y. Crowell, 1969. i–xxv.

MacCannell, Dean. *The Tourist: A New Study of the Leisure Class*. 1976. Berkeley: U of California P, 1999.

Marryat, Frederick. "How to Write a Book of Travels." *Olla Podrida. The Works of Captain Marryat*. Vol. 1. New York: Peter Fenelon Collier, 1900. 525–38.

"Modern Tourism." *Blackwood's Magazine* August 1848: 185–89.

Moran, Benjamin. "Contributions towards a History of American Literature." *Trubner's Bibliographical Guide to American Literature*. Ed. Nicolas Trubner. London: Trubner, 1859. xxxvii–civ.

Paine, Albert Bigelow, ed. *Mark Twain's Letters*. 2 vols. New York: Harpers, 1917.

Parkman, Francis. *The California and Oregon Trail*. 1849. New York: Viking/Library of America, 1991.

Percy, Walker. "The Loss of the Creature." *The Message in a Bottle*. New York: Noonday Press, 1997. 46–63.

Pratt, Mary Louise. *Imperial Eyes: Travel Writing and Transculturation.* New York: Routledge, 1992.

Salamo, Lin. Introduction. *The Prince and the Pauper.* The Works of Mark Twain. Ed. Victor Fischer and Lin Salamo. Berkeley: U of California P, 1979.

Smith, Harold F. *American Travellers Abroad: A Bibliography of Accounts Published before 1900.* Carbondale-Edwardsville: Southern Illinois UP, 1969.

Smith, Henry Nash. *Mark Twain: The Development of a Writer.* Cambridge: Belknap/Harvard UP, 1962.

Smith, Henry Nash, and William M. Gibson, eds. *Mark Twain-Howells Letters: The Correspondence of Samuel L. Clemens and William Dean Howells, 1872–1910.* 2 vols. Cambridge: Belknap/Harvard UP, 1960.

Stanley, Hiram. Rev. of *Following the Equator. Dial* 16 Mar. 1898: 186–87.

Taylor, Bayard. *A Journey to Central Africa.* 1854. New York: Greenwood-Negro Press, 1970.

———. *At Home and Abroad, First Series.* 1859. New York: Putnam, 1862.

———. *At Home and Abroad, Second Series.* 1862. *Prose Writings of Bayard Taylor.* Rev. ed. New York: Putnam, 1869.

———. *Eldorado: or, Adventures in the Path of Empire.* 1850. Glorietta, NM: Rio Grande Press, 1967.

———. *The Lands of the Saracen.* New York: Putnam, 1855.

———. *Views A-Foot; or Europe Seen with Knapsack and Staff.* 1846. New York: Putnam, 1848.

Thoreau, Henry David. *Walden.* 1854. Princeton: Princeton UP, 1971.

Thorp, Willard. "Pilgrim's Return." *Literary History of the United States.* Vol. 2. 3rd ed. Ed. Robert Spiller et al. New York: Macmillan, 1969. 827–42.

Tuckerman, Henry T. "The Philosophy of Travel." *United States Magazine and Democratic Review* 14 (1844): 527–39.

Twain, Mark. *Following the Equator.* 1897. The Oxford Mark Twain. Ed. Shelley Fisher Fishkin. New York: Oxford UP, 1996.

———. *The Innocents Abroad.* 1869. The Oxford Mark Twain. Ed. Shelley Fisher Fishkin. New York: Oxford UP, 1996.

———. *Life on the Mississippi.* 1883. The Oxford Mark Twain. Ed. Shelley Fisher Fishkin. New York: Oxford UP, 1996.

———. *Roughing It.* 1872. The Oxford Mark Twain. Ed. Shelley Fisher Fishkin. New York: Oxford UP, 1996.

———. *A Tramp Abroad.* 1880. The Oxford Mark Twain. Ed. Shelley Fisher Fishkin. New York: Oxford UP, 1996.

Veblen, Thorstein. *The Theory of the Leisure Class.* 1899. Boston: Houghton Mifflin, 1973.

Wegelin, Christof. "The Rise of the International Novel." *PMLA* 77 (1962): 305–10.

Willis, Nathaniel Parker. *Pencillings by the Way.* 1836. *The Prose Works of N. P. Willis.* Philadelphia: Carey & Hart, 1849.

Ziff, Larzer. *Return Passages: Great American Travel Writing, 1780–1910.* New Haven: Yale UP, 2000.

Selected Bibliography

Adams, Percy G. *Travelers and Travel Liars, 1660–1800.* Berkeley: U of California P, 1962.

——. *Travel Literature and the Evolution of the Novel.* Lexington: UP of Kentucky, 1983.

Adler, Judith. "Origins of Sightseeing." *Annals of Tourism Research* 16 (1989): 7–29.

——. "Travel as Performed Art." *American Journal of Sociology* 94.6 (1989): 1366–91.

Ahluwalia, Harsharan Singh. "Mark Twain's Lecture Tour in India." *Mark Twain Journal* 18.1 (1976–77): 4–7.

Baetzhold, Howard G. "The World Tour and After (1895–1897)." *Mark Twain and John Bull: The British Connection.* Bloomington: Indiana UP, 1970. 179–95.

Baker, Paul. *Fortunate Pilgrims: Americans in Italy, 1800–1860.* Cambridge: Oxford UP, 1964.

Batten, Charles L., Jr. *Pleasurable Instruction: Form and Convention in Eighteenth-Century Travel Literature.* Berkeley: U of California P, 1978.

Beatty, Richmond Croom. *Bayard Taylor: Laureate of the Gilded Age.* Norman: U of Oklahoma P, 1936.

Beauchamp, Gorman. "The American Vandal in Italy." *Centennial Review* 40 (1996): 69–79.

Beidler, Philip D. "Realistic Style and the Problems of Context in *The Innocents Abroad.*" *American Literature* 52 (1980): 33–49.

Bendixen, Alfred. "Americans in Europe before 1865: A Study of the Travel Book." Diss., U of North Carolina, 1979.

Berkove, Lawrence I., ed. "'An Irregular Correspondent': The European Travel Letters of Mark Twain's Editor and Friend, Joe Goodman." *Mark Twain Journal* 35.2 (1997): 1–43.

Bird, John Christian, Jr. "'One Right Form for a Story': Mark Twain and the Narrative I." Diss., The University of Rochester, 1986.

Bird, John R. "Structure in Mark Twain's Art and Mind: *Life on the Mississippi.*" *Mississippi Quarterly* 34 (1981): 91–112.

Blair, Walter. *Horse Sense in American Humor.* Chicago: U of Chicago P, 1942.

Blanton, Casey. *Travel Writing: The Self and the World.* New York: Twayne, 1997.

Boorstin, Daniel. *America and the Image of Europe.* Gloucester, MA: Peter Smith, 1976.

———. *The Image: A Guide to Pseudo-Events in America.* New York: Atheneum, 1985.

Branch, Edgar M. *The Literary Apprenticeship of Mark Twain.* Urbana: U of Illinois P, 1966.

Brazil, John R. "Structure in Mark Twain's Art and Mind: *Life on the Mississippi.*" *Mississippi Quarterly* 34 (1981): 91–112.

Bredeson, Robert C. "Landscape Description in Nineteenth-Century American Travel Literature." *American Quarterly* 20 (1968): 86–94.

Brodwin, Stanley. "The Useful and Useless River: *Life on the Mississippi* Revisited." *Studies in American Humor* 2 (1976): 196–208.

Brooks, Van Wyck. *The Dream of Arcadia: American Writers and Artists in Italy, 1760–1915.* New York: Dutton, 1958.

Brown, David. "Genuine Fakes." *The Tourist Image: Myths and Myth Making in Tourism.* Ed. Tom Selwyn. New York: Wiley, 1996. 33–47.

Budd, Louis. *Our Mark Twain.* Philadelphia: U of Pennsylvania P, 1983.

Butor, Michael. "Travel and Writing." *Mosaic* 8.1 (1974): 1–16.

Buzard, James. *The Beaten Track: European Tourism, Literature, and the Ways to Culture, 1800–1918.* New York: Clarendon/Oxford UP, 1993.

———. "A Continent of Pictures: Reflections on the 'Europe' of Nineteenth-Century Tourists." *PMLA* 108 (1993): 30–44.

Caesar, Terry. *Forgiving the Boundaries: Home as Abroad in American Travel Writing.* Athens: U of Georgia P, 1995.

Cardwell, Guy. "*Life on the Mississippi:* Vulgar Facts and Learned Errors." *ESQ* 29 (1973): 283–93.

Carter, Paul J. "Olivia Clemens Edits *Following the Equator.*" *American Literature* 30 (1958): 194–209.

"Carter's *Letters from Europe.*" *American Quarterly Review* 2 (1827): 539–84.

Channing, William Ellery. "Address on Self-Culture." *The Works of William Ellery Channing, D.D.* 4th ed. Vol. 2. Boston: James Munroe, 1845. 347–411.

Clemens, Cyril. "Contract for *Roughing It.*" *Mark Twain Quarterly* 6.3 (1944): 5.

Cohen, Erik. "Authenticity and Commoditization in Tourism." *Annals of Tourism Research* 15.3 (1988): 371–86.

————. "A Phenomenology of Tourist Experiences." *Sociology* 13 (1979): 179–201.

————. "The Sociology of Tourism: Approaches, Issues, and Findings." *Annual Review of Sociology* 10 (1984): 373–92.

————. "Who Is a Tourist?: A Conceptual Clarification." *Sociological Review* 22 (1974): 527–55.

Cohen, Erik, and Robert L. Cooper. "Language and Tourism." *Annals of Tourism Research* 13 (1986): 533–64.

Cook, Nancy. "Finding His Mark: Twain's *The Innocents Abroad* as a Subscription Book." *Reading Books: Essays on the Material Text and Literature in America*. Ed. Michele Moylan and Lane Stiles. Amherst: U of Massachusetts P, 1996. 151–178.

Covici, Pascal, Jr. *Mark Twain's Humor: The Image of a World*. Dallas: Southern Methodist UP, 1962.

Cox, James. *Mark Twain: The Fate of Humor*. Princeton: Princeton UP, 1966.

Craig, Jennifer. "The Culture of Tourism." *Touring Cultures: Transformations of Travel and Theory*. Ed. Chris Rojek and John Urry. New York: Routledge, 1997. 113–36.

Crawshaw, Carol, and John Urry. "Tourism and the Photographic Eye." *Touring Cultures: Transformations of Travel and Theory*. Ed. Chris Rojek and John Urry. New York: Routledge, 1997. 176–95.

Culler, Jonathan. "The Semiotics of Tourism." *Framing the Sign: Criticism and Its Institutions*. Norman: U of Oklahoma P, 1989. 153–67.

Dahl, Curtis. "Mark Twain and the Moving Panoramas." *American Quarterly* 13 (1961): 20–32.

Davis, John. *The Landscape of Belief: Encountering the Holy Land in Nineteenth-Century American Art and Culture*. Princeton: Princeton UP, 1996.

Dickinson, Leon T. "Marketing a Best Seller: Mark Twain's *Innocents Abroad*." *Papers of the Bibliographical Society of America* 41 (1947): 107–22.

————. "Mark Twain's Revisions in Writing *The Innocents Abroad*." *American Literature* 19 (1947): 139–57.

Dolmetsch, Carl. *"Our Famous Guest": Mark Twain in Vienna*. Athens: U of Georgia P, 1992.

Dulles, Foster Rhea. *Americans Abroad: Two Centuries of European Travel*. Ann Arbor: U of Michigan P, 1964.

Earnest, Ernest. *Expatriates and Patriots: American Artists, Scholars, and Writers in Europe*. Durham: Duke UP, 1968.

Edwards, Justin D. *Exotic Journeys: Exploring the Erotics of U.S. Travel Literature, 1840–1930*. Hanover: UP of New England, 2001.

Emerson, Everett. *The Authentic Mark Twain*. Philadelphia: U of Pennsylvania P, 1984.

———. *Mark Twain: A Literary Life*. Philadelphia: U of Pennsylvania P, 2000.

Fairbanks, Mary Mason. "The Cruise of the *Quaker City*, with Chance Recollections of Mark Twain." *Chataugua* July 1892: 429–32.

Feifer, Maxine. *Tourism in History*. New York: Stein & Day, 1986.

Fender, Stephen. "'The Prodigal in a Far Country Chawing of Husks': Mark Twain's Search for a Style in the West." *Modern Language Review* 71 (1976): 737–56.

Fiedler, Leslie A. "An American Abroad." *Partisan Review* 33 (1966): 77–91.

Florence, Don. *Persona and Humor in Mark Twain's Early Writings*. Columbia: U of Missouri P, 1995.

Frear, Walter Francis. *Mark Twain and Hawaii*. Chicago: Lakeside Press, 1947.

Frederick, Bonnie, and Susan H. McLeod, eds. *Women and the Journey: The Female Travel Experience*. Pullman: Washington State UP, 1993.

Frow, John. "Tourism and the Semiotics of Nostalgia." *October* 57 (1991): 123–51.

Fussell, Paul. "Travel, Tourism, and International Understanding." *Thank God for the Atom Bomb and Other Essays*. New York: Summit, 1988. 151–76.

Ganzel, Dewey. *Mark Twain Abroad: The Cruise of the* Quaker City. Chicago: U of Chicago P, 1968.

———. "Samuel Clemens, Guidebooks, and *The Innocents Abroad. Anglia* 83 (1965): 78–88.

———. "Samuel Clemens, Sub Rosa Correspondent." *English Language Notes* 1 (1964): 270–73.

———. "Twain, Travel Books, and *Life on the Mississippi*." *American Literature* 34 (1962): 40–55.

Gerber, John C. "Mark Twain's Use of the Comic Pose." *PMLA* 77 (1962): 297–98.

"Going Abroad." *Putnam's Magazine* 1 (1868): 530–38.

Goluboff, Benjamin. "The Problems of the Picturesque: Nineteenth-Century American Travelers in Britain." *New Orleans Review* 18.2 (1991): 5–16.

Gribben, Alan. "Mark Twain, Business Man: The Margins of Profit." *Studies in American Humor* 1 (1982): 24–43.

———. *Mark Twain's Library: A Reconstruction*. 2 vols. Boston: G. K. Hall, 1980.

Gunn, Drewey Wayne. "The Monomythic Structure of *Roughing It. American Literature* 61.4 (1989): 563–85.

Hale, Sarah. "The Romance of Travelling." *Traits of American Life*. Philadelphia: E. L. Carey and A. Hart, 1835. 187–208.

Hardack, Richard. "Water Pollution and Motion Sickness: Rites of Passage in Nineteenth-Century Slave and Travel Narratives." *ESQ* 41 (1995): 1–40.

Henderson, Heather. "The Travel Writer and the Text: 'My Giant Goes With Me Wherever I Go.'" *New Orleans Review* 18.2 (1991): 30–40.

Hill, Hamlin. *Mark Twain and Elisha Bliss.* Columbia: U of Missouri P, 1964.

———. "Mark Twain: Audience and Artistry." *American Quarterly* 15 (1963): 25–40.

———. *Mark Twain: God's Fool.* New York: Harper & Row, 1973.

Hirst, Robert Hart. "The Making of *The Innocents Abroad:* 1867–1872." Diss., U of California–Berkeley, 1975.

Howe, Lawrence. Afterword. *Life on the Mississippi.* The Oxford Mark Twain. Ed. Shelley Fisher Fishkin. New York: Oxford UP, 1996. 1–18.

Howells, William Dean. "Mark Twain's New Book." *Atlantic* May 1880: 686–88.

James, Henry. "Americans Abroad." *Nation* 3 Oct. 1878: 208–09.

Jehlen, Myra. "The American Landscape as Totem." *Prospects* 6 (1981): 17–36.

Kaplan, Amy. "Imperial Triangles: Mark Twain's Foreign Affairs." *Modern Fiction Studies* 43 (1997): 236–48.

Kaplan, Caren. *Questions of Travel.* Durham: Duke UP, 1996.

Kaplan, Fred. Afterword. Following the Equator *and Anti-Imperialist Essays.* The Oxford Mark Twain. Ed. Shelley Fisher Fishkin. New York: Oxford UP, 1996. 1–16.

Kaplan, Justin. *Mr. Clemens and Mark Twain: A Biography.* New York: Simon & Schuster, 1966.

Kolb, Harold J., Jr. "Mark Twain and the Myth of the West." *The Mythologizing of Mark Twain.* Ed. Sara de Saussure Davis and Philip D. Beidler. Tuscaloosa: U of Alabama P, 1984. 119–35.

Krauth, Leland. *Proper Mark Twain.* Athens: U of Georgia P, 1999.

Krippendorf, Jost. *The Holiday-Makers.* Oxford: Heinemann, 1987.

Kruse, Horst H. *Mark Twain and* Life on the Mississippi. Amherst: U of Massachusetts P, 1982.

Leed, Eric J. *The Mind of the Traveler.* New York: Basic Books/Harper-Collins, 1991.

Leonard, James S. Afterword. *A Tramp Abroad.* The Oxford Mark Twain. Ed. Shelley Fisher Fishkin. New York: Oxford UP, 1996. 1–14.

Lettis, Richard. "The Appendix of *Life on the Mississippi.*" *Mark Twain Journal* 21.2 (1982): 10–12.

Lowry, Richard S. "Framing the Authentic: The Modern Tourist and *The Innocents Abroad.*" *New Orleans Review* 18.2 (1991): 18–28.

———. *"Littery Man": Mark Twain and Modern Authorship.* New York: Oxford UP, 1996.

Lueck, Beth L. *American Writers and the Picturesque Tour: The Search for National Identity, 1790–1860.* New York: Garland, 1997.

Lynn, Kenneth S. *Mark Twain and Southwestern Humor.* Boston: Little & Brown, 1959.

Lyons, Paul. "From Man-Eaters to Spam-Eaters: Literary Tourism and the Discourse of Cannibalism from Herman Melville to Paul Theroux." *Arizona Quarterly* 51.2 (1995): 33–62.

MacCannell, Dean. *Empty Meeting Grounds.* New York: Routledge and Kegan Paul, 1992.

———. *The Tourist: A New Study of the Leisure Class.* 1976. Berkeley: U of California P, 1999.

Marryat, Frederick. "How to Write a Book of Travels." *Olla Podrida.* The Works of Captain Marryat. Vol. 1. New York: Peter Fenelon Collier, 1900. 525–38.

McCarthy, Harold T. "Mark Twain's Pilgrim's Progress: *The Innocents Abroad.*" *Arizona Quarterly* 26 (1970): 249–58.

McKee, John DeWitt. "*Roughing It* as Retrospective Reporting." *Western American Literature* 5 (1970): 113–19.

Melton, Jeffrey Alan. "Adventurers and Tourists in Mark Twain's *A Tramp Abroad.*" *Studies in American Humor* 3.5 (1998): 34–47.

———. "Keeping the Faith in Mark Twain's *The Innocents Abroad.*" *South Atlantic Review* 64.2 (1999): 58–80.

———. "Touring Decay: Nineteenth-Century American Travel Writers in Europe." *Papers on Language and Literature* 35 (1999): 206–22.

———. "The Tourist as Art Critic: Mark Twain and the Old Masters." *Studies in American Culture* 22.2 (1999): 61–69.

———. "The Trouble with Tourists: Authenticity and the Failure of Tourism." *Popular Culture Review* 10.2 (1999): 9–19.

———. "The Wild Teacher of the Pacific Slope: Mark Twain, Travel Books, and Instruction." *Thalia* 16 (1996): 46–52.

Metwalli, Ahmed M. "Americans Abroad: The Popular Art of Travel Writing in the Nineteenth Century." *America: Exploration and Travel.* Ed. Steven E. Kagle. Bowling Green: Bowling Green UP, 1979. 68–82.

Michelson, Bruce. "Ever Such a Good Time: The Structure of Mark Twain's *Roughing It.*" *Dutch Quarterly Review of Anglo-American Letters* 17 (1987): 182–99.

———. *Mark Twain on the Loose: A Comic Writer and the American Self.* Amherst: U of Massachusetts P, 1995.

————. "Mark Twain the Tourist: The Form of *The Innocents Abroad*." *American Literature* 49 (1977): 385–98.

Mills, Sara. *Discourses of Difference: An Analysis of Women's Travel Writing and Colonialism*. New York: Routledge, 1991.

"Modern Tourism." *Blackwood's Magazine* August 1848: 185–89.

Montgomery, Marion. "The Old Romantic vs. the New: Mark Twain's Dilemma in *Life on the Mississippi*." *Mississippi Quarterly* 11 (1958): 79–82.

Moran, Benjamin. "Contributions towards a History of American Literature." *Trubner's Bibliographical Guide to American Literature*. Ed. Nicolas Trubner. London: Trubner, 1859. xxxvii–civ.

Mulvey, Christopher. "Anglo-American Fictions: National Characteristics in Nineteenth-Century Travel Literature." *American Literary Landscapes*. Ed. F. A. Bell and D. K. Adams. New York: St. Martins, 1988. 61–77.

————. *Anglo-American Landscapes: A Study of Nineteenth-Century Anglo-American Travel Literature*. New York: Cambridge UP, 1983.

————. *Transatlantic Manners*. New York: Cambridge UP, 1990.

Nash, Denison. "Tourism as a Form of Imperialism." *Hosts and Guests: The Anthropology of Tourism*. Ed. Valene L. Smith. Philadelphia: U of Pennsylvania P, 1977. 33–47.

Obenzinger, Hilton. *American Palestine: Melville, Twain, and the Holy Land Mania*. Princeton: Princeton UP, 1999.

Paine, Albert Bigelow, ed. *Mark Twain's Letters*. 2 vols. New York: Harpers, 1917.

Papovich, J. Frank. "Popular Appeal and Sales Strategy: The Prospectus of *The Innocents Abroad*." *English Language Notes* 19 (1981): 47–50.

Parsons, Coleman O. "Down the Mighty River with Mark Twain." *Mississippi Quarterly* 22 (1969): 1–18.

————. "Mark Twain: Sightseer in India." *Mississippi Quarterly* 16 (1963): 76–93.

————. "Mark Twain: Traveler in South Africa." *Mississippi Quarterly* 29 (1975): 3–41.

Percy, Walker. "The Loss of the Creature." *The Message in a Bottle*. New York: Noonday Press, 1997. 46–63.

Perry, Lewis. *Boats against the Current: American Culture between Revolution and Modernity, 1820–1860*. New York: Oxford UP, 1993.

Porter, Carolyn. "Social Discourse and Non-Fictional Prose." *Columbia Literary History of the United States*. Ed. Emory Elliott et al. New York: Columbia UP, 1988. 345–63.

Pratt, Mary Louise. *Imperial Eyes: Travel Writing and Transculturation*. New York: Routledge, 1992.

Regan, Robert. "Mark Twain, 'the Doctor,' and a Guidebook by Dickens." *American Studies* 22 (1981): 35–55.

——. "The Reprobate Elect in *The Innocents Abroad*." *American Literature* 54 (1982): 240–57.

——. *Unpromising Heroes: Mark Twain and His Characters.* Berkeley: U of California P, 1966.

Rennie, Neil. *Far-Fetched Facts: The Literature of Travel and the Idea of the South Seas.* New York: Oxford UP, 1996.

Robinson, Forrest G. "Patterns of Consciousness in *The Innocents Abroad*." *American Literature* 58 (1986): 46–63.

——. " 'Seeing the Elephant': Some Perspectives on Mark Twain's *Roughing It*." *American Studies* 21.2 (1980): 43–64.

Rogers, Franklin R. "Burlesque Travel Literature and Mark Twain's *Roughing It*." *Bulletin of the New York Public Library* 67 (1963): 155–68.

——. *Mark Twain's Burlesque Patterns as Seen in the Novels and Narratives, 1855–1885.* Dallas: Southern Methodist UP, 1960.

——. *The Pattern for Mark Twain's* Roughing It*: Letters from Nevada by Samuel and Orion Clemens, 1861–1862.* Berkeley: U of California P, 1961.

——. "The Road to Reality: Burlesque Travel Literature and Mark Twain's *Roughing It*." *Literature as Mode of Travel.* Ed. Warner G. Rice. New York: New York Public Library, 1963. 85–98.

Rojek, Chris, and John Urry. "Transformations of Travel and Theory." *Touring Cultures: Transformations of Travel and Theory.* New York: Routledge, 1997. 1–19.

Ryan, Chris. "The Tourist Experience." *Recreational Tourism.* New York: Routledge, 1991. 35–49.

Schriber, Mary Suzanne. "Women's Place in Travel Texts." *Prospects* 20 (1995): 161–79.

——. *Writing Home: American Women Abroad, 1830–1920.* Charlottesville: U of Virginia P, 1997.

Scott, Arthur L. "*The Innocents Abroad* Reevaluated." *Western Humanities Review* 7 (1953): 215–23.

——. "Mark Twain Looks at Europe." *South Atlantic Quarterly* 52 (1953): 399–413.

——. "Mark Twain Revises 'Old Times on the Mississippi,' 1875–1883." *Journal of English and Germanic Philology* 54 (1955): 634–38.

——. "Mark Twain's Revisions of *The Innocents Abroad* for the British Edition of 1872." *American Literature* 25 (1953): 43–61.

Shillingsburg, Miriam Jones. *At Home Abroad: Mark Twain in Australasia.* Jackson: UP of Mississippi, 1988.

Sloan, James Murphy. "Mark Twain's Travel Books: A Study in Form." Diss., Yale U, 1979.

Sloane, David E. E. Afterword. *The Innocents Abroad*. The Oxford Mark Twain. Ed. Shelley Fisher Fishkin. New York: Oxford UP, 1996. 1–18.

Smith, Harold F. *American Travellers Abroad: A Bibliography of Accounts Published before 1900*. Rev. ed. Lanham, MD: Scarecrow Press, 1999.

Smith, Harriet Elinor. Introduction. *Roughing It*. The Works of Mark Twain. Ed. Harriet Elinor Smith and Edgar Marquess Branch. Berkeley: U of California P, 1993. 797–911.

Smith, Henry Nash. "Mark Twain's Images of Hannibal." *Texas Studies in English* 37 (1958): 3–23.

———. *Mark Twain: The Development of a Writer*. Cambridge: Belknap/Harvard UP, 1962.

Smith, Valene, ed. *Hosts and Guests*. Philadelphia: U of Pennsylvania P, 1989.

Spengemann, William C. *The Adventurous Muse*. New Haven: Yale UP, 1977.

Stafford, Barbara. *Voyage into Substance: Art, Science, Nature, and the Illustrated Travel Account, 1760–1840*. Cambridge: MIT Press, 1984.

Stanley, Hiram. Rev. of *Following the Equator*. *Dial* 16 Mar. 1898: 186–87.

Steinbrink, Jeffrey. *Getting to Be Mark Twain*. Berkeley: U of California P, 1991.

———. "Mark Twain and Joe Twichell: Sublime Pedestrians." *Mark Twain Journal* 20.3 (1980–81): 1–6.

———. "Why the Innocents Went Abroad: Mark Twain and American Tourism in the Late Nineteenth Century." *American Literary Realism* 16 (1983): 278–86.

Stone, Albert E. "The Twichell Papers and Mark Twain's *A Tramp Abroad*." *Yale Library Gazette* 29 (1955): 151–64.

Stout, Janis. *The Journey Narrative in American Literature*. Westport, CN: Greenwood Press, 1973.

Stowe, William W. *Going Abroad: European Travel in Nineteenth-Century Culture*. Princeton: Princeton UP, 1994.

Stowell, Robert F. "River Guide Books and Mark Twain's *Life on the Mississippi*." *Mark Twain Journal* 16.4 (1973): 21.

Tenney, Thomas Asa. "Mark Twain's Early Travels and the Travel Tradition in Literature." Diss., U of Pennsylvania, 1971.

Thorp, Willard. "Pilgrim's Return." *Literary History of the United States*. Vol. 2. 3rd ed. Ed. Robert Spiller et al. New York: Macmillan, 1969. 827–42.

Tuckerman, Henry T. "The Philosophy of Travel." *United States Magazine and Democratic Review* 14 (1844): 527–39.

Turner, Lewis, and John Ash. *The Golden Hordes*. New York: St. Martins, 1976.

Urry, John. *The Tourist Gaze: Leisure and Travel in Contemporary Societies.* London: Sage, 1990.

Veblen, Thorstein. *The Theory of the Leisure Class.* 1899. Boston: Houghton Mifflin, 1973.

Walker, Franklin D. *Irreverent Pilgrims: Melville, Browne, and Mark Twain in the Holy Land.* Seattle: U of Washington P, 1974.

Wecter, Dixon, ed. *The Love Letters of Mark Twain.* New York: Harpers, 1949.

Wegelin, Christof. "The Rise of the International Novel." *PMLA* 77 (1962): 305–10.

Welland, Dennis. *Mark Twain in England.* Atlantic Highlands, NJ: Humanities Press, 1978.

———. "Mark Twain's Last Travel Book." *Bulletin of the New York Public Library* 69 (1965): 31–48.

West, Gary V. "The Development of the Mark Twain Persona in the Early Travel Letters." *Mark Twain Journal* 20.3 (1980–81): 13–16.

Whitford, Kathryn. "Rough Spots in *Roughing It.*" *Mississippi Quarterly* 16 (1963): 94–96.

Wonham, Henry B. Afterword. *Roughing It.* The Oxford Mark Twain. Ed. Shelley Fisher Fishkin. New York: Oxford UP, 1996. 1–17.

———. *Mark Twain and the Art of the Tall Tale.* New York: Oxford UP, 1993.

Ziff, Larzer. *Return Passages: Great American Travel Writing, 1780–1910.* New Haven: Yale UP, 2000.

Index

Alta California, 79

American Quarterly Review, on romantic reveries, 37–38

American West: as myth, 98–100, 102, 148; natural beauty of, 103–4; reality of desert, 104–6

Athens, 68–69

Blackwood's Magazine, "Modern Tourism," 7

Bliss, Frank, Twain letter to, 82, 180n. 2

Boorstin, Daniel, *The Image,* 7, 10, 12, 170n. 12, 171n. 18

Bridgman, Richard, *Traveling in Mark Twain,* 2–3

Browne, John Ross: *Adventures in Apache Country,* 29, 53–54, 178n. 6; *An American Family in Germany,* 41; *Etchings of a Whaling Cruise,* 28, 32, 41, 175n. 32; *The Land of Thor,* 29–30, 173n. 20

Catholicism, negative references to. *See* Travel-book conventions: anti-Catholicism; Travel-book conventions, Twain's use of: anti-Catholicism

Channing, William Ellery, "Address on Self-Culture," 19

Claude Glass, 63, 103

Clemens, Olivia, Twain letter to, 125

Clemens, Samuel Langhorne. *See* Twain, Mark

Cohen, Erik: on experimental tourists, 107–8; on tourist experience, 13, 146–47; and tourist theory, 170n. 13, 170n. 14, 171n. 18, 179n. 11

Coleridge, Samuel Taylor, 61, 176n. 3

Como, Lake, 46–47

Concord, Massachusetts, 11–14

Culler, Jonathan, 9, 170n. 13

Damascus, 70–71

Dana, Richard Henry, Jr., *Two Years before the Mast,* 28

DeQuille, Dan, Twain letter to, 34, 170n. 11

Dimsdale, Thomas J., *The Vigilantes of Montana,* 102, 178n. 8

Emerson, Ralph Waldo, "Self-Reliance," 56

Fisk, Wilbur, *Travels in Europe,* 25

Franklin, Benjamin, 118

Galilee, Sea of, 69–70

Grand Canyon, the, 8

Greeley, Horace, *An Overland Journey,*
174n. 24
Gribben, Alan, *Mark Twain's Library,*
177n. 11

Hall, Adelaide, *Two Travelers in
Europe,* 57
Hannibal, Missouri, 132–37
Harper's Magazine, "Editor's Table," 123
Hawthorne, Nathaniel, *The House of
the Seven Gables,* 67
Hill, Hamlin, on Twain's sales figures,
1–2, 167n. 2
Hinchliff, Thomas, *Summer Months
among the Alps,* 87–88, 177n. 16
Howells, William Dean: on *A Tramp
Abroad,* 58; Twain letter to, 83

Irving, Washington: as travel writer,
20–22; *The Sketch-Book,* 20–22,
45–46, 67, 172n. 9, 172n. 10

James, Henry, "Americans Abroad," 7
Jarves, James Jackson: *History of the
Sandwich Islands,* 120, 179n. 12,
179n. 15, 179n. 16; *Parisian Sights
and French Principles Seen through
American Spectacles,* 27, 29, 42–43,
56; *Scenes and Scenery in the Sandwich Islands,* 21, 38, 52–53
Jerusalem: church of the Holy Sepulcher, 74–77; grotto of the annunciation, 72–73

Kaplan, Justin, *Mr. Clemens and Mark
Twain,* 2, 167–68n. 3, 168n. 7
Kirkland, Caroline, *Holidays Abroad,*
26–27, 47–48
Kruse, Horst, *Mark Twain and* Life
on the Mississippi, 122–23, 132,
179n. 13, 180n. 19

Lang, Andrew, Twain letter to, 2, 4

MacCannell, Dean, *The Tourist,* 6, 9–
11, 170n. 13, 170n. 17, 171n. 18,
176n. 8
Marryat, Frederick, on travel writing,
23–24
Melville, Herman, *Moby-Dick,* 122,
138, 148, 173n. 21
Moran, Benjamin, 17

Napoleon, as tourist, 93–94
New World, American tourists in: as
destiny, 20–21, 52–56, 98–101;
"civilization" versus "savagery,"
52–55

Old World, American tourists in:
American identity, 18, 55–56;
anti-Catholicism of, 49–52;
confidence in democracy, 47–49;
confidence in natural beauty, 45–
47; interest in macabre, 41–44;
motivations for, 17–20
"Oriental Pictures," 61–66

Paris, 66
Paris Morgue, the, 42–44
Parkman, Francis, *The California and
Oregon Trail,* 31, 52
Percy, Walker, "The Loss of the Crea-
ture," 8, 10, 13
Pratt, Mary Louise, *Imperial Eyes,* 147
Prime, William, 39, 50, 75; *Tent Life
in the Holy Land,* 40
Putnam's Magazine, "Going Abroad," 17

Quaker City, 1, 14–15, 48, 60, 64, 68,
74, 77, 96, 100, 108, 121

San Francisco, 119–21
Smith, Harold, *American Travellers
Abroad,* 18
Smith, Henry Nash: on romantic
reveries, 174n. 25; on *Roughing It,*

99; on *The Innocents Abroad,*
169n. 11

Stanley, Hiram, on *Following the Equator,* 169n. 11

Tahoe, Lake, 46–47, 109–14
Tangier, as "foreign," 63–64
Taylor, Bayard, 34, 80–81, 172n. 11,
174n. 24, 176n. 9, 177n. 11,
177n. 14; *At Home and Abroad*
(first series), 56–57; *Eldorado,* 21;
A Journey to Central Africa, 25–26,
27; *The Lands of the Saracen,* 31;
Views A-Foot, 46, 48, 81–83, 174–
75n. 31
Tenney, Thomas, 172n. 8, 174n. 26
Territorial Enterprise (Virginia City),
118, 120
Thoreau, Henry David, *Walden,* 10–
11, 14
Thorp, Willard, on travel-writing
conventions, 23–24
Tourism, as "great popular movement," 5
Tourist, American identity as, 19–22,
55–56. *See also* New World, American tourists in; Old World, American tourists in
Tourist, Twain as, xiv–xv, 4–5
Tourist Age, xv, 2, 5, 7, 8, 11, 13, 14–
15, 58, 59–60, 72, 78, 83, 92, 93–
94, 95, 98, 125, 139, 144
Tourist experience, 5–14, 66–69,
77–78; authenticity, 5–14, 61,
102–4, 116–17; by proxy, 86–92;
imagination, 64, 71–76, 77–78, 79;
memory, 76–78, 79
Touristic faith, 12–13, 61–78, 79
Travel-book conventions: 2, 3, 4; adventurers, 80–81; anti-Catholicism,
49–52; comfort, 44–56; coming
home, 56–58; criticism of, 22–24,
defined, 22–58; entertainment,

37–44; expectation versus reality,
60; humility, 24–26; instruction,
30–37; macabre interests, 41–44;
narrative asides, 32–33; narrator
introductions, 24–30; romantic
reveries, 37–41; travel partners,
24–30; truth and honesty, 26–28
Travel-book conventions, Twain's use
of: anti-Catholicism, 49–52; "civilization" versus "savagery," 54–55;
comfort, 44–56; entertainment,
37–44; instruction, 33–37; local
anecdotes and legends, 36–37;
macabre, 43–44; narrative asides,
36–37, 173n. 22; romantic reveries, 39–41
Travel books: popularity of, 16–19; as
genre, 3–4
Travel channel, the, 5–6
"Travelers" versus "tourists," 6–14
Travel writer, Twain as, xiv–xv
Travel writers: attraction to travel
writing, 21–22; going home,
96–97; as professional authors,
173n. 17
Travel writing: definition of, 22–
23; popularity of, 16–18, Twain's
theory of, 157–66
Trubner's Bibliographic Guide to American Literature, 17–18
Tuckerman, Henry, 16
Twain, Mark: adventurer, 80–94; experimental tourist, 108–22; impressionist reader, 160–61; popularity
of his travel books, 1; split personality, xiii; tourist, xiv, xv, 4, 14;
travel writer, xiv, xv, 1–2, 14
Twain, Mark, works of: *Adventures of
Huckleberry Finn,* 1, 128–29, 138,
179n. 16, 180n. 5; *Adventures of
Tom Sawyer,* 1, 2; *Following the
Equator,* xiii, xiv, xv, 1, 54, 128,
138–40, 140–57, 180n. 6, 180n. 7,

180–81n. 8; *The Gilded Age*, 2; *The Innocents Abroad*, xiii, xiv, xv, 1, 2, 4, 8, 14–15, 26, 27, 33, 34, 35–36, 39–40, 43–44, 46, 48, 50–51, 57, 60–78, 79, 93, 95, 96, 98, 108, 114, 121, 128, 133, 135, 138–40, 173n. 19, 174–75n. 31; *Life on the Mississippi*, xiv, 1, 95–97, 122–37; "Old Times on the Mississippi," 96, 129; *The Prince and the Pauper*, 2; *Roughing It*, xiv, 1, 33–34, 35, 40, 54, 57, 95–122, 123, 128, 177–78n. 1; *The Tragedy of Pudd'nhead Wilson*, 180; A *Tramp Abroad*, xiv, 1, 36, 57, 58, 59, 78–94, 96, 98, 114, 128

Twichell, Joseph, 82, 177n. 12

United States Magazine and Democratic Review, 16

Veblen, Thorstein, *The Theory of the Leisure Class*, 79–80, 85, 170n. 15
Venice, 66–67

Wegelin, Christof, 17, 171n. 3
Whymper, Edward, *Scrambles amongst the Alps*, 89–90, 177n. 17
Willis, Nathaniel Parker, *Pencillings by the Way*, 42, 48, 49–50
Wonham, Henry B., *Mark Twain and the Art of the Tall Tale*, 178n. 10

Ziff, Larzer, *Return Passages*, 2–3, 168n. 9, 172n. 11, 180n. 6, 181n. 9

About the Author

Jeffrey Alan Melton (PhD, University of South Carolina) is Associate Professor of English at Auburn University Montgomery. He lives in Tuscaloosa, Alabama, with his wife and daughter.